W9-ARN-167

The Time-Life Gardener's Guide

BULBS

A

BOOK

This book is one of a series of guides to good gardening.

The Time-Life Gardener's Guide

BULBS

TIME-LIFE BOOKS, ALEXANDRIA, VIRGINIA

CONTENTS

1

BULBS AND THEIR CARE

2

INDOOR DELIGHTS

3

INCREASING YOUR COLLECTION

The term "bulb," as used in this book, refers to any plant that stores food underground in specially modified leaves, stems or roots; besides true bulbs, the term includes some that are, strictly speaking, corms, tubers, rhizomes and tuberous roots. All of them stockpile everything needed for a new growth cycle, and most of them can outlast adverse climatic conditions—and then burst into bloom as soon as the weather improves. They are among the easiest and most reliable plants that a gardener can grow.

On the following pages you will learn how to select and care for different kinds of bulbs, how to plant them outdoors for dazzling spring and summer displays, how to force bulbs to bloom indoors in virtually any season. A chapter on propagation takes you step by step through a number of methods that make it easy to multiply your stock of bulbs.

To help you choose bulbs that will flourish in your garden, there's a zone map on pages 78-79; locate your zone, then consult the Dictionary of Bulbs, which starts on page 88, for plants suited to where you live. You'll also find a monthly maintenance checklist, a troubleshooting guide to help you diagnose and combat diseases and pests, and tips to enhance your enjoyment of the explosive beauty that nature has packed into bulbs.

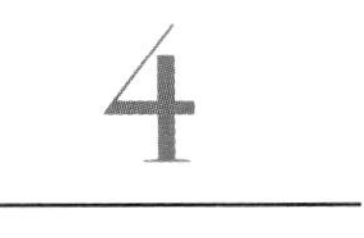

WORKING IN TANDEM WITH NATURE

DICTIONARY OF BULBS

1

BULBS AND THEIR CARE

Few garden plants mark the passage of seasons more clearly than the flowering bulbs. Crocuses pushing through the snow herald the coming of spring, and tulips and daffodils announce that spring has truly arrived. By late spring, ornamental onions have appeared; and lilies, in all their myriad versions, are a sure sign of midsummer. Finally, as leaves fall and winds sharpen with the coming of autumn, the spectacular blossoms of dahlias grow ever more brilliant.

Happily for gardeners, it is easy to incorporate this cyclical display into a garden plan, for flowering bulbs are among the most rewarding of plants. Whether they are true bulbs, corms, tubers, rhizomes or tuberous roots, they carry within their underground structures all the nutrients needed to bring them into flower: in effect, they are self-perpetuating. They are also adaptable, equally effective in formal beds and naturalized settings, in modest-sized lawns and grandly conceived landscapes. And as a group they are, with a few exceptions, undemanding. Their needs can be ticked off on the fingers of one hand.

Flowering bulbs are partial to a loamy soil, especially one that is rich in compost or similar organic material. They are fussy about the depth at which they are planted, which varies, naturally enough, with the size of the bulb. When the flowers fade, they should ideally be beheaded. Although this is not essential, beheading concentrates the plants' energy back into the bulbs, ensuring more abundant flowering in the future. For some tall-growing varieties, such as dahlias and gladioli, stakes may be needed. And though most bulbs survive winter handily, because in fact they depend on cold as an element in their regenerative process, a mulch is sometimes helpful to protect them from sudden temperature changes.

Detailed descriptions of these simple tasks are given on the following pages, along with helpful advice on where to buy bulbs and how to pick good ones, and how to sort out the difference between true bulbs and their near cousins—the corms, tubers, rhizomes and tuberous roots.

PATCHES OF COLOR IN THE MIDST OF SPRING GREENERY

Nothing more cheerfully signals the coming of spring than the bright blooms of crocuses and daffodils, and nowhere do they look better than poking their heads up through an expanse of lawn that is just turning green. The flowers, growing from bulbs planted under the grass, often shoot up with what seems foolhardy speed, right into an icy, late-season snowfall. But these uniquely hardy blooms and their bulbs somehow survive winter's last blasts to proclaim that the sun is high again and a season of rebirth has arrived.

This dramatic annual show is not hard to produce. Choose an open stretch of lawn that gets plenty of sunlight. Then select the bulbs and get them into the ground in the fall. (For more exact planting times, see the dictionary entries in this volume.) The planting itself *(opposite)* should look casual and informal, as if nature, rather than human hands, had done the job.

Once planted, the bulbs will repeat their performance season after season. Crocuses, daffodils, scilla and other early-season bulbs can remain in the ground for years. They do not need to be dug up and divided like many other plants; in fact they multiply freely on their own underground. They also need a bare minimum of care: a sprinkling of fertilizer each spring as the foliage begins to appear and another application in the autumn.

The lawn where the bulbs are planted should not be mowed, of course, while the plants are blooming and their foliage is young and fresh; the leaves manufacture food that is vital to the bulbs' survival and flowering. So wait to trim the grass until the foliage has turned yellow and begun to die back —about six weeks after the flowers have peaked. Gardeners anxious to mow should choose the earliest-blooming bulbs, which should have flowered and faded before the grass gets out of hand.

Clouds of white and yellow daffodils shoot up in an orchard beneath gnarled fruit trees. The daffodils flourish, their bulbs reproducing and spreading underground, because they bloom early in the spring, before the trees leaf out and cast too much shade.

1 To give the spring blooms in your lawn a natural look, grab a handful of bulbs of the same sort and gently toss them on the grass. Some should fall in rough clusters, some singly. Take care not to mix different cultivars in the same cluster; they may bloom at different times and make the cluster look ragged. But it is a good idea to plant different cultivars in separate areas, so that some clusters will bloom early, some late.

2 Use a trowel to cut a round plug of grass everywhere that a bulb or a cluster of bulbs has fallen. The opening should be slightly larger in diameter than the bulb or the cluster. Set the plug aside, then dig a hole that is two or three times as deep as the bulb is wide—about 6 inches deep for most daffodils but shallower for miniatures and for crocuses and scilla.

3 As you dig the holes, set the soil aside on a sheet of newspaper. For each hole's worth of soil, mix in a tablespoon of a balanced fertilizer such as 10-10-10. Drop some of the amended soil in the bottom of each hole—an inch or so of the mix per hole should be enough.

4 Place the bulbs, nose side up, in the holes and cover them with the remaining soil. Firm the soil with your hands and water it lightly. Replace the grass plug, tamp it down and water again. Repeat the scattering and planting in as many places as you wish until you have the spring display you want. □

SETTING BULBS IN A BED OF THEIR OWN

Not all bulbs lend themselves to naturalizing as daffodils and crocuses do *(pages 8-9)*; some flourish best in sunny beds of good-textured loamy soil that drains well, is rich in nutrients and is also chemically balanced. This sounds like a pretty tall order, but with a little thought and planning—followed, inevitably, by a bit of good old-fashioned digging—it is not that hard to create these optimum conditions.

First, choose the bed's location. A few bulbs can tolerate shade, but most like it sunny and warm. So select an area that has full sun and is protected from harsh winds by shrubs or a wall.

Then analyze the soil's pH level—that is, its acid-alkaline balance. One reason bulbs grow so well in Holland is that the soil is full of crushed seashells, which make it alkaline. Collect a soil sample from the proposed bed and send it to the nearest soil testing laboratory or agricultural extension office. If the lab report indicates the soil tends toward acidity (a pH of 5.9 or below), be ready to add some lime. And be ready to enrich the soil with a 10-10-10 fertilizer—the so-called complete fertilizer.

Then consider the soil's texture. The ideal is a dark, crumbly loam that holds moisture—but not too much. Light, sandy soil drains too swiftly; heavy, clayey earth can become sodden and rot bulbs planted in it. Both can be much improved, though, by adding organic matter—compost, peat moss, shredded leaves—which opens and aerates clayey areas and both adds substance and aids moisture retention in sandy soil.

Once these various supplements have been collected—fertilizer, organic matter and lime if needed—it is time to dig up the bed, mix in the additives and plant the bulbs *(opposite)*. Most of them should be planted at a depth about three times their width, but for variations, see the Dictionary of Bulbs *(pages 88-137)*.

In a sunny bed alongside a white dowel fence, rows of white tulips and cream-colored daffodils nod their heads above a rank of massed grape hyacinths. The bulbs are somewhat shielded from spring breezes by the fence.

1 Determine where you want your bed of flowering bulbs and how large it should be; then turn the earth to a depth of 9 to 12 inches. As you dig, turn over each spadeful of earth and chop up the clods. Remove all weeds, old roots and rocks as you go.

2 After turning the bed, pour a layer of organic matter on top. A 1-inch layer is enough for good soil, but use at least 3 inches to improve the composition of earth that is sandy or clayey. Work the organic matter into the bed with your spade. Sprinkle some 10-10-10 fertilizer on the amended soil—about ¾ pound for every 25 square feet. Work it into the soil along with any required lime.

3 When the earth is ready, dig individual holes in it for your bulbs. Plant them growing end up *(box, below)*. Larger bulbs such as daffodils should be spaced 6 to 12 inches apart, depending on how close you want the blooms, but tiny bulbs (crocus, grape hyacinth) can be far closer—2 or 3 inches. Cover the bulbs with soil and water well. □

WHICH WAY IS UP

Many bulbs have quite obvious top sides and bottom ones. Daffodils, for example, have flat undersides with remnants of roots attached, and pointed tips from which growth will come. But some plants are harder to be sure about, such as dahlias, which grow from tuberous roots, and anemones, which spring from wrinkled, odd-shaped tubers. With such anomalous bulbs, look first for the remains of roots, then for the beginnings of growing points, to determine which way is up. If you are still unsure, plant the bulb sideways; the growing stems will seek light and head upward while the roots will descend in search of moisture and food.

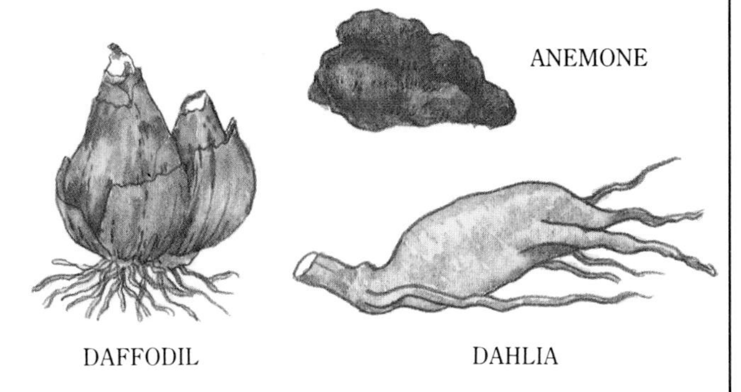

SOME RULES OF THUMB FOR BUYING BULBS

Unless the bulbs themselves are first-rate, no amount of careful soil preparation will guarantee a sparkling display of blooms. Happily, there are a couple of easy rules to keep in mind when going bulb shopping in the fall.

Rule No. 1 is this: as you look through the bins of bulbs that garden centers display each autumn, select the largest examples you can find. The reason is that big bulbs are packed with reserve food energy, which can be counted on to produce luxuriant foliage and bright flowers when the spring growing season arrives. Small bulbs may not bloom at all, at least not the first year. Of course, bulb sizes differ from plant to plant; hyacinth bulbs, for example, run about twice as large as crocuses. And bulb sizes also vary between cultivars. But the rule still stands: choose the largest ones available for each type.

Rule No. 2 is to make sure the bulbs are heavy and feel solid. Lightness means a bulb has dried out inside. Similarly, softness indicates disease—and nicks may mean damage. Also, except for paperwhite narcissus *(page 40)* and autumn crocuses, avoid bulbs that have begun to sprout; a show of growth means that bulbs have been in the store too long.

It follows from these handy axioms that it is risky to buy unexamined bulbs packaged in bags or boxes labeled "mixed bulbs" or "bargain assortment." The bulbs inside may be fine; on the other hand they could be low-grade leftovers hardly worth the trouble to plant.

Instead of going to a nursery, you can of course choose bulbs from the catalogs sent out by mail-order houses. Bulbs bought by mail tend to be more costly than the assortments in nursery bins, but those shipped by top-line firms are usually of high quality. The rule here is to deal only with reputable firms. Beware of catalogs touting very low prices; there is probably a good reason for the astonishing bargains, namely a large admixture of inferior bulbs.

Large, firm and still wearing their papery protective jackets, three dozen top-grade bulbs lie together with fallen leaves on a patch of soil, ready for planting. Clockwise from lower left, they include purplish hyacinths, double-nosed narcissus, plump tulips and some irises in the center.

BEWARE: VANISHING SPECIES

A number of bulbs grow in the wild. Unfortunately, some of them—cyclamen and snowdrops from abroad, and jack-in-the-pulpits and trout lilies from the United States—are threatened with extinction, because it is easier and quicker to dig them up than to propagate them. Some unprincipled nurseries stock bulbs collected in the wild by unethical suppliers. The best way to help save these plants is to buy bulbs only from reputable sources that sell propagated plants, not ones collected in the wild.

MEASURING SIZE, COUNTING NOSES

Several kinds of bulbs, like the daffodils pictured here, vary not only in size, but also in the number of growing points, or "noses," they have. Double-nosed and triple-nosed bulbs are choicer than singles because, with more growing points, they will produce extra foliage and flowers. Still, size remains a key factor, especially of the main member of the cluster, the so-called mother bulb. Given a choice, always select the cluster with the most sizable mother bulb.

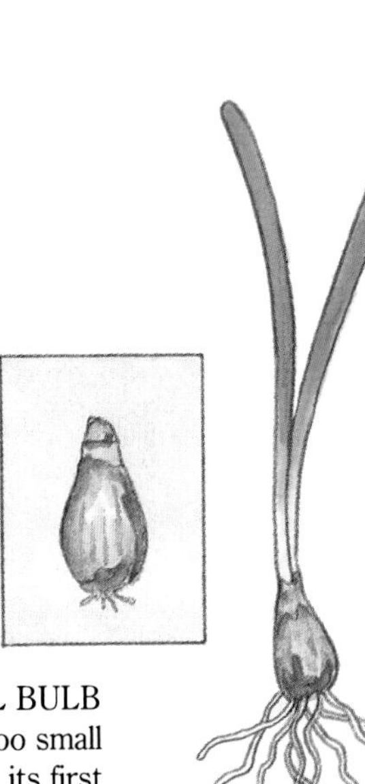

SMALL BULB
This undersized daffodil is too small to send up anything but foliage its first year, but may with care flower in its second season.

MIDSIZE BULB
The mother bulb of this double-nosed daffodil is big enough to bloom the first year. The daughter will send up foliage the first year but no bloom until a year later.

LARGE BULB
This large, choice triple-nosed bulb will produce two flowers the first season. The smaller daughter will add its bloom in the second season. □

QUICK AND EASY SOIL-ENRICHING COMPOST

Like virtually all growing things, bulbs prosper best in rich, good-textured soil—and nothing improves a garden plot more effectively than old-fashioned homemade compost. The usual way to manufacture compost is to pile leaves, grass clippings and other garden wastes in a big backyard bin of some sort. But a simpler method is to shred the same natural ingredients and pack them in an inexpensive garbage can of heavy plastic, as shown on the opposite page. The wastes turn into usable compost with amazing speed—usually in a matter of weeks—and the neat, discrete can takes up little room. The method is ideal, in fact, for gardeners who have limited outdoor space and need only modest amounts of compost at any one time.

The first requirement for the composting process, aside from finely ground organic wastes, is oxygen—thus the holes that need to be drilled in the plastic can. Oxygen promotes the decay of the organic matter, spurring bacteria to break down its tissues into rich, nutritious and odorless compost. The second necessity is a source of nitrogen—liquid fertilizer or manure—that further helps the bacteria to do their job. A third is the periodic stirring of the can's contents *(bottom, opposite),* which again introduces oxygen and speeds decomposition. So does heat. When the bacteria are hard at work and the whole composting process is in full swing, the pile will emit steam, indicating that the interior has reached 140° F or more.

A good time to start a garbage can compost pile is August or early September. That way an initial supply of compost can be used as a soil amendment in midautumn, to enrich the soil and protect the bulbs through the winter. Then the can, reloaded with more autumn leaves, will easily produce a second batch of compost that can be used as a winter mulch.

With crisp foliage and bright shiny blooms, a border of orange and yellow Greigii tulips thrives in a bed of good soil that has been enriched with a thick layer of well-aged compost.

1 Gather several small piles of leaves and other organic wastes—hay, plant prunings and grass trimmings. Grind them up thoroughly with a horticultural shredder, if you have one, or by running a power lawn mower back and forth over the piles *(below).* A shredder can also handle twigs and small branches, but it is best not to try chopping up such tough items with a mower.

2 Drill or punch holes in the side, top and bottom of a 3-foot-tall plastic garbage can. The holes, which are needed for drainage and ventilation, should be at least 1 inch in diameter and spaced about 6 inches apart.

3 To prevent the waste matter from falling through the holes, line the can with screening. Cut the screen with utility shears or with wire cutters, using the can's lid and bottom as templates *(above, left)* for those pieces. Then cut a rectangular sheet as long as the container is high and as wide as its circumference. Bend the sheet and attach it to the can's inside wall with a staple gun.

4 Place the can on some bricks to keep the bottom off the ground and allow for ventilation. Fill the container with your shredded material. Add 3 cups of manure or 1 cup of 20-20-20 liquid fertilizer. Moisten the mixture and stir it well. Then stir again every two or three days. The compost should be rich, dark and crumbly in about four weeks. □

COMBINING BULBS WITH OTHER PLANTINGS

Bulbs look especially handsome when put in a bed that is already planted with perennials. The bulbs' bright, waxy blooms show up dramatically against a background of mixed flowers and foliage. They will also lengthen a bed's yearly color display, since a number of bulbs pop up before winter is over, and others are the last to bloom in the fall.

The trick to mixing bulbs in a bed with other plants is to put suitable bulbs in the right places—to achieve a season-long display and to be sure the bulbs thrive. Before you start, note the exposure of the site. Most bulbs need at least four hours of direct sun each day, and they will get it if the bed faces south or west. Then measure the bed in question, noting its present occupants, and make a scale drawing *(opposite)*. With such a chart in hand, you can sketch in the places where the bulbs should go *(pages 18-19)*. Any scale will do; on the graph shown here, two squares equal 1 foot.

The main things to consider when spotting bulbs are their season of bloom, their colors, and their heights and shapes. Naturally, some early-season bloomers like crocuses should be included and some autumnal bulbs as well. Then add some bulbs that flower in mid-spring, late spring and midsummer, planting them to fill gaps where other plants will not be in full bloom at those times. For choices, see the dictionary in this volume.

As to color, plant bulbs whose blooms will harmonize (or at least not clash) with neighboring clumps of flowers. Finally, consider plant height. Tall plants like lilies should go at the back of a border, looking over the heads of shorter plants, and low growers such as grape hyacinth in front. This rule can be broken, though, with small plants that bloom so early, or so late, that no other, taller plants are present to compete for attention.

A bed artfully designed to show steady, eye-pleasing color combines bulbous agapanthus sporting its summer show of blue flowers with four perennials: yellow coneflowers and purple-pink asters, which bloom all summer, and silvery artemesia and rosy sedums, which flower until the first frost.

1 Using a tape measure, determine the dimensions of your bed or border, and the spacing of the existing trees and plants—here a dogwood and an azalea bush and several perennials. Include dormant plants hiding underground if you have marked their locations or recall where they are.

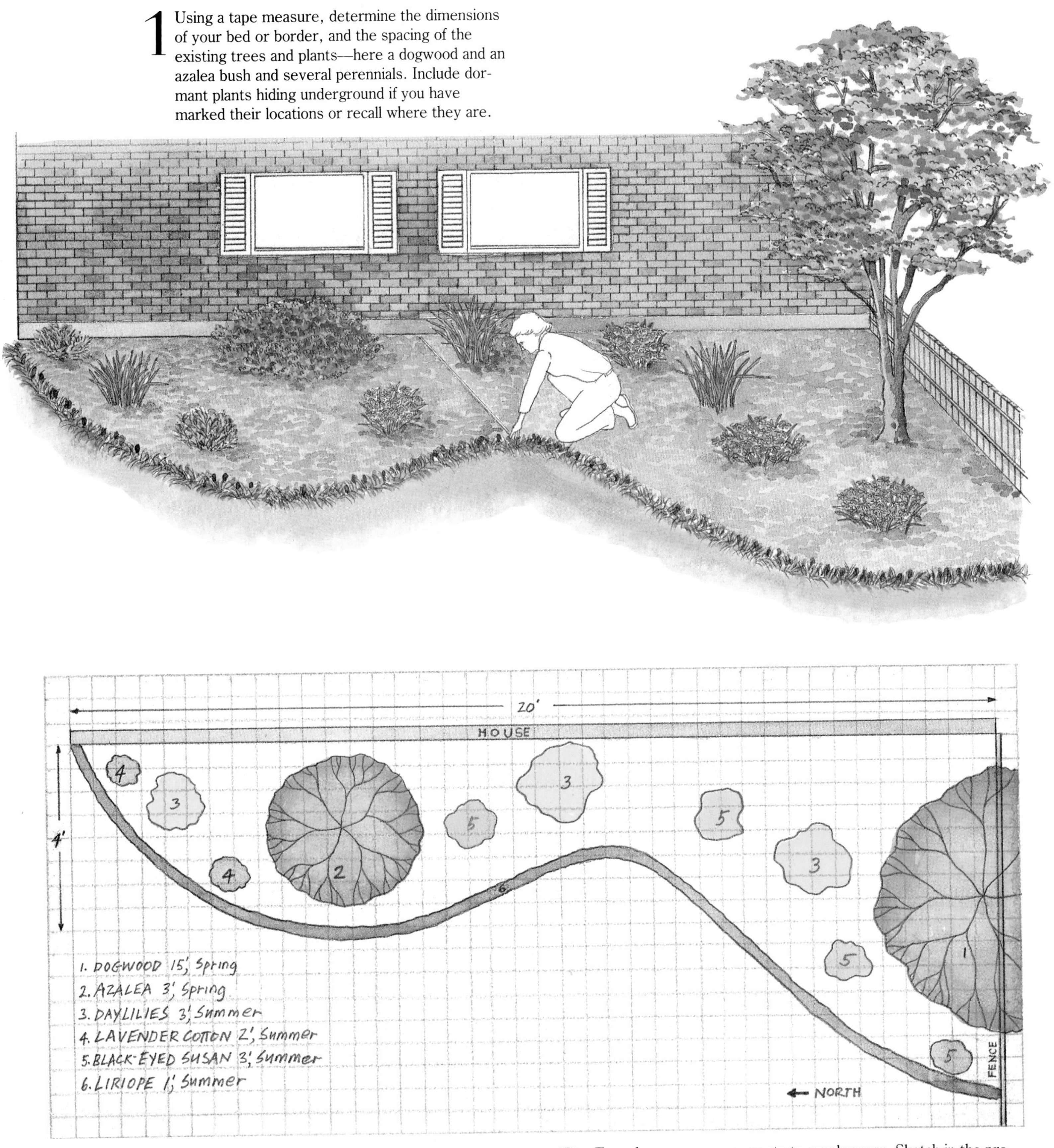

Transfer your measurements to graph paper. Sketch in the present plants, coding them by number as shown. Note their heights, colors and seasons of bloom. Also draw in any walkways or other architectural features, in this case the brick foundation of a house and a picket fence, and indicate the direction of exposure.

3 Tape a sheet of tracing paper over your graph-paper plan. Sketch on it where you think clusters of various bulbs will best fit, listing your candidates below. Remember to take into account the grown plants' heights, colors and times of flowering. Locate bulbs that bloom simultaneously along the length of the border and not in a single area; otherwise you will have odd-looking, isolated little patches of bloom. □

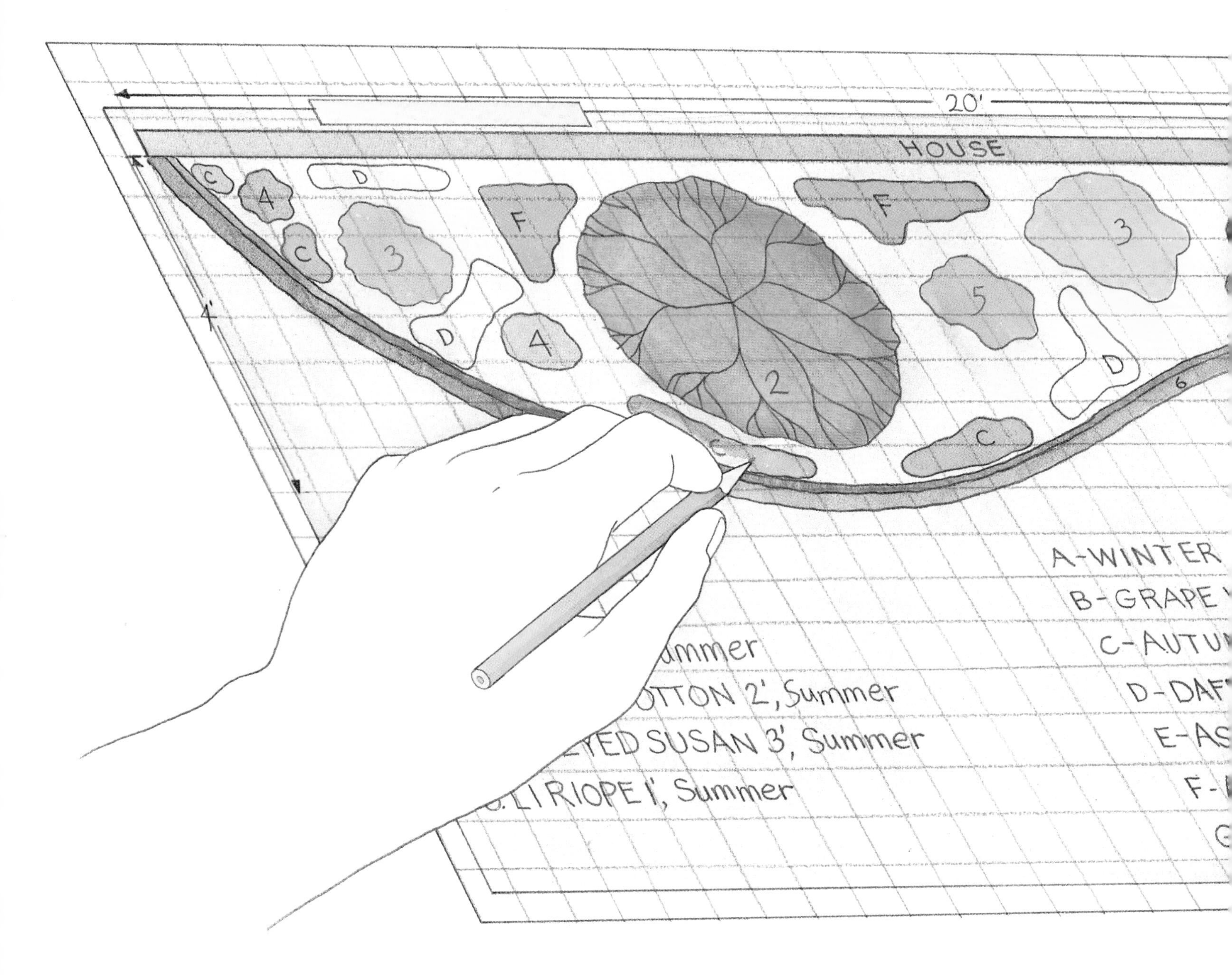

G
5
D
3
C
A
I
5
C
5
FENCE
TE 8", Spring
NTH 9", Spring
OCUS 1', Fall
THALIA' 16", Spring
HYBRID LILY 2'-5', Summer
CAN HYBRID LILY 4'-6', Summer
NTAL HYBRID LILY 2½'-7', Summer
← NORTH

A GALLERY OF BULBS AND HOW THEY GROW

The word "bulb" is commonly used to describe plants having five different kinds of food storage structures. In addition to true bulbs, there are corms, tubers, rhizomes and tuberous roots. What they have in common is that they grow from underground storage structures that are made up of modified plant parts. True bulbs store food in modified leaf tissue; corms, tubers and rhizomes store it in modified stem tissue; tuberous roots store it in roots. All five storage structures serve the same purpose; by building up a reserve of nutrients during the growing season, they enable the plant to survive a long dormant period—and then put out fresh foliage and flowers as soon as weather conditions permit.

Once they have done so, photosynthesis, the process whereby plants manufacture food, takes place only in green tissue. As long as it remains alive and green, the foliage of a bulbous plant will continue to make food needed for the underground storage structure to produce next year's flower. That is why the foliage of a bulbous plant should not be removed from the plant when the flower fades; it should be allowed to die back naturally.

Most bulbs available from garden centers and mail-order sources are designated winter-hardy. Examples include tulips, lilies and daffodils. These natives of temperate climes normally go dormant when the weather turns cold and are ready to blossom in the spring. Other bulbs, among them amaryllis, are known as tender bulbs; they come from the tropics, where dry weather triggers dormancy and wet weather prompts renewed growth. Whichever kind they are, bulbs are usually purchased in their dormant phase.

In addition to storing food, bulbs have in common a capacity for generating buds that either split off or can be split off from the parent to develop into independent plants. By understanding and exploiting the natural life cycles of different bulbs, you can help them flourish—and expand your stock by propagating your own plants.

Around the shapely trunk of a crape myrtle, blue spring starflowers, pink and purple anemones, and yellow daffodils herald spring. All these flowers are classed as bulbs, though they arise from different structures: anemones from tubers, daffodils and spring starflowers from tunicate bulbs.

TRUE BULBS

A true bulb has a basal plate that consists of compressed stem tissue. Roots descend from the bottom, and modified leaves (scales) grow upward from it. The scales store food. One kind of true bulb, which includes daffodils *(left)* and tulips, is called tunicate; such bulbs have an outer tunic of dry, papery scales covering fleshy inner scales and a tiny flower bud. The flower bud and inner scales will elongate and emerge to form the flower and foliage. The other kind of bulbs are scaly bulbs, like the lily *(below)*. They consist of overlapping fleshy scales that surround an apical bud that will develop into flowers and foliage, and they have no common covering. Both kinds of true bulbs produce offspring bulbs from lateral buds located near the basal plate.

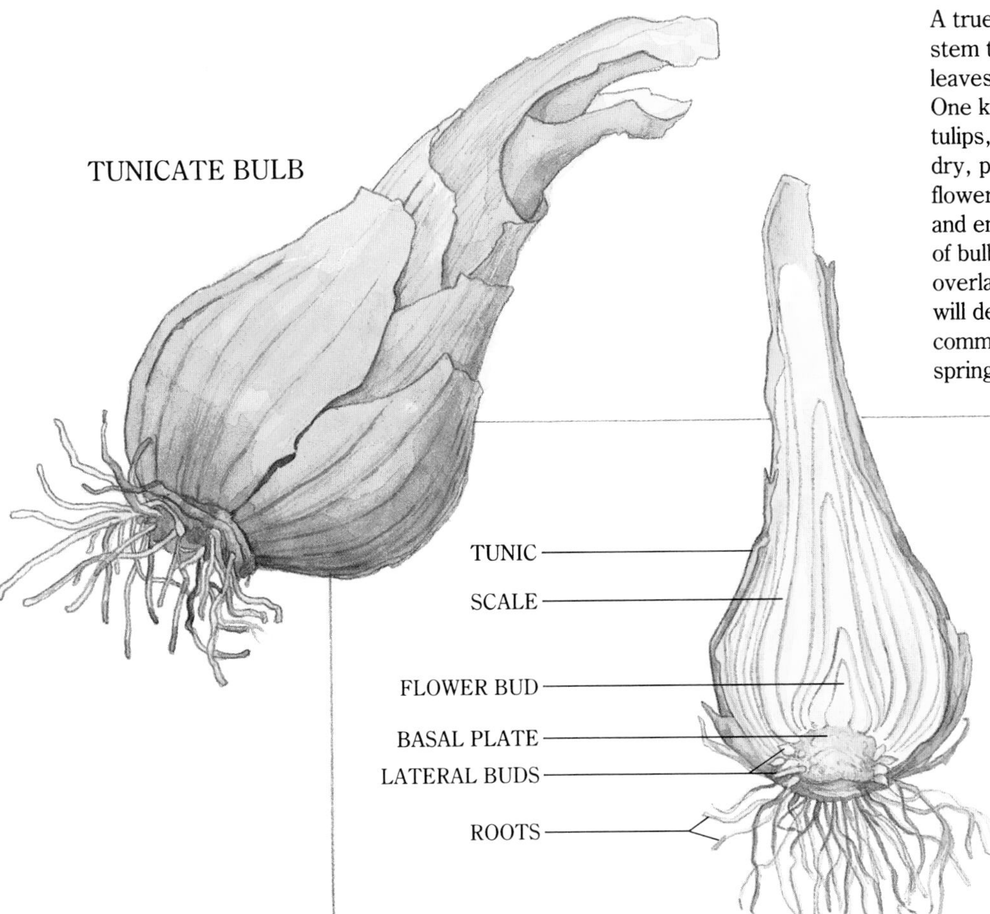

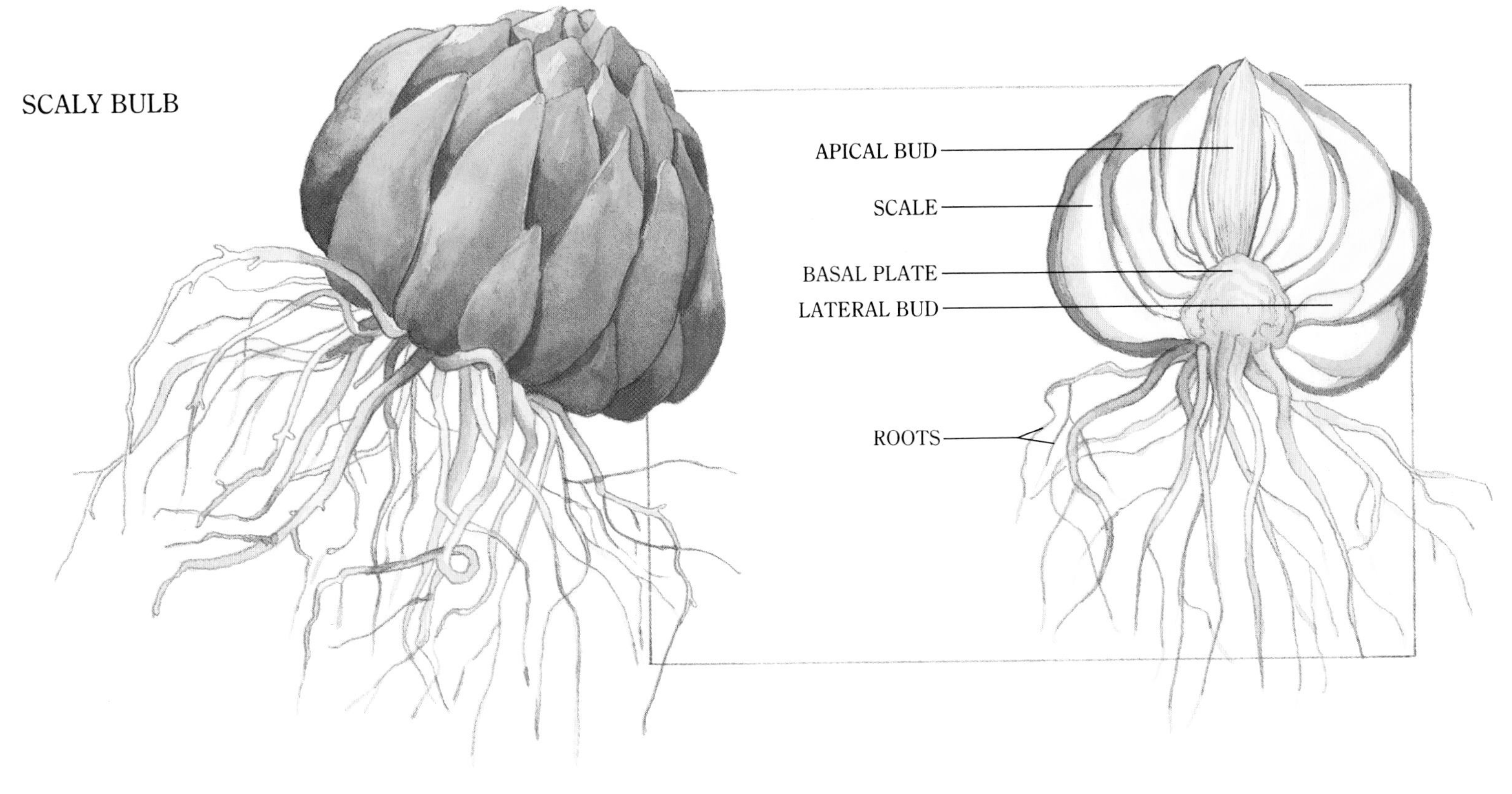

CORMS

A corm is a swollen stem base (as on the peacock orchid shown at left and directly below). On the bottom it has roots; at or near the top it has an apical bud, or growth bud, that will develop both foliage and flowers. Like a tunicate bulb, a corm has a papery covering (a tunic) that protects food that is stored in the stem tissue inside. At the base of the corm, lateral buds (which are not visible to the naked eye) will produce tiny corms called cormels.

APICAL BUD
TUNIC
STEM TISSUE
ROOTS

TUBERS

A tuber consists of thickened stem tissue with a cluster of growth buds protruding from its top. Foliage and flowers grow from these buds. Roots extend from the bottom of the tuber. Most tubers (like the tuberous begonia illustrated below) simply grow larger from year to year and produce more and more growth buds.

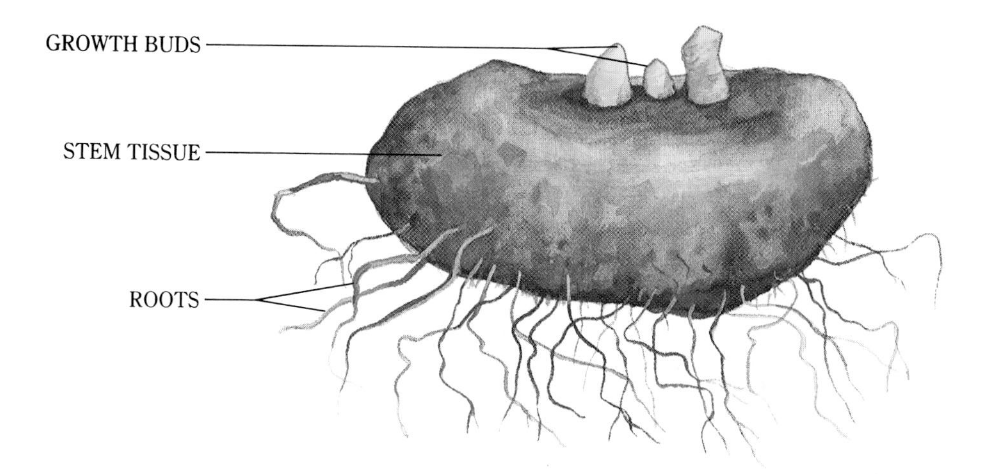

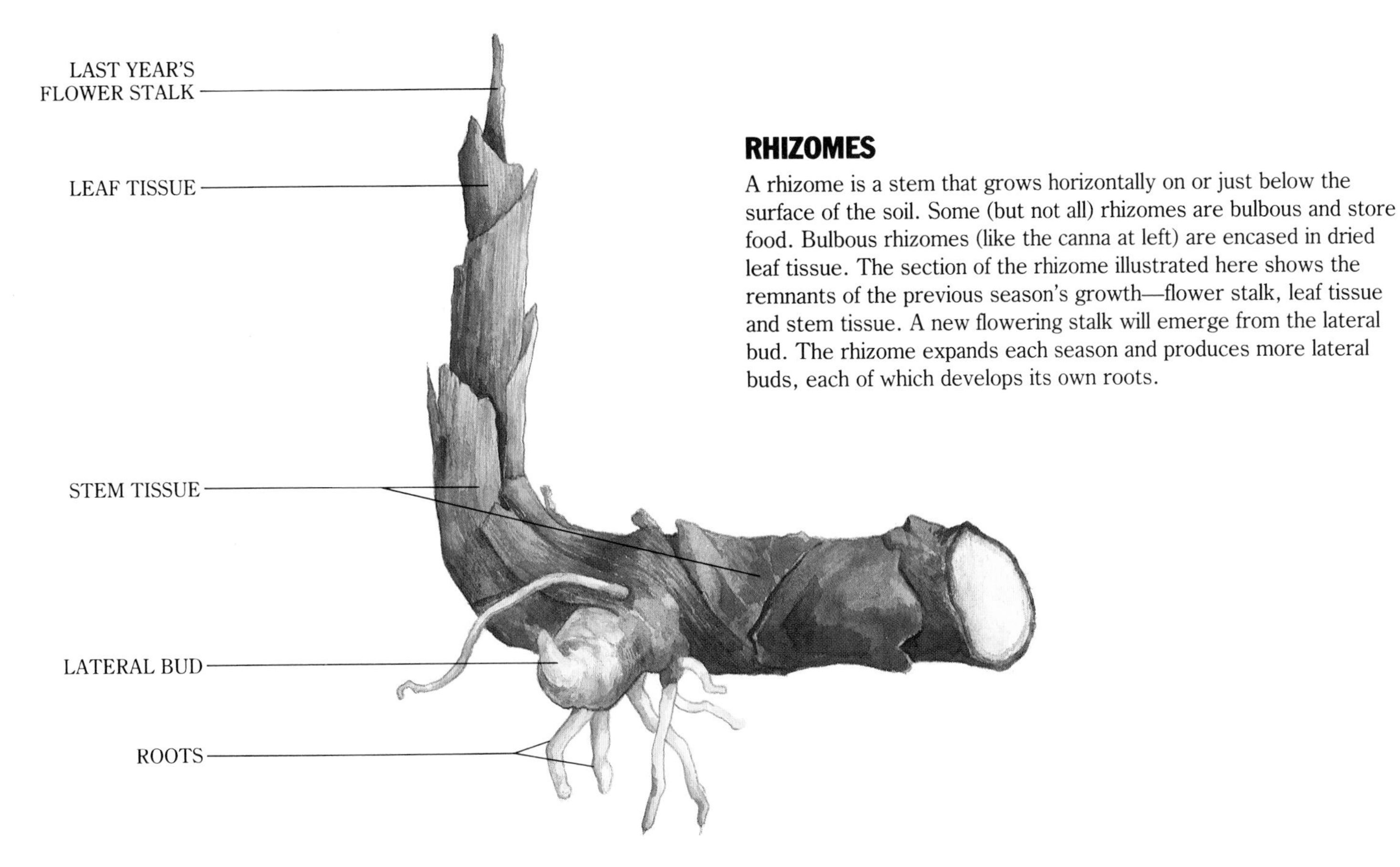

RHIZOMES

A rhizome is a stem that grows horizontally on or just below the surface of the soil. Some (but not all) rhizomes are bulbous and store food. Bulbous rhizomes (like the canna at left) are encased in dried leaf tissue. The section of the rhizome illustrated here shows the remnants of the previous season's growth—flower stalk, leaf tissue and stem tissue. A new flowering stalk will emerge from the lateral bud. The rhizome expands each season and produces more lateral buds, each of which develops its own roots.

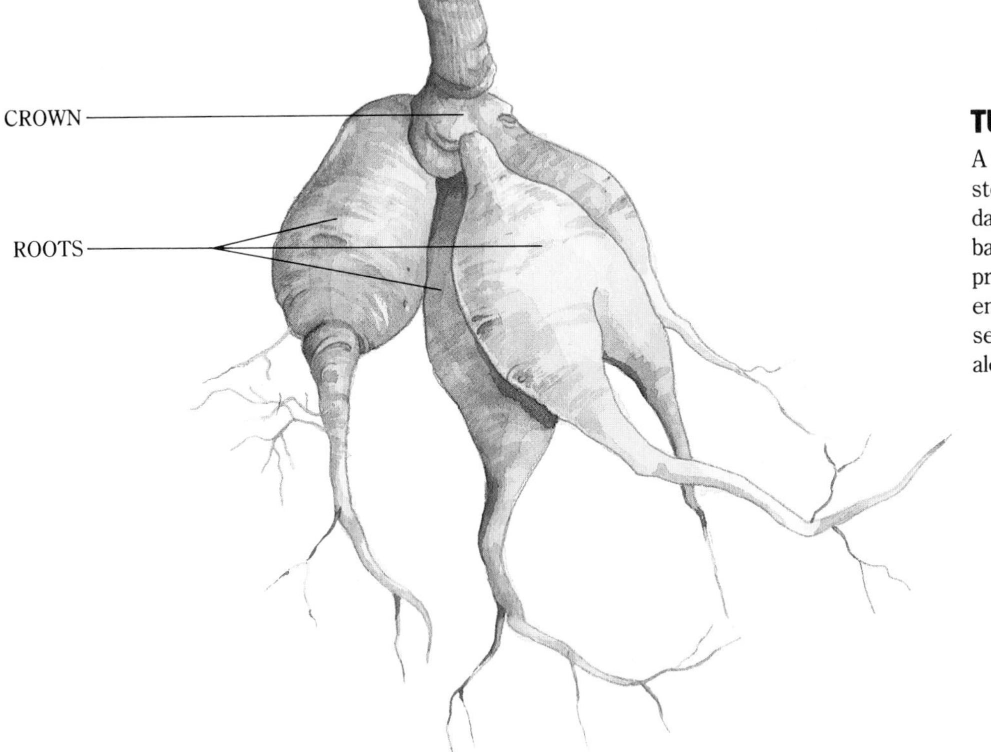

TUBEROUS ROOTS

A tuberous root is a specialized root that stores food. Tuberous roots, like the dahlia shown at left, join a stem at its base, which is called a crown and which produces new buds. Tuberous roots are entirely depleted during the growing season, and new tuberous roots form alongside the old ones.

LIFE CYCLES OF BULBS

Illustrated here and on the following two pages are the life cycles of four bulbous plants, all of which change in form, both above and below the ground, as the seasons change. The daffodil, a tunicate bulb, blooms in the spring. The others—the lily, a scaly bulb; the peacock orchid, a corm; and the dahlia, a tuberous root—bloom in the summer. Not shown here are tubers and rhizomes, which do not change significantly below the ground; they simply get larger and produce more growth buds from year to year.

TUNICATE BULBS

A tunicate bulb, such as a daffodil, is planted in fall and blooms in spring. The embryonic flower is fully formed inside the bulb, which is protected by a papery outer covering, or tunic. During the growing season lateral buds form inside the bulb; after increasing in size they eventually emerge and split from the mother bulb.

FALL

EARLY SPRING

SCALY BULBS

A scaly bulb, such as a lily, is planted in fall for summer bloom. In addition to the main flowering stem, a shorter stem without flowers emerges from a large lateral bud. The following year this stem will mature enough to produce flowers; eventually it will split from the mother bulb to become an independent plant.

FALL

SPRING

MIDSPRING

SUMMER

FALL

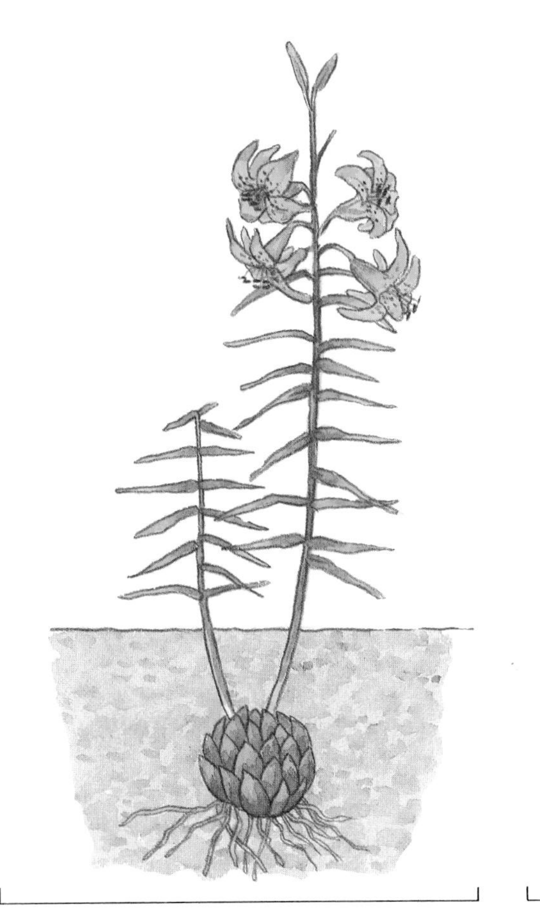

MIDSUMMER

LATE SUMMER

FALL

CORMS

A corm, such as a peacock orchid, is planted in spring for summer bloom. During the growing season the corm is gradually depleted. While this is happening, a new corm forms on top of the old one, and tiny offspring called cormels form between the old and new corms.

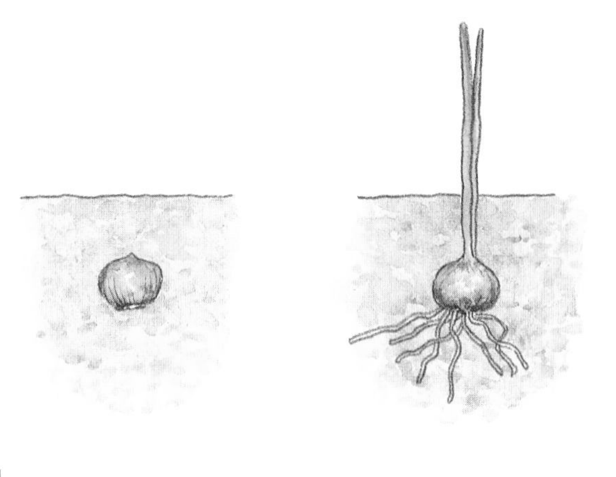

SPRING

TUBEROUS ROOTS

A tuberous root, such as a dahlia, is planted in spring for summer bloom. As the dahlia grows, the original tuberous root withers, as a corm does. At the same time, new tuberous roots develop alongside the old one; by the end of the season the new roots are mature and can be separated to form new plants. □

SPRING

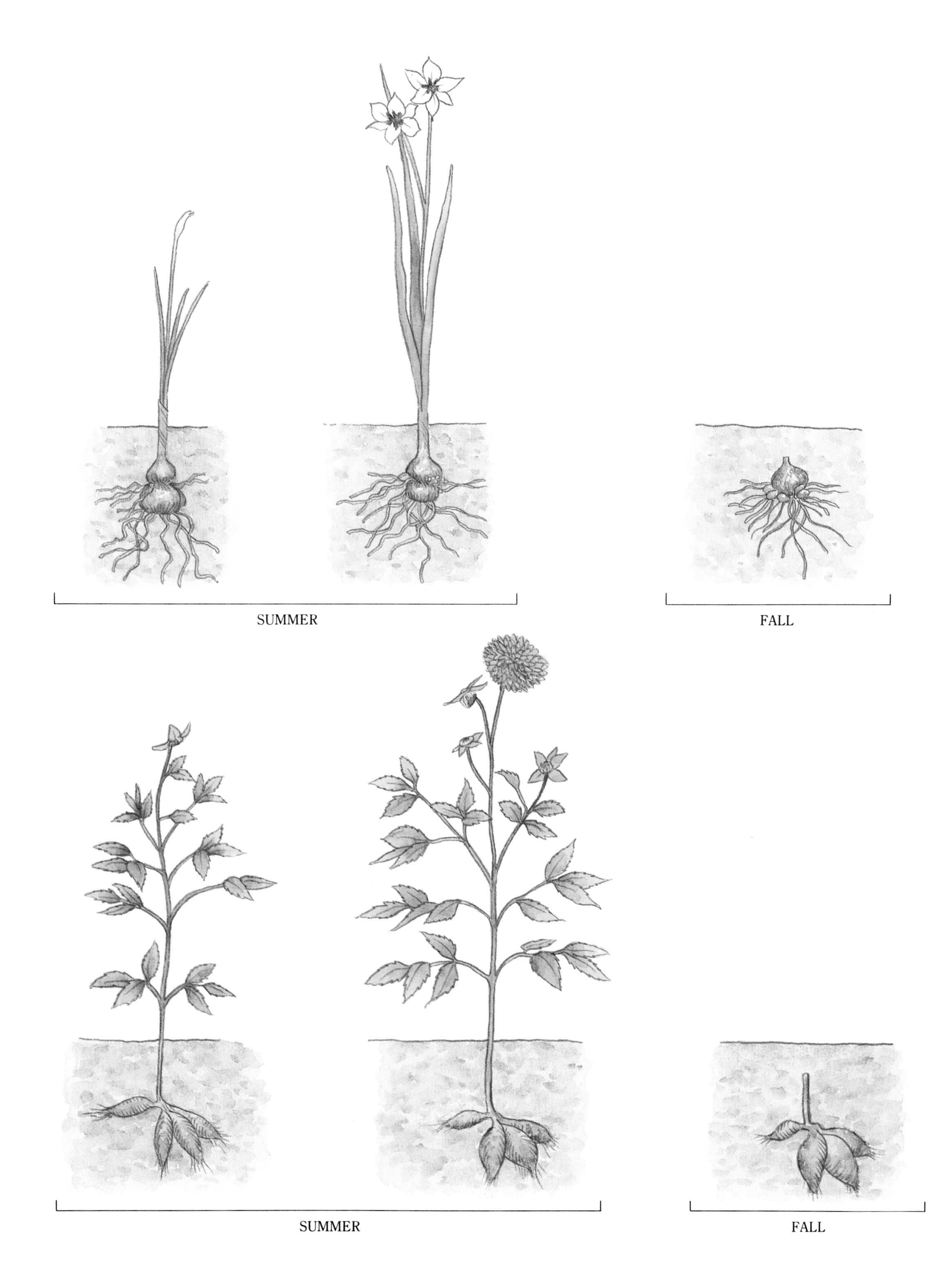
SUMMER
FALL
SUMMER
FALL

GROWING AND NURTURING OUTSIZED BLOOMS

Several of the larger bulbous plants, most especially dahlias, can be made to produce outsized blooms that look superb in a garden or as cut flowers in a vase—or even may qualify for entry in flower shows. The only drawback is that these plants become top-heavy. The solution to this problem is staking. The drawings opposite show both how to cultivate superblooms and the best way to shore them up with stakes.

The key is to put the stakes in the ground at the same time the planting is done. This way there is no danger of spearing and mutilating the dahlias' tuberous roots, as there would be if the stakes were shoved into the ground later on, when the plants have already sent up their swiftly growing stems. And of course the stakes are in place when the plants need them. The least conspicuous stakes are those of green-painted bamboo. The least abrasive material to use for tying is soft twine or raffia. This sort of staking is needed not only for dahlias, but also for lilies, gladioli and other tall plants.

For those that, like dahlias, are tender, the planting should be done in the spring, when the danger of frost is past, so the plants and their blossoms have a long season to grow. Ideally the soil should be a rich, well-drained loam and the location a sunny one protected from harsh winds.

Making the growing plants produce extra-large blooms requires only some simple pruning of side branches and their flower buds, then the extra buds on the main stem. Once these have been removed, the plant can put all its growing energy into the remaining two or three buds—which will open to form the desired spectacular flowers. To be sure of healthy growth through the season, keep the soil around the dahlias moist, and apply a balanced fertilizer a couple of times a season.

A giant salmon-colored blossom with a touch of yellow in the center tops the stem of a hybrid dahlia. Similar large blooms are produced by selective pinching of the taller dahlias.

1 To stake a tall-growing dahlia safely at planting time, push one end of a 3-foot length of bamboo into the bottom of the planting hole, right next to the tuberous roots. The holes for large dahlias should be about 10 inches deep. When the roots and the stake are both in place, fill in the hole with good soft loam.

2 When flower buds form, pinch them off from the sides of the main stem *(above).* Leave only two or three buds at the top of the main stem, which will then benefit from a large measure of the plant's sugars and other stored nutrients.

3 When the main stem has grown 1½ feet high, begin tying it to the stake with string or raffia. Knot the ties firmly around the stake, but leave a loose loop around the stem, so as not to bruise or strangle it. Continue tying at intervals as the stem reaches its full height and the blossoms mature. □

. . . AND SMALLER ONES IN PROFUSION

Another technique produces the opposite effect on dahlias. If you want bushier plants with lots of blossoms rather than a few big ones, pinch off the terminal foliage buds, but leave the flower buds alone. This will encourage more branches to grow, and the result will be a lower, wider-spreading plant. All branches will send forth flowers, making the dahlia a bower of small blooms. This method works especially well with dwarf dahlias, which are naturally low-growing.

A SIMPLE REGIME TO MAKE BULBS FLOURISH

Once put in the ground, most bulbs will remain there year after year, sending up new stalks and foliage and flowers each spring with impressive energy. The trick is to make sure they stay healthy and strong. And they will, provided they are given the simple sorts of regular, seasonal care illustrated on the opposite page. Bulbs are perennials, programmed to grow and bloom lavishly for many seasons. They just need some encouragement to do it right.

One vital task is deadheading, that is, pinching off faded blooms before they produce seeds. The making of seeds costs plants considerable energy, which can better be channeled into the bulbs themselves. Foliage, though, should be left intact until it has faded and dried; through photosynthesis, the leaves manufacture the sugars and other nutrients the bulbs require. To hide unsightly yellowing foliage, design the garden so that other, later-leafing plants grow up to hide it.

Bulbs need water, of course—a good amount when the flower buds appear, then regular supplements during rainless periods. Many bulbs need extra watering in the fall, to send them into the winter with a reserve of moisture in their tissues. A few, however, should remain dry through winter dormancy; check the dictionary in this volume to see which ones need late-season watering and which don't.

The next requirement is fertilizer. Apply it when the bulbs are first planted, when the first shoots begin to emerge in the spring, and every succeeding spring and fall.

Finally, bulbs should be covered with a blanket of mulch year round, as insulation against winter cold and summer heat. Mulch also conserves moisture in the soil and prevents the growth of weeds.

Plantings of low-growing violets and vinca provide a handsome setting for a clutch of vivid orange-red tulips. Later, when the spent tulip blossoms have been pinched off and the mottled green foliage has begun to dry up, the violets will act as camouflage, hiding the unsightly yellowing leaves.

DEADHEADING

To conserve energy needed by a bulb while it is blooming, pinch off flower heads as they wither and before they produce seeds. Do not, however, remove the flower stalk; as long as it remains green, the stalk, like the foliage, manufactures food the bulb needs for its future growth.

FERTILIZING

In fall, after the stalks and foliage have died, break them off and discard them. Place markers so you will later know where there are bulbs underground. Then hand-sprinkle some 10-10-10 granular fertilizer on the soil *(right);* and fertilize again in spring as new greenery appears.

WATERING

Water your bulbs well after fertilizing them—the moisture will carry the nutrients to the bulbs' roots. For small areas, you can use a hose nozzle as shown at left; for large areas, employ a soaker hose that oozes water into the ground. Long slow soakings are better than frequent sprinklings, which encourage diseases and shallow rooting.

MULCHING

Spread a 3- to 4-inch layer of mulch over the area where your bulbs are planted *(right)* to keep soil temperatures stable through the winter. Organic mulches such as compost and shredded bark are best; they add nutrients to the soil as they decompose. The layer of mulch should be renewed in the spring, to keep the soil cool and hold in moisture. □

2

INDOOR DELIGHTS

For avid gardeners who suffer through the long winter months deprived of a chief source of pleasure, bulbs can be a godsend. With a little tender care they can be encouraged to speed up their normal cycle of growth and bloom indoors long before nature intended. The technique is called forcing, and its result is the now-familiar sight of a bowl of paperwhite narcissus or a giant amaryllis in flower among the Christmas greenery.

Not all bulbs respond equally well to forcing, and for those that do, the forcing procedure has different requirements. Some bulbs, after being potted, need a mandatory chilling period of anywhere from six to 15 weeks at temperatures barely above freezing. Others need eight to 12 weeks at 50° to 60° F. The differences are dictated by the bulbs' places of origin; those that were originally tropical plants need shorter and less chilly periods of dormancy. In addition, while some forced bulbs require a facsimile of garden soil, others, such as paperwhites, tulips and hyacinths, are so self-reliant that they will bloom in a dish of moistened pebbles, taking all their nutrients from their own reserves of stored food.

The fascinating procedures involved in forcing are explained on the following pages. Included are instructions for chilling the potted bulbs in an outdoor trench when, as generally happens, the family refrigerator is not large enough to accommodate both potted plants and foods. There are also instructions for getting more than a single year of pleasure from an amaryllis bulb, and suggestions for using forced bulbs as cut flowers. Perhaps most helpful of all, there is a chart, on pages 48-49, showing the forcing times and special handling required for 29 different kinds of bulbs.

FORCING SPRING BULBS TO BLOOM IN WINTER

Bulbs can be a cornucopia of color for your home, brightening winter days with a display of spring blossoms. You can force them to flower out of season indoors by exposing them to a speeded-up version of their normal growth cycle. Among the hardy spring-blossoming bulbs that respond well to forcing are tulips, daffodils, crocuses and hyacinths.

The bulbs of these flowers need to experience a dormant season of cold (but not freezing) temperatures before they are ready to bloom. The easiest way to satisfy this requirement is to store them in a refrigerator.

Most suppliers ship bulbs to arrive for fall planting, usually in late September or early October. To ensure a good selection and to allow ample forcing time for winter blossoming, order early. And look for cultivars that are especially recommended for forcing.

As soon as the bulbs arrive, plant them in a container of potting mix. Don't combine different cultivars in the same container; they may bloom at different times, adulterating the effect you are trying to achieve.

Before refrigerating the container of bulbs, check the temperature. The ideal is 40° F, but anything between 35° and 48° is satisfactory. Depending on the variety, bulbs require from 12 to 14 weeks of chilling.

Some ripening fruits give off an odorless gas called ethylene, which causes tulip bulbs to grow in contorted, twisted shapes and to produce discolored flowers. Apples are the worst culprits, so never put apples and tulip bulbs in the same refrigerator.

Forcing produces beautiful flowers, but it weakens bulbs. Enjoy their burst of midwinter color, then discard them—and start planning what you will order for next year's display.

After three months of chilling on cellar steps, these tulips are ready to be brought in out of the cold for forcing into bloom. The shoots are pale because they have not yet been exposed to sunlight.

1 Prepare a potting mix of 3 parts peat, 1 part vermiculite and 1 part perlite. Mix in a tablespoon of 10-10-10 fertilizer. Cover the bottom of a shallow container with the mixture to a depth of 2 to 3 inches. Water to moisten.

2 Insert each tulip bulb in the soil with its pointed end up and its flattened side *(inset)* against the wall of the pot. The first leaves will emerge from the flattened sides and will grow over the edge of the pot.

3 Add more potting mix until just the tips of the bulbs are visible *(left)*. Tamp the soil down. Water with a weak fungicide solution. Sufficient water in the soil not only stimulates growth but helps conduct the cool temperature of the refrigerator to the bulbs.

4 Place the potted bulbs in the refrigerator or some other dark place with temperatures between 35° and 48° F. Chill them for at least 12 weeks; then check for growth. If roots have developed and are protruding through the drainage holes, or if the bulbs are sending up shoots, remove them from the refrigerator and place them in a bright, warm location to encourage the growth of foliage and buds. When the tulips bloom, you can prolong the display by returning the container to the refrigerator each night; the warmer they are kept, the faster they will finish flowering. □

A TRENCH FOR OUTDOOR CHILLING

One good way to force potted bulbs into early bloom—especially when you have a large number of bulbs that would be a nuisance to store indoors in a refrigerator or a cellar—is to expose them to winter's chill in a covered outdoor trench.

The challenge is to get your bulbs cold —but not too cold. Any temperature lower than 32° F can kill bulbs. The answer is to chill them in an outdoor trench that is dug below the frost line—that is, 6 to 12 inches deep, depending on the area in which you live. To ensure adequate drainage, site the trench on a slight slope. If the weather is very dry, water occasionally; moisture in the soil stimulates root growth. But don't overwater; constant dampness can cause bulbs to rot.

Not all bulbs are ready to flower at the same time. By taking advantage of nature's own schedule, you can provide a steady supply of colorful accents for your home all winter long. Before you bury potted bulbs, divide them into groups according to their natural blooming times. Label each pot with the name of the bulb and the date for removal from the trench. Then load the pots into the trench by groups so that you can easily dig out the earliest bloomers first. Draw a rough diagram indicating the location of the various pots; mark a calendar to remind you when to lift each group; and post the diagram and the calendar together in some convenient spot. The bulbs must remain chilled for at least 12 weeks; after that you can bring them in whenever you like.

The bulbs can be planted in any kind of container so long as it has drainage holes. Strawberry jars—cylindrical pots with holes around the sides for plants to grow through *(opposite)*—make attractive containers for unusual displays of several bulbs at once.

A weathered wooden box bursts with sprays of dark pink hyacinths. Such a box can be planted with hardy bulbs, buried in an outdoor trench to keep the bulbs chilled, then dug up and brought indoors when top growth emerges from the soil.

1 Fill a strawberry jar up to the lowermost holes with a potting mix made of 3 parts peat, 1 part vermiculite and 1 part perlite. Place one crocus corm in each hole with the growing tip angled up and slightly outward. Add more potting mix and corms until all holes are filled. Place several corms across the top of the container and cover them with 1 inch of mix. Water well.

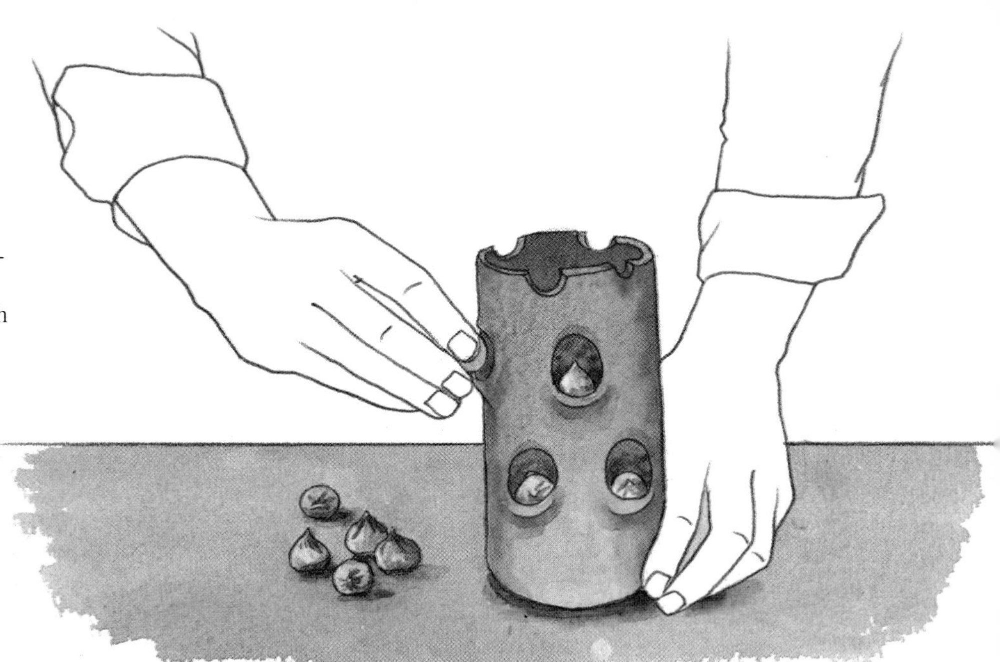

2 With a garden spade, dig a trench *(left)* on a site that has good drainage. Make sure the trench is big enough and deep enough to allow you to bury a number of pots in the ground.

3 Place the containers in the trench and fill in around them with loose soil. Tamp the soil down lightly with your foot. Cover with mulch. In 12 to 15 weeks, move away some of the mulch; if shoots are beginning to emerge in the containers, the crocus corms are ready to lift. Dig up the containers and place them indoors in a bright, warm location. Flowers should appear in three to six weeks. □

ENCOURAGING AN AMARYLLIS TO STAGE REPEATED COMEBACKS

The great popularity of amaryllis bulbs is well earned. These tropical bulbs are easily forced and, with proper care, will provide many years of extravagantly sized and spectacularly colored flowers. Amaryllis bulbs can be purchased from late fall to early spring. Always choose the largest bulbs available; they will not only produce the largest flowers but are most likely to give rise to multiple flower stalks with many blossoms that will open over a three-week period. Good-sized bulbs may be as large as medium grapefruits.

The bulbs should be planted soon after you purchase them. Amaryllis likes a "tight fit," so choose a pot that is only 2 to 4 inches wider than the diameter of the bulb. Make sure the pot drains well.

Bulbs should bloom in four to six weeks. The flowers are short-lived and should be cut off as soon as they fade. When the flower display is completely spent, remove the flower stalk, but continue watering the plant to keep the foliage alive through the spring and summer months. During this period, the plant will store nutrients needed for the next growing season.

Stop watering in late fall to induce dormancy. The foliage will turn yellow and wilt. When the leaves are totally dry and dead, cut them. Then store the bulb, in the same pot and in the same soil, in a dark, cool place at about 50° to 60° F for about eight weeks.

Check the pot periodically. When new growth emerges, replace the top layer of old soil with fresh soil and add a spoonful of 10-10-10 fertilizer. Move the pot to a bright location. To make sure the flower stalk grows straight, rotate the pot regularly so that all sides get equal amounts of sun.

An amaryllis bulb can remain in the same pot through several growth cycles. There is no need to transfer it to a larger container until the bulb begins to press against the wall of the pot.

Four brilliant red amaryllis blossoms bloom in a terra-cotta pot that is hardly bigger than the bulb. With proper care, such a bulb will generate flowers year after year.

1 Before potting an amaryllis bulb for forcing, use sharp scissors to snip off all dead or unhealthy roots *(right);* these will look dry and brown. Be careful not to damage any living roots, which are lighter in color and have a moist, swollen appearance.

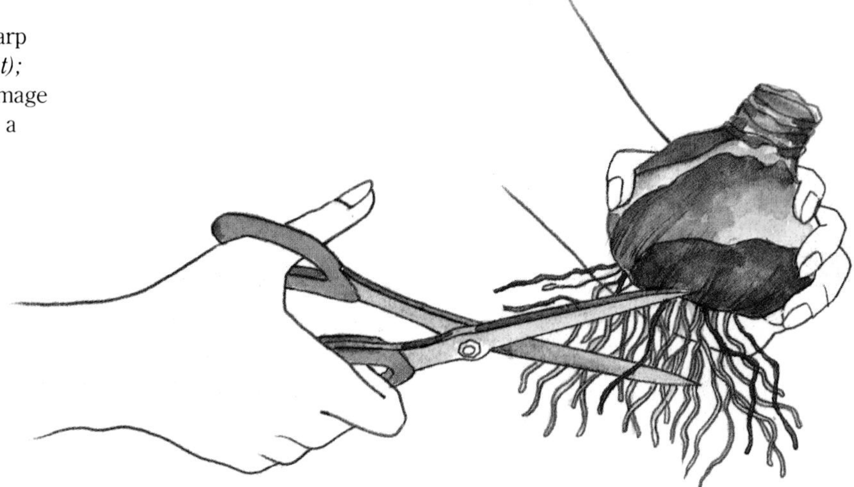

2 Half-fill a pot with potting mix (3 parts peat, 1 part vermiculite, 1 part perlite) to which you have added a tablespoon of 10-10-10 fertilizer. Set the bulb on top of the soil. Fill in around the bulb with more potting mix for support, but leave about half of the bulb exposed. The tip should rise above the rim of the pot *(left).*

3 Water well. Place the pot in a warm, bright location. Flowers will appear within four to six weeks. As they fade, cut them off. When the flowers cease to bloom, cut off the flower stalk where it emerges from the bulb. Water as before until late fall; then allow the plant to dry out. Remove all foliage when it is totally dead. Leave the pot in a cool, dark place until new growth appears next season. □

FRAGRANT PAPERWHITES IN WATER AND PEBBLES

Some early-spring-blooming bulbs store so much food inside them that they can be forced to bloom in a container without any soil; all they need to grow is water—and some pebbles to keep the stems upright. Among them are daffodils, hyacinths and tulips. The daffodil known as the paperwhite narcissus has a further advantage; since it comes from a warm climate, the bulb does not require a long chilling period before it is ready to bloom. It is likely already to be showing new shoots when you buy it.

When forced under proper conditions, paperwhite narcissus will bloom in five to six weeks. If you want to enjoy the flowers during the Christmas season, start the bulbs in the middle of November.

The best containers for forcing paperwhites are bulb pans, leakproof shallow dishes that have no drainage holes. Containers made of clay should be glazed—at least on the inside—to ensure that they will hold water.

Although paperwhites do not need chilling, they grow best at relatively cool temperatures—50° to 60° F. Warmer temperatures stimulate stem growth at the expense of root growth; the elongated stems may flop over later under the weight of their flowers.

After paperwhites bloom, too much warmth will cause the flowers to fade quickly. You can prolong the blooming period by putting the entire container in the refrigerator each night. When all the flowers have faded, discard the bulbs; they can seldom be successfully forced again.

For information on the chilling periods required by other daffodils, hyacinths and tulips, see the chart on pages 48-49. These bulbs are sometimes available prechilled and ready to be forced.

A cluster of paperwhite narcissus bulbs, anchored in pebbles that stand in water, grows in a shallow bowl alongside a pot of wax begonias (to the left) and some geraniums (to the rear). The paperwhite bulbs need no soil; they can be forced to bloom in water in about six weeks' time.

1 On the bottom of a waterproof container, arrange a 2- to 3-inch layer of pebbles. Over the pebbles sprinkle a pinch of horticultural charcoal; the charcoal will absorb any odors from the water the paperwhites grow in.

2 Position the bulbs on top of the pebbles with the growing tips facing up *(right)*. You can space them as close as ½ inch apart; since the bulbs will be discarded after a single growing season, they do not need room to spread.

3 Add more pebbles so that the bulbs are firmly positioned. Pour in water until it just reaches the bottom of the bulbs; bulbs entirely submerged in water are susceptible to rot. Place the container in a cool, dark place for about two weeks. When growth emerges from the bulb tips, move the container to a cool, bright location; flowers should appear in another three to four weeks. For even growth, rotate the container daily to expose all sides of the plants to the sun. Keep the water level constant. □

GROWING BULBS BY THE TRAYFUL FOR EARLY SPRING BOUQUETS

White cottage tulips and red parrot tulips, harvested from forced bulbs before they were fully open, unfold into a glorious display. If the water is changed daily and the flowers are kept cool at night, they may last up to 10 days.

You can't keep cut flowers from fading. But bulbs forced into bloom in indoor flats will provide you with long-lasting bouquets in early spring—if you follow a few simple do's and don'ts.

First, determine whether or not the bulbs you are forcing have been prechilled; if they have not, consult the chart on pages 48-49 to find out how long they need to be chilled before they are planted. Then, take care to harvest the flowers at the proper time. Don't wait until the blooms are fully open; check frequently and start cutting as soon as they show a little color.

There is nothing static about cut flowers; the stems continue to take in water, and anything that interferes with this process shortens their life.

Since stems hold the most water in the early morning or evening, these are the best times of day to harvest them. The moment you cut each flower, plunge it into a pail of tepid water so that the stem is completely submerged.

Air bubbles trapped in stems can block water uptake; to prevent this, recut each stem underwater, then place them all in a fresh pail of water and let them stand until you are ready to arrange the flowers for display.

Fill a container with water and add a commercial floral preservative or a combination of liquid laundry bleach and sugar. The bleach will inhibit the growth of bacteria that can clog the cut ends of the stems, and the sugar will provide food for the flowers.

Flowers grown from bulbs are often displayed in tall glass vases that support and show off their long, slender stems. If you use a shallow container, you'll probably need some kind of "frog"—a wire, ceramic or glass device with holes—to hold up individual stems.

To keep your arrangement looking attractive as long as possible, remove fading flowers and add fresh ones. Change the water often—once a day if possible. And try to keep the ambient temperature on the cool side; flowers fade faster in warm rooms.

1 Fill a flat with 2 to 3 inches of potting mix. Add ¼ cup of 10-10-10 fertilizer and mix well. Set daffodil bulbs in the growing medium, nose side up and 4 inches apart. Cover with more potting mix until just the noses of the bulbs are visible. Water with a fungicide solution. Place the flat in a brightly lit location and keep it moist.

2 When the flowers are just beginning to show some color (don't wait until they are fully open), use scissors or a sharp, clean knife to cut each flower at the base of the stem, where it emerges from the bulb. Immediately after cutting, submerge the stem in a pail of tepid water.

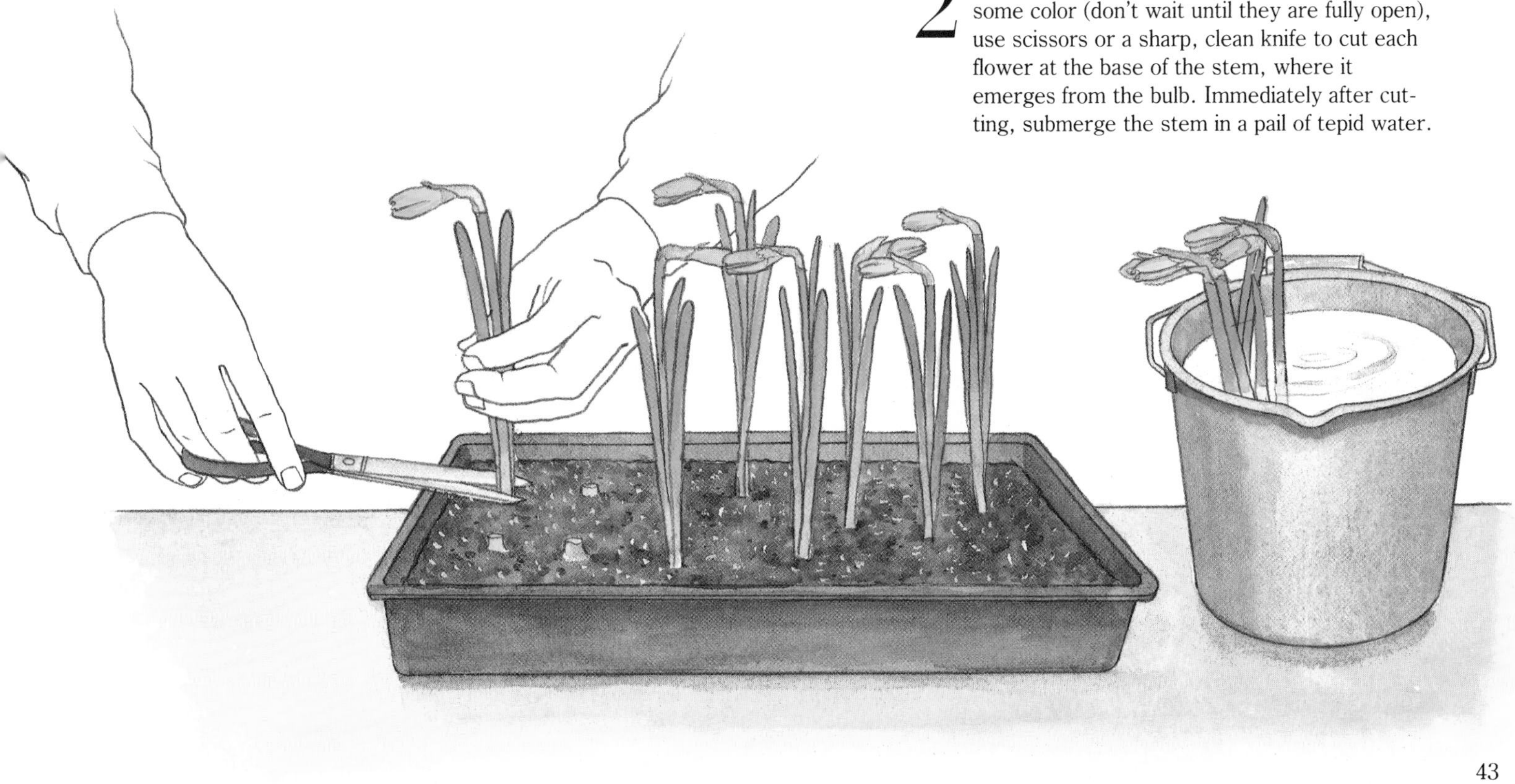

3 After harvesting the flowers, remove the foliage and recut each stem to the desired length underwater; making the second cut underwater ensures that no air bubbles are trapped in the stem. Let the recut stems soak in the pail of water for about three hours. Since daffodil stems discharge a colorless sap that can harm other types of flowers, limit the pail to daffodils only.

4 When you are ready to display the cut flowers, fill a vase or a bowl with fresh water. Stir in ¼ teaspoon of liquid laundry bleach (to inhibit the growth of bacteria) and 1 teaspoon of sugar (to provide food); or add a commercial floral preservative according to instructions on the label. Add the flowers.

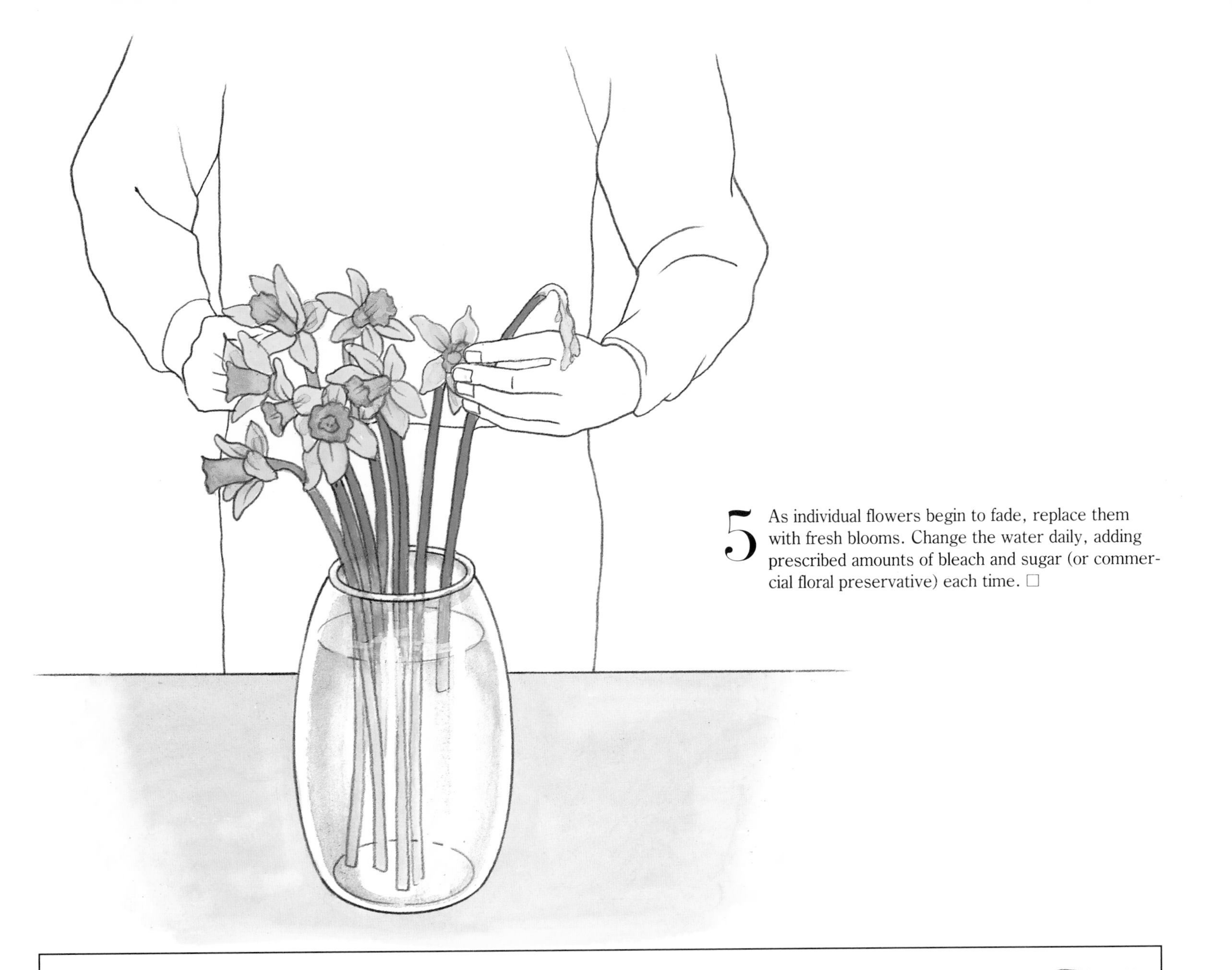

5 As individual flowers begin to fade, replace them with fresh blooms. Change the water daily, adding prescribed amounts of bleach and sugar (or commercial floral preservative) each time. □

CUT FLOWERS THAT REQUIRE EXTRA CARE

The flowers of some bulbs need special attention after they are cut. Daffodil stems exude a slimy substance that is toxic to irises, roses, tulips and a number of other flowers. Fortunately, the substance dissipates completely when the stems are allowed to sit in a pail of water for three hours; after this, daffodils can be safely combined in arrangements with any other flower. The stamens of lilies carry abundant pollen that can rub off on other flowers, causing messy stains; after cutting lily stems, carefully snip off the stamens. Certain cut flowers, including tulips and anemones, continue growing when placed in water; they may have to be repositioned periodically to maintain a balanced formal arrangement.

REST AND REHABILITATION FOR TROPICAL BULBS

Tropical bulbs—those that come from the world's warmest regions—will not survive the cold temperatures that hardy bulbs need to start growing. Yet given the right conditions, bulbs from the tropics make excellent, long-lived houseplants—provided they are allowed to dry out periodically. A long dry period causes them to go dormant; when they emerge from dormancy, they are ready for a vigorous growing season. Unlike most hardy bulbs, which are so weakened by forcing that they usually need to be discarded after a single growing season, tropical bulbs behave more like perennials; they can be reforced successfully year after year.

One of the most popular tropical bulbs for forcing is the caladium tuber, which is raised not for its flowers, which are insignificant, but for its large, many-colored leaves.

To start newly purchased caladium tubers, plant them indoors in a pot with a drainage hole. The green or pinkish points—the buds from which new growth will come—must face up. Strong sunlight and cold drafts can kill growing caladiums; give them a warm, humid environment with bright but indirect sun.

To hasten growth after dormancy, the tubers can be soaked in a solution of gibberellic acid—a substance derived from plant growth hormones. Gibberellic acid is available from camellia societies and orchard supply houses. Other tropical bulbs that respond to treatment with gibberellic acid include calla lilies and elephant's ear.

A potful of several cultivars of caladium show off their brightly colored and patterned leaves. Given proper care, caladium tubers can be forced to grow new foliage year after year with equally beautiful results.

1 To grow caladium tubers as houseplants, start the tubers indoors in late winter or early spring. Half-fill a pot with a mix of 3 parts peat, 1 part vermiculite and 1 part perlite. Lay the tubers on the surface, 3 inches apart, with the growth buds facing up. Cover them with ½ to 1 inch of potting mix. Water them thoroughly. To encourage the tubers to grow, pinch off flowers as they form.

2 In the fall, place the pot of caladiums outdoors until the top growth is killed by frost; this will send the tubers below the soil into dormancy. Once the foliage dies, bring the pot indoors immediately to ensure that the tubers themselves do not freeze.

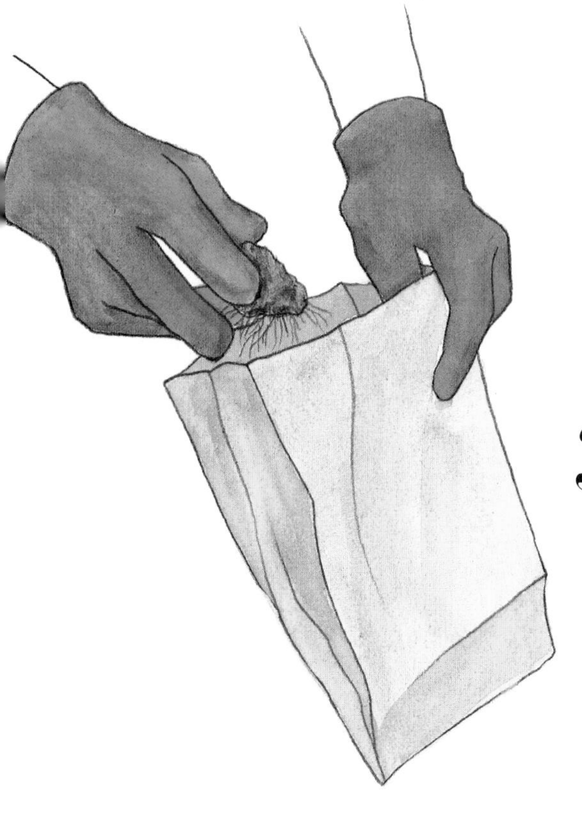

3 Remove the tubers from the pot, rinse them with water, and spread them out on paper or a rack to dry. Wearing gloves to protect your fingers, place 2 to 3 tablespoons of fungicide powder in a paper bag; add the tubers, close the bag and shake it until the tubers are coated with powder.

4 Store the caladium tubers in a flat container filled with dry peat moss. Keep the container in a warm, dark place; ideally, the temperature should remain between 55° and 60° F.

5 After about two months, remove the caladium tubers from the container and soak them overnight (12 hours) in a solution of gibberellic acid—approximately ⅛ teaspoon per gallon of water. Then pot the tubers as in Step 1 to start a new growing season. □

SCHEDULING BULBS TO BLOOM ON DEMAND

Like all growing things, individual bulbs have their idiosyncrasies. Though almost any bulb can be forced to bloom indoors, different bulbs need different environments to produce the best results. For example, all bulbs need to be stored in darkness, but the length of time and the temperature they require while in storage varies from bulb to bulb.

The chart below lists 29 bulb genera and species that are commonly grown indoors and that can generally be counted on to produce showy flowers or foliage with a minimum of maintenance. The chart tells you when and how to give specific bulbs the type of storage and growing environment they need.

BULB	BLOOM SEASON	WHEN TO STORE	HOW TO STORE	WHEN TO GROW	HOW TO GROW
ACHIMENES	Summer	Winter	Potted in dry soil at 50° to 60° F for 8 to 12 weeks	Spring	In bright light at 65° to 75° F
AGAPANTHUS	Summer	Winter	Potted in dry soil at 50° to 60° F for 8 to 12 weeks	Spring	In bright light at 50° to 60° F
AMARYLLIS	Late summer or fall	Winter	Potted in dry soil at 50° to 60° F for 8 to 12 weeks	Spring	In bright light at 65° to 75° F
BEGONIA × TUBERHYBRIDA	Fall	Winter	Boxed in dry peat moss at 50° to 60° F for 8 to 12 weeks	Spring or summer	In limited light at 65° to 75° F
CALADIUM	Summer	Winter	Boxed in dry peat moss at 50° to 60° F for 8 to 12 weeks	Spring	In limited light at 65° to 75° F with high humidity
CANNA × GENERALIS	Summer	Winter	Potted in dry soil at 50° to 60° F for 8 to 12 weeks	Spring	In bright light at 65° to 75° F
CROCUS	Winter or spring	Fall	Potted in moist soil at 35° to 48° F for 15 to 16 weeks	Winter or spring	In bright light at 65° to 75° F
CYCLAMEN PERSICUM	Winter	Late spring or summer	Potted in dry soil at 50° to 60° F for 8 to 12 weeks	Fall	In limited light at 50° to 60° F
EUCHARIS	Summer	Winter	Potted in dry soil at 50° to 60° F for 8 to 12 weeks	Spring	In bright light at 65° to 75° F with high humidity
FREESIA	Winter or spring	Summer	Potted in dry soil at 50° to 60° F for 8 to 12 weeks	Fall	In bright light at 50° to 60° F
FRITILLARIA	Late winter or early spring	Summer	Potted in dry soil at 50° to 60° F for 8 to 12 weeks	Fall	In bright light at 50° to 60° F

BULB	BLOOM SEASON	WHEN TO STORE	HOW TO STORE	WHEN TO GROW	HOW TO GROW
GLORIOSA	Summer or fall	Winter	Potted in dry soil at 50° to 60° F for 8 to 12 weeks	Spring	In bright light at 50° to 60° F
HIPPEASTRUM	Winter or early spring	Late summer or fall	Potted in dry soil at 50° to 60° F for 8 to 12 weeks	Late fall or winter	In bright light at 65° to 75° F
HYACINTHUS	Spring	Fall	Potted in moist soil at 35° to 48° F for 13 to 15 weeks	Winter	In bright light at 65° to 75° F
HYMENOCALLIS	Late spring or summer	Fall or winter	Potted in slightly moist soil at 50° to 60° F for 8 to 12 weeks	Spring	In bright light at 65° to 75° F
IRIS *(danfordiae, histrio, histrioides, reticulata)*	Late winter or spring	Fall	Potted in moist soil at 35° to 48° F for 15 to 16 weeks	Winter	In bright light at 65° to 75° F
IXIA	Spring or early summer	Late summer	Potted in dry soil at 50° to 60° F for 8 to 12 weeks	Winter	In bright light at 50° to 60° F
LILIUM	Late winter or spring	Fall	Potted in moist peat moss at 40° to 45° F for 6 weeks	Winter	In bright light at 65° to 75° F
MUSCARI ARMENIACUM	Late winter or early spring	Fall	Potted in moist soil at 40° to 48° F for 15 to 16 weeks	Winter	In bright light at 65° to 75° F
NARCISSUS (Tazetta species and hybrids)	Late winter or early spring	Do not store		Winter	In bright light at 65° to 75° F
NARCISSUS (all other species)	Late winter or early spring	Fall	Potted in moist soil at 40° to 48° F for 13 to 15 weeks	Winter	In bright light at 65° to 75° F
NERINE	Late summer or early fall	Winter	Potted in dry soil at 50° to 60° F for 8 to 12 weeks	Spring	In bright light at 50° to 60° F; keep soil moist
OXALIS ADENOPHYLLA	Winter	Summer	Boxed in dry peat moss at 50° to 60° F for 8 to 12 weeks	Fall	In bright light at 65° to 75° F
SPARAXIS	Spring or summer	Winter	Potted in dry soil at 50° to 60° F for 8 to 12 weeks	Spring	In bright light at 50° to 60° F
SPREKELIA	Spring	Winter	Potted in dry soil at 50° to 60° F for 8 to 12 weeks	Spring	In bright light at 50° to 60° F
TULIPA (single and double early hybrids)	Late winter or early spring	Fall	Potted in moist soil at 40° to 48° F for 13 to 15 weeks	Winter	In bright light at 65° to 75° F
VALLOTA	Late summer or fall	Winter	Potted in dry soil at 50° to 60° F for 8 to 12 weeks	Spring	In bright light at 50° to 60° F
VELTHEIMIA	Spring	Summer	Potted in slightly moist soil at 50° to 60° F for 8 to 12 weeks	Fall or winter	In bright light at 50° to 60° F
ZANTEDESCHIA	Spring or summer	Late summer	Potted in dry soil at 50° to 60° F for 8 to 12 weeks	Winter	In bright light at 65° to 75° F; keep soil moist

3
INCREASING YOUR COLLECTION

Bulbs, especially exotic hybrids, can be expensive. It is one thing to splurge on a single splendid amaryllis to grace a winter windowsill, but quite another to invest in a host of golden daffodils to nod in an April breeze. One way to bypass the expense is to propagate new plants from existing plants or from purchased seed. Bulbs acquired in this way are not only less costly, but they can duplicate exactly a much-loved flower or, with luck, combine the qualities of two much-loved flowers. And when grown from seed they greatly expand the limited range of choices offered by local nurseries or even by specialists in bulbs.

Probably the most fascinating technique for creating new bulbs is the process of hybridizing, that is, cross-pollinating two related flowers. Admittedly a delicate operation, requiring patience and the instincts of a gambler (there is no guarantee of the desired outcome), hybridizing is likely to appeal only to dedicated bulb fanciers. Less demanding and more predictable are such techniques as starting new plants from stem cuttings, and starting them from the tiny bulblets that form around the base of the parent bulb or, in some species, bulbils at the base of the leaves.

Other methods of propagation, such as scaling, scoring, scooping and sectioning, are operations performed on the bulbs themselves. In scaling, used for bulbs that look somewhat like artichokes, as many as six outer leaves, or scales, are removed to serve as genetic material for the production of new plants. Scoring, scooping and sectioning, all applicable to bulbs that are shaped like onions, in effect interrupt the bulb's natural development, forcing the bulb to redirect its energies into the creation of new bulbs.

These and other techniques of bulb propagation are explained on the following pages. They are best done when the bulb is at its prime, full of the nutrients it has been collecting all summer long. And gardeners should not expect immediate results. Most young bulbs do not reach flower-bearing age for two or three years.

STARTING FROM SEED FOR ECONOMY AND VARIETY

Not many gardeners grow bulbs from seed, largely because most bulbs take several years to progress from seed to flowering. But some bulbous plants—the tubers, the tuberous roots and the rhizomes such as dahlias *(right),* tuberous begonias and achimenes—are easy to grow from seed and will produce flowers in their first summer.

There are several good reasons to start from seed. One advantage is cost. Seeds are cheaper than bulbs; the bulbs you buy at a garden center all have to be grown by nurserymen before being offered for sale, and the time and effort expended by the nurserymen goes into the final price. A second advantage is variety; nurseries and mail-order houses generally stock a wider range of unusual seeds than they do of unusual tubers, rhizomes and tuberous roots. Specialty plant societies expand the choice, offering seeds of plants that are rare.

The time to start dahlia seeds is in early spring, so that the plants will be ready to flower in summer. They should be started in flats indoors. After seedlings have sprung up, they should be transplanted into individual pots and then, when all danger of frost is past, transplanted into the garden *(pages 54-55).* They will bloom in the summer. In fall (because dahlias are tender) the tuberous roots must be dug up and stored for the winter; they can be replanted outdoors next spring. Hardy bulbous plants can be started from seed and transplanted as seedlings in the same way, but then they can remain in the ground for as many seasons as it takes them to bloom.

Small but already vigorous dahlias, started from seed and then nurtured in small, individual pots, are ready to be transplanted into a prepared bed in a garden.

1 To get a small flat or planting pan ready for seeding, fill it to within ½ inch of the top with vermiculite. Then place the flat (which should have small holes in the bottom) in a larger pan of water to moisten the vermiculite. When the surface looks thoroughly soaked, lift the flat from the pan and let it drain until water ceases to drip through the drainage holes.

2 Make shallow furrows in the vermiculite about an inch apart with the pointed end of a plastic plant label or the tip of a knife. Drop seeds into the furrows, spacing them 1 inch from one another. Cover the seeds with a thin layer of vermiculite.

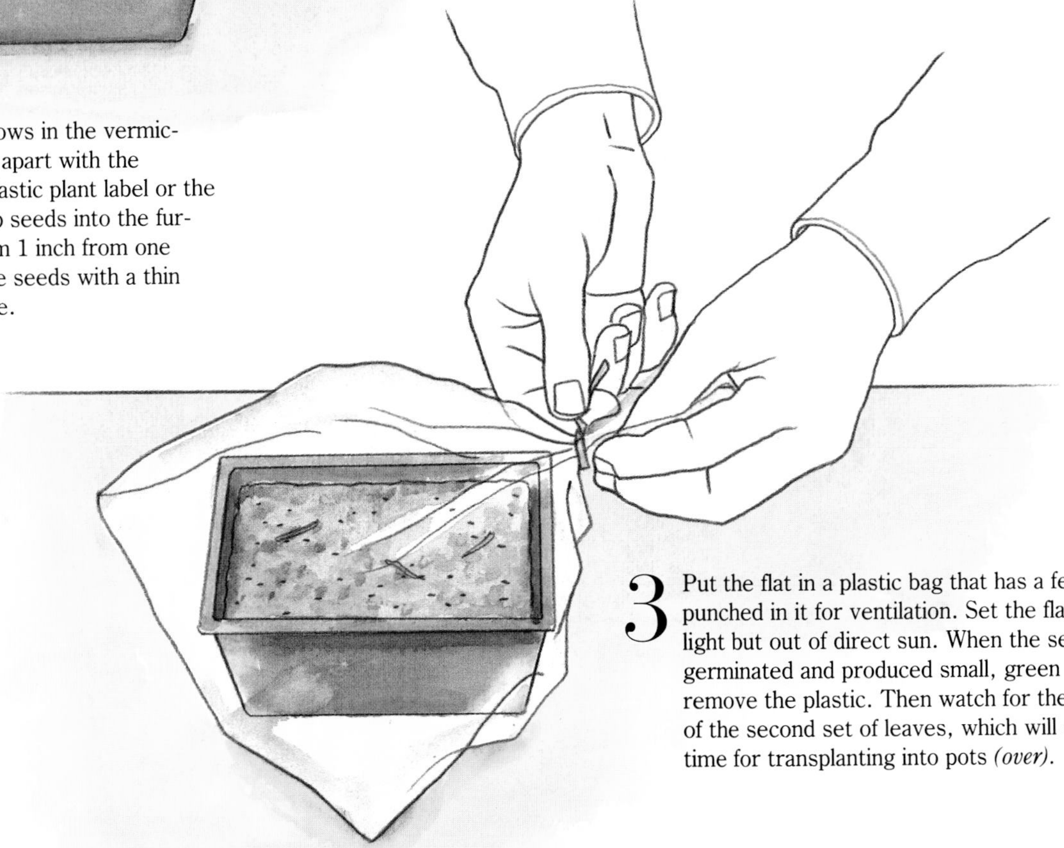

3 Put the flat in a plastic bag that has a few holes punched in it for ventilation. Set the flat in good light but out of direct sun. When the seeds have germinated and produced small, green leaves, remove the plastic. Then watch for the appearance of the second set of leaves, which will signal the time for transplanting into pots *(over)*.

4 Fill a set of small peat pots with a moist mixture of 3 parts peat moss, 1 part perlite and 1 part vermiculite. Punch a hole in the mixture in each peat pot, then transplant the seedlings, lifting each one gently from the flat with a plastic label, as shown, and planting it at the same depth as before. Be careful not to handle the stems, which are fragile.

5 When the seedlings—young dahlias are shown here—have grown 6 inches or so, they can be transplanted into the garden. The outdoor bed should be prepared as shown on pages 10-11. For each seedling, dig a hole deep enough for it to sit at the same depth as it sat in its pot. Fill in around the roots with the soil you dug up, and tamp it down gently with your fingers.

6 In the fall, when the growing season is over, let the first frost kill back the new plants' foliage. This will send the plants into dormancy. Then, with a knife that has been sterilized in a solution of 1 part household bleach to 9 parts water, slice off the dead top growth at the soil line.

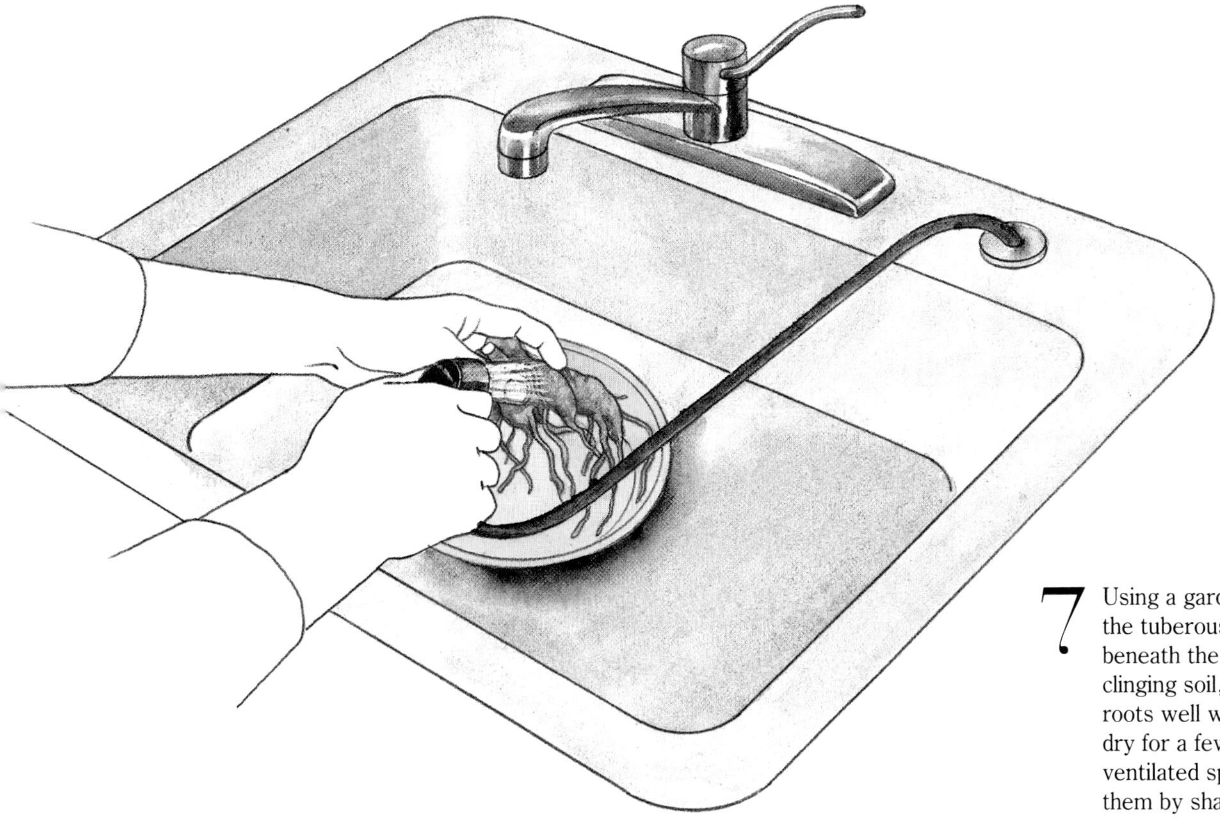

7 Using a garden fork, carefully dig up the tuberous roots that have grown beneath the soil. Shake off most of the clinging soil, then rinse the tuberous roots well with water at a sink. Let them dry for a few days in a shady, well-ventilated spot. Once they are dry, dust them by shaking them in a paper bag containing fungicide powder.

8 Store the tuberous roots over the winter in dry peat moss in a cool, dark area at 55° to 60° F. In the spring, take them from the moss and, if the plants have multiple tuberous roots, separate them with a sterile knife *(right)*. Make sure each new root has at least one growth bud and is firm and healthy; discard any that are mushy or shriveled. Plant the root sections outdoors in a freshly turned bed. □

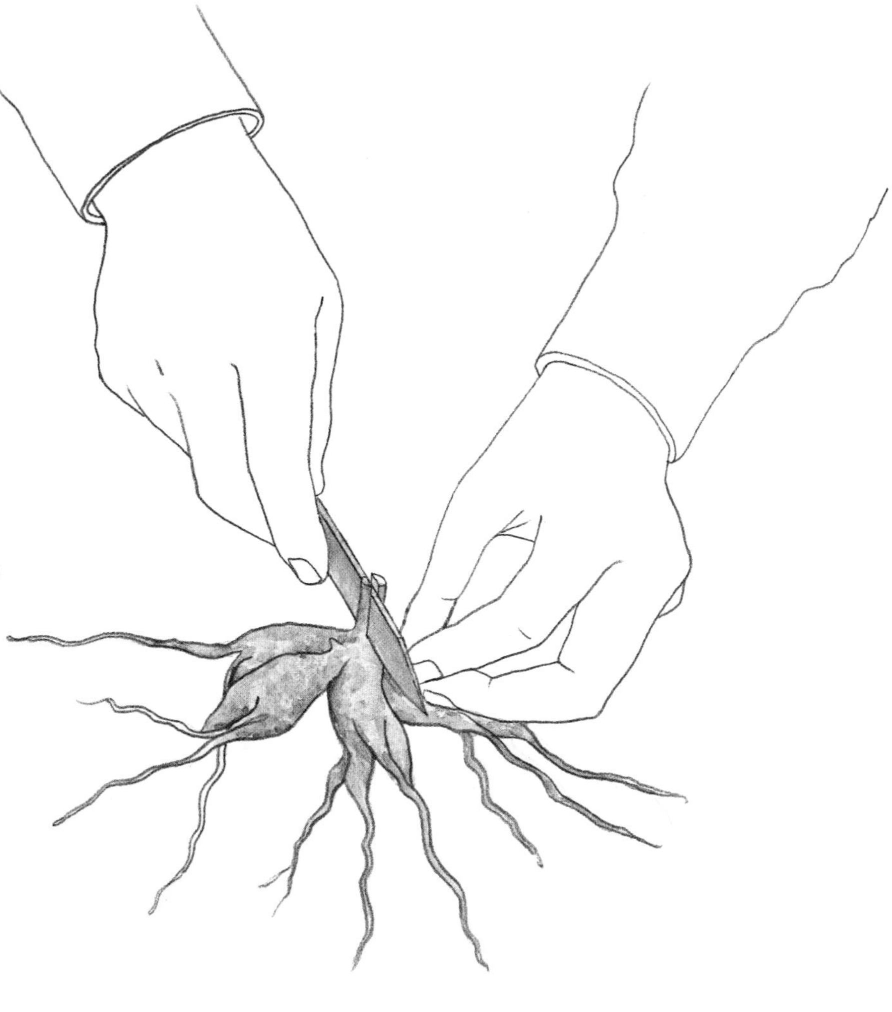

POLLINATING LILIES TO MAKE YOUR OWN HYBRIDS

Most of the bulbs you buy at garden centers or by mail order are hybrids. They have been selectively bred to enhance desirable characteristics, such as bigger and brighter flowers, more luxuriant foliage, or sweeter fragrance. Some plants, like lilies, are relatively easy to hybridize because their sexual parts are large and readily identifiable. With a little knowledge of plant anatomy, you can try your hand at creating your own lily hybrids.

Each lily flower contains a female organ (called a pistil) and several male organs (called stamens). To make a hybrid you must first prevent the plant from pollinating itself; then you transfer pollen from the stamen of one plant (the male parent) to the pistil of another plant (the female parent).

Fertilization takes place when pollen travels down the pistil to the ovary of the female parent. Not every pollination results in fertilization, so it pays to make several attempts at the same time.

When fertilization occurs, seeds develop inside the ovary. The plants that grow from these seeds will show characteristics inherited from both parents, but the exact appearance of the offspring is hard to predict. The fun comes from gambling that nature will produce a new plant that combines the features you like best—say, a certain mix of color, petal shape, perfume and hardiness.

Be sure to keep good records of all your crosses in case you want to repeat or build on a particular success. Always list the female parent first: "Female Plant Name × Male Plant Name—Date."

In the fall, collect seeds from the ripening seedpod before it splits open, and plant the seeds immediately. Don't expect them all to germinate. Those that do may take several years before they flower.

This soft pink Oriental Hybrid lily is ready to act as the male parent in a hybridization. The ripe anthers on the tips of its stamens have split open to reveal the powdery, bright orange pollen.

ANATOMY OF A LILY

The female part (pistil) consists of a tip (the stigma), which receives the pollen, and a tube (the style), which connects to the ovary. Inside the ovary are the ovules, which become seeds after they have been fertilized. There are six male parts (stamens), each consisting of a tip (the anther), where pollen is produced, and a stemlike filament, which holds the anther away from the flower. The petals and sepals protect the inner flower parts and attract insects to aid in pollination.

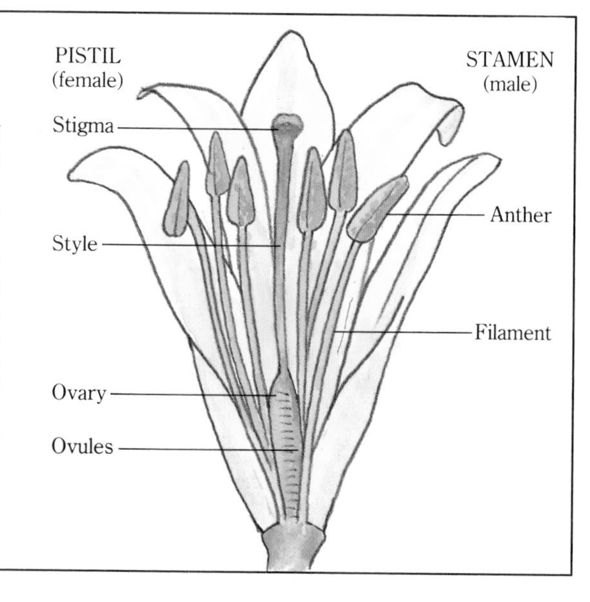

1 For the female parent, choose a bud that is on the verge of opening—one that has begun to show color. Make a careful incision around the middle of the bud with a sharp, sterile knife *(left)*. The blade should cut through the petals but go no deeper.

2 With your fingers, carefully lift off the top half of the petals to expose the interior of the flower *(right)*. You will find all the flower parts—anthers and filaments, stigma and style—standing close together. Gently separate them.

3 Use your fingers or a knife to remove all the anthers. In an unopened flower the anthers will be unripe and so no pollen will be visible, but removing the anthers now will prevent later contamination of the female parts (the stigma and the style). Take care not to damage them.

4 On the plant you have chosen to be the male parent (here colored deep pink), find a flower with anthers that have already split and are beginning to expel their powdery pollen. Pull or cut off a filament with its anther *(left)*.

5 Holding the filament between your fingers, brush the anther across the stigma of the female parent (here colored yellow). The pollen from the anther will adhere to the stigma's sticky surface.

6 Label a glassine envelope with the names of the parent plants (female first) and include the date. Carefully cover the pollinated flower with the envelope and secure it loosely with a twist tie *(left)*; this will prevent contamination of the flower by wind- or insect-borne pollen from other plants.

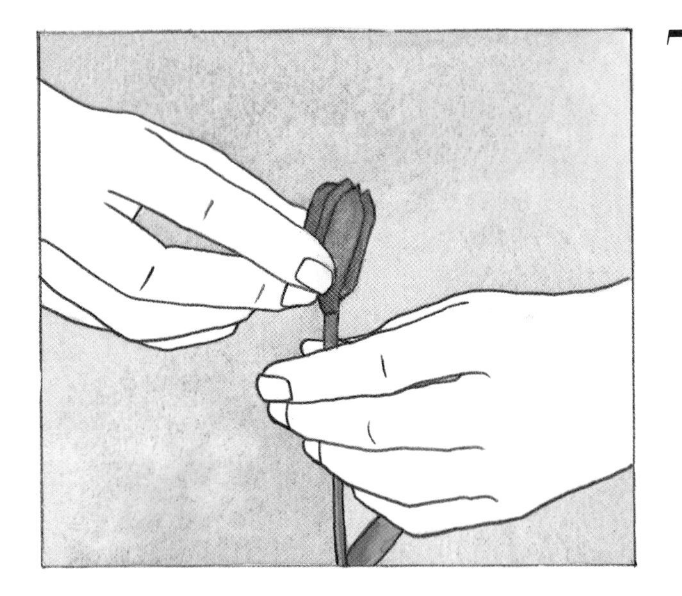

7 In late summer, after the petals have opened and fallen off, remove the glassine envelope. If fertilization has been successful, you will see a large seedpod. Check its appearance daily. When the seedpod begins to turn brown (but before it splits open), snap it off where it joins the stem *(left)*.

8 Cut open the seedpod lengthwise along a seam and shake out the seeds. Spread them on a paper towel to dry. Sow them in a well-prepared bed *(pages 10-11)* in a protected part of the garden. Seeds sown in the fall will germinate the following spring. □

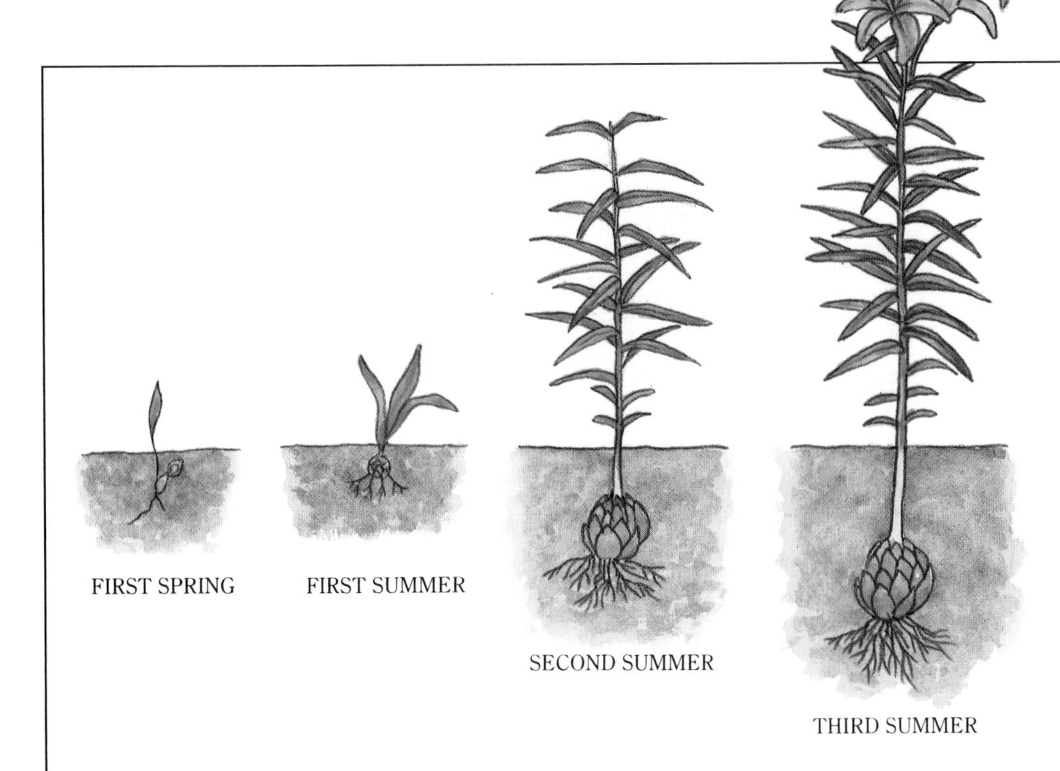

HOW THE LILY GROWS

A lily grown from seed will take two or three years to reach flowering size. After the seed germinates, a tiny bulb forms. In the first spring, this bulb will send up a single tiny leaf; in the first summer more leaves will appear. In the second summer, the plant may be four or five times higher and will have a central stem with many leaves issuing from it, but will produce no flowers. Only in the third summer can flowers be expected. As the bulb grows to full size, its roots will gradually pull it deeper and deeper beneath the soil surface.

PROPAGATING BULBS THAT HAVE STEMS TO SPARE

A bed of tuberous begonias shows near uniformity of flower shape and color—made possible by propagating stem cuttings from a single parent. The bed is edged with lobelia.

Plants seize every possible opportunity to propagate themselves. Under the right conditions, pieces of stems removed from certain bulbous plants will sprout roots and develop into mature plants on their own. Propagation by stem cutting works especially well with plants that have multiple branches and need to undergo a period of dormancy; examples include dahlias, achimenes and tuberous begonias. The plants that grow from the stem cuttings will be exact replicas of their parents.

Cuttings should be made in the late summer or early fall, and raised indoors until the following spring. Be sure to include a growing point on every cutting you make. You can get good results with either a tip cutting, that is, the end of a branch with the terminal growth bud attached, or a medial cutting, a piece from the middle of a branch with one or more lateral growth buds *(box, opposite)*. Look for lateral buds in the leaf axils, where leaves join the stem.

Precautions should be taken to keep stem cuttings from drying out. Each cutting needs at least one pair of leaves to allow the new plant to manufacture food by photosynthesis—but since moisture is readily lost through foliage, remove the lowermost leaves.

To guard against fungus and other infections, always use sterile tools and containers. It's easy to sterilize knives and pots; just dip them in a solution of 1 part household bleach to 9 parts water.

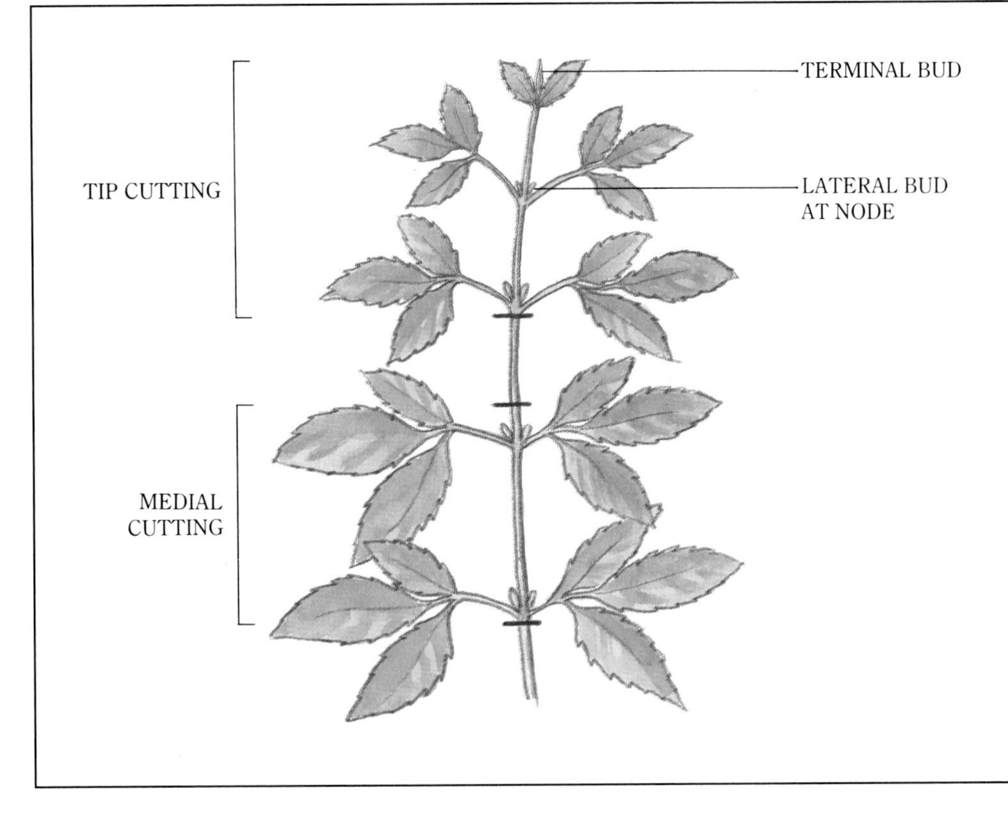

ANATOMY OF A STEM

A growing stem has several distinct parts, as shown on the dahlia at left. At the very tip is a terminal bud, from which new upward growth emerges. Lateral buds, which produce growth from the sides, are found in nodes at the leaf axils, where leaves join the stem. In the illustration, the dark lines across the stem show where cuts should be made for a tip cutting and for a medial cutting. To root, a cutting must have a node at the base (for roots to grow) and either a bud or a node at the top (for new upward growth). The nodeless section of stem between cuttings should be discarded.

1 To prepare a rooting flat for stem cuttings, fill a shallow, sterilized container with several inches of potting mixture that is half peat and half perlite. Moisten the mixture by setting the container in a pan of water. Remove it when the mixture is damp but not soaking wet.

2 With a sharp, sterilized knife, cut off a section of stem 6 to 8 inches long *(above, left)* from a healthy, vigorous plant. Then, holding the cutting gently between your fingers, cut the stem section in half just below a leaf node *(above, right)*.

3 For a tip cutting, take the upper half of the section you have just cut; strip off the lowermost leaves, keeping just a few leaves on top. Then pinch off any flowers or flower buds. The bottom half of the original stem section will be the medial cutting; cut off the nodeless section of stem *(box, page 61)* and remove the lowermost leaves.

4 Sprinkle a small amount of rooting hormone powder on a piece of paper and dip the bottom ends of the cuttings in the powder. Poke holes in the potting mixture with your fingertip. Insert the cuttings in the holes and gently firm the potting mixture around them. Water the flat by spraying with a mister.

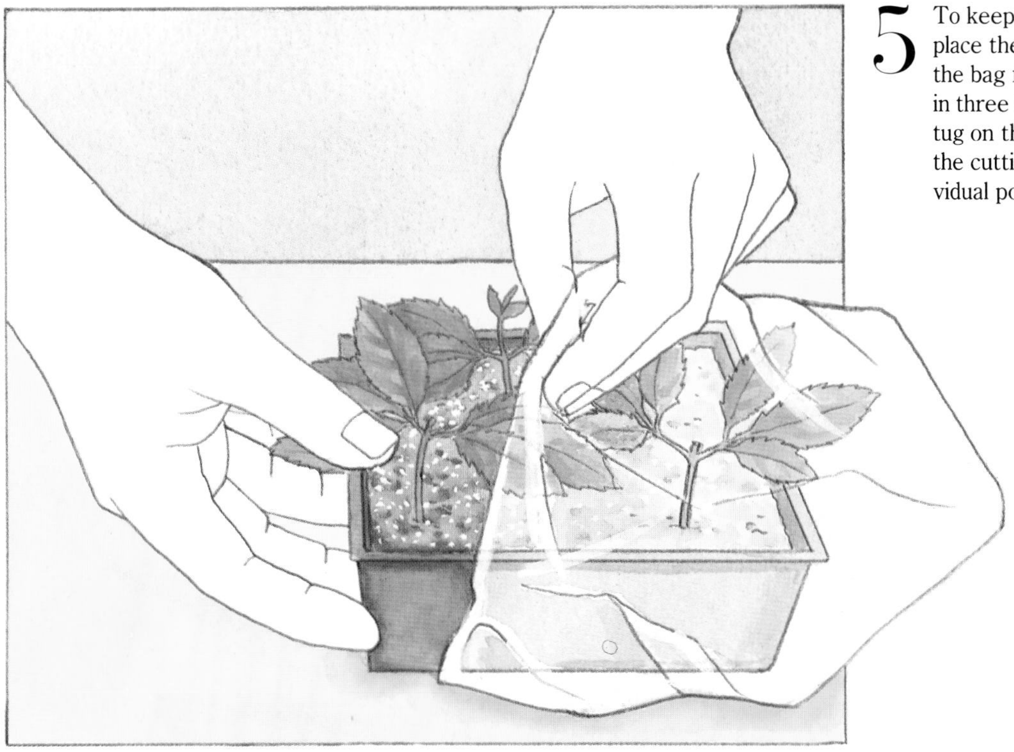

5 To keep the cuttings in a humid atmosphere, place the flat inside a plastic bag. Cut a few slits in the bag for ventilation. Roots should start to form in three to four weeks. To check progress, gently tug on the cuttings; once you feel resistance, the cuttings are ready to be transplanted to individual pots *(page 54)*. □

DIVIDING BULBS FOR NEW PLANTS AND NEW VIGOR

These clumps of autumn crocus will be ready for division as soon as their pink flowers fade. In general, fall-blooming bulbs like these are divided after they have flowered; spring bloomers are divided after their foliage dies.

Division is a form of multiplication in the plant kingdom. When you divide a plant, you separate it into two or more sections so that each section is capable of independent growth. Division not only produces new plants; it rejuvenates old plants and prompts them to flower more abundantly. Most bulbous plants need division every three or four years; the only exceptions are cultivars that naturalize well without overcrowding (see the Dictionary of Bulbs).

Many bulbous plants divide naturally as the original, or "mother," bulb splits into two or more "daughter" bulbs. In some cases, the daughter bulbs will separate entirely from the mother and mature on their own. But with many cultivars, underground crowding becomes a problem: the daughters fail to mature and the mother bulb has so much trouble competing with its offspring for nutrients that its own capacity to flower is diminished.

To take full advantage of natural division among bulbous plants, dig up an overcrowded clump, separate the bulbs into viable sections and replant the sections where each has room to grow and flower.

The ideal time to divide bulbous plants is after they have entered their dormant period. But since it is difficult to locate bulbs when no foliage is showing, you can do the next best thing: wait until the plants have finished flowering, then dig them up as soon as their top growth dies.

Tender bulbs like dahlias should be stored for the winter undivided, since cut and torn surfaces are likely to rot during storage. They should be divided right before being replanted in spring. Hardy bulbs like daffodils should be replanted immediately after being divided and allowed to winter in the ground.

Whatever the bulb, make sure that each division has some roots and at least one growth bud. The offsets that often appear around mature bulbs can also be separated and planted independently.

1 With a spading fork or a pitchfork, carefully dig up a clump of bulbous plants. Holding the clump in one hand, brush loose soil and stones from the bulbs *(right)* with your fingers. Be careful not to damage the roots.

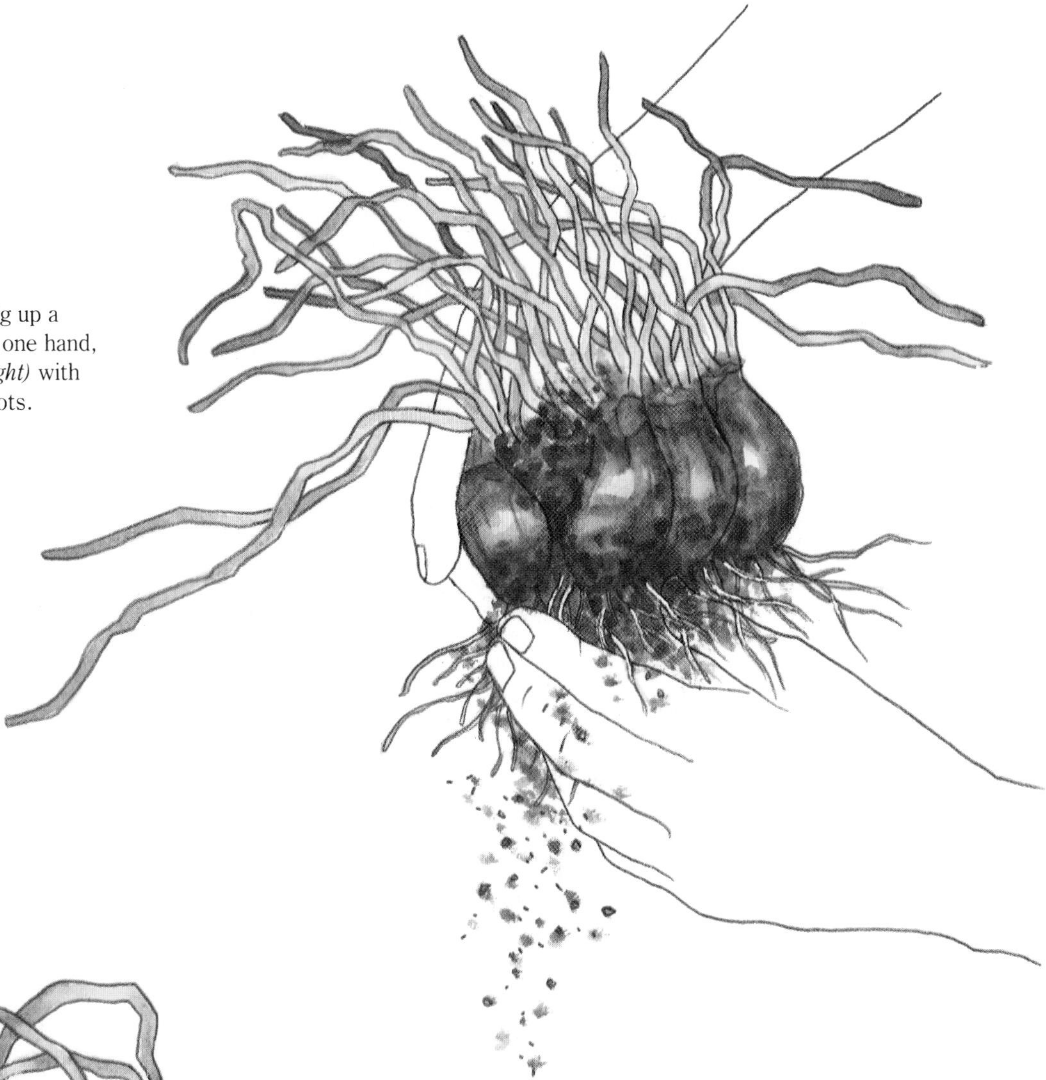

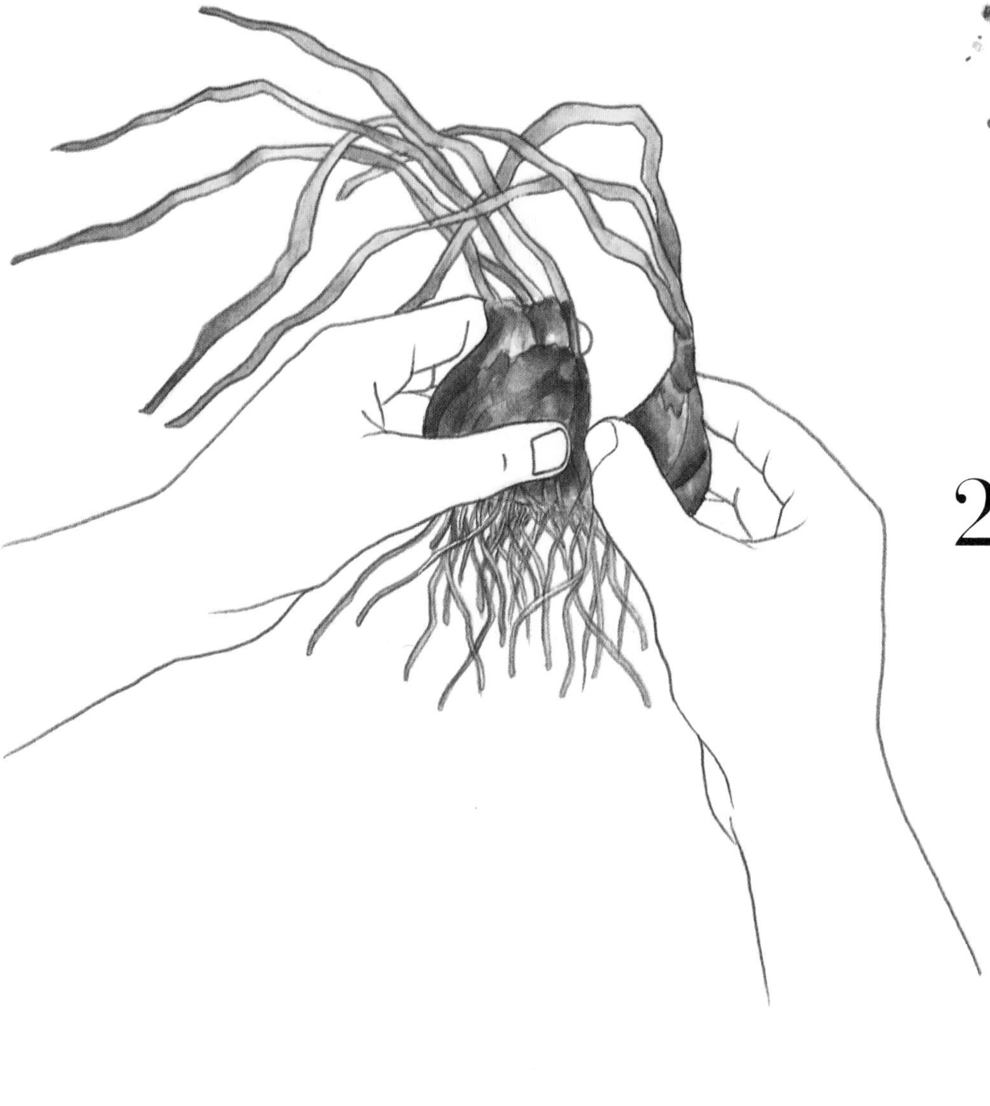

2 Separate the clump into individual bulbs, and pry apart any roots that are tangled. Look for small offset bulbs attached to the mother bulbs. If the offsets can be easily separated, pick them off; otherwise, leave them in place to mature further. Make sure that each new bulb includes a piece of basal plate—the area near the bottom of the bulb where new roots grow. Replant the divisions in new or newly amended and fertilized soil. □

BULBLETS—OFFSPRING OF TRUE BULBS

One of the easiest and most economical ways to increase some bulbs—lilies, fritillaries and ornamental onions among them—is to take advantage of their propensity for generating offspring bulbs. These small bulbs, each of which can be separated from the parent and raised as an independent plant, are of two sorts: bulblets and bulbils. Bulblets appear spontaneously on the sides of the parent bulb or along the underground portion of the stem. Bulbils form in the leaf axils or flower heads *(opposite)*.

You can encourage the formation of bulblets and bulbils by removing flower buds and flowers from a lily plant. Deprived of its flowers and hence of its seeds, the plant is unable to reproduce sexually, and is therefore more likely to turn its energies to asexual reproduction.

If left on the parent, few bulblets or bulbils will survive to develop into mature plants. They should be "harvested" in the late summer or early fall, and planted immediately—to prevent their drying out.

All lily bulbs need a period of chilling before they are ready to grow again. You can give offspring bulbs the necessary chilling by planting them in a raised nursery bed in your garden in a sheltered corner that receives plenty of light. The soil should be rich in organic matter and well turned *(pages 10-11)*. Cover the bulblets to a depth of 2 to 3 inches; as they increase in size, their roots will pull them deeper below the soil surface.

Mulch after planting and water well to keep the soil moist. The plants will take up to three years to mature and reach flowering size.

A clump of majestic fritillaries stands tall in a sunny bed. Fritillaries are among a few bulbs that form small bulblets underground; harvested, planted and carefully nurtured for a few years, the bulblets will give rise to another generation of beautiful flowering plants.

1 To harvest lily bulblets, dig up a mature lily; carefully work a spading fork around the plant until it begins to heave from the soil. Gently remove the soil; look for bulblets on the side of the parent bulb or on the stem between the top of the bulb and the soil surface.

2 With your fingers, carefully pick the bulblets off the stem *(right),* and set them aside. If the bulblets have formed roots of their own, be especially careful not to damage them.

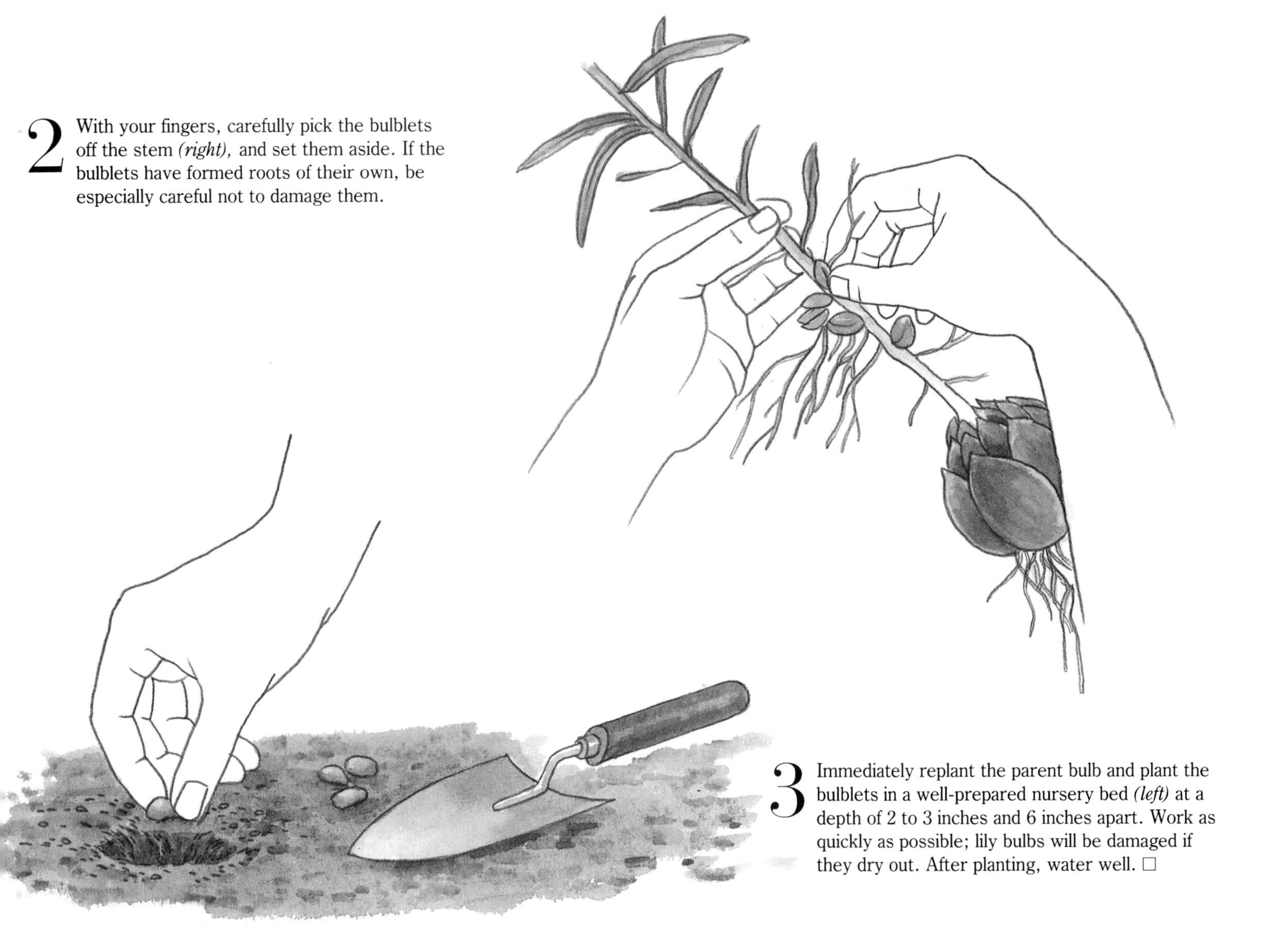

3 Immediately replant the parent bulb and plant the bulblets in a well-prepared nursery bed *(left)* at a depth of 2 to 3 inches and 6 inches apart. Work as quickly as possible; lily bulbs will be damaged if they dry out. After planting, water well. □

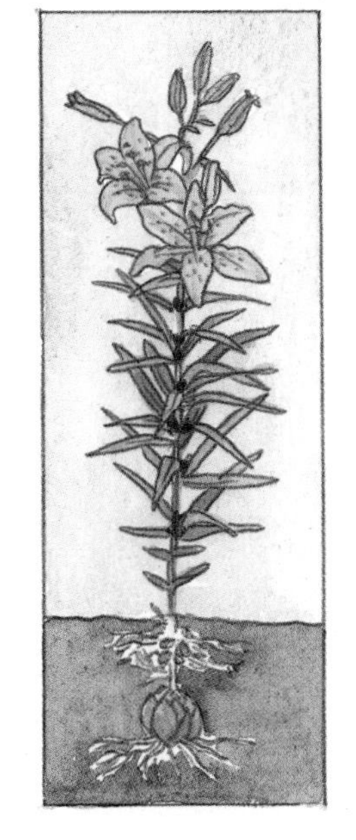

BULBILS: THE LITTLEST BULBS

Even smaller than bulblets are the tiny reproductive structures called bulbils. They form in the leaf axils of tiger lilies and in the flower heads of some ornamental onions. They are typically dark in color (in some cases almost black) and look like tiny beads. Bulbils ripen in late summer or early fall; they are ready to be harvested as soon as you can easily separate them from the parent. After removing them, plant and nurture the bulbils as you would bulblets.

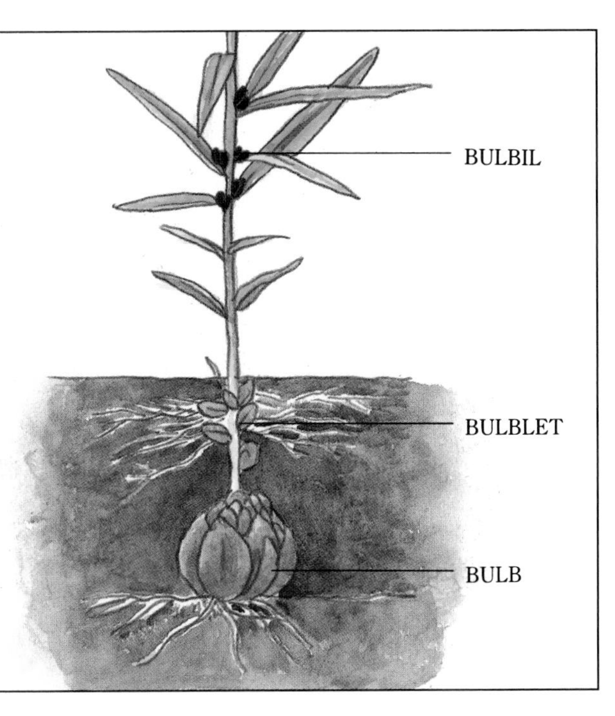

CORMS AND THEIR PROGENY: LITTLE CORMELS

Gladioli, freesias, bugle lilies and some other flowering plants that grow from the fleshy underground stems known as corms *(page 22)* are peculiarly easy to propagate. The corms themselves wither each year, and in the process make new corms to replace the old ones. While engaged in this odd self-reproduction, they also give birth to small offspring called cormels. In nature, most cormels die for lack of space to grow. But if human hands collect and nurture them, they will produce in turn an extra new generation of plants. It usually takes two years for these plants to flower; after that they will be just as colorful and vigorous as those started from full-fledged, nursery-bought corms.

Digging up mature corms and picking off their cormels, shown below and opposite, should be done in the fall, after the growing season is over. Hardy cormels need to be planted right away, like the bulblets described on the previous pages; tender cormels should be stored over the winter and put in the ground the following spring. The best place to do the storing is in an unheated garage or basement or other cool place where the temperature hovers around 50° F.

When spring comes, the cormels should be planted first in the sort of nursery bed described on pages 66-67. After about two years of this pampered existence, when they start to produce flower buds, they will be strong enough for transplanting into a garden bed of well-prepared soil.

The startlingly bright and complex blooms of an unusual cormous plant called montebretia seem to explode amid the plants' bright green, spiky foliage. Montebretia can be propagated easily by separating small cormels from the plants' corms and nurturing these offspring.

1 To start collecting cormels, dig up a cormous plant—here a gladiolus—with a spading fork when the foliage has yellowed in the autumn.

2 Gently work the soil from the new corm with your fingers; the old one will be a withered structure attached to the bottom, and will probably come off with the soil. Locate the tiny cormels clinging to the new corm's base. Carefully pick off the cormels *(right)* and set them aside for the moment.

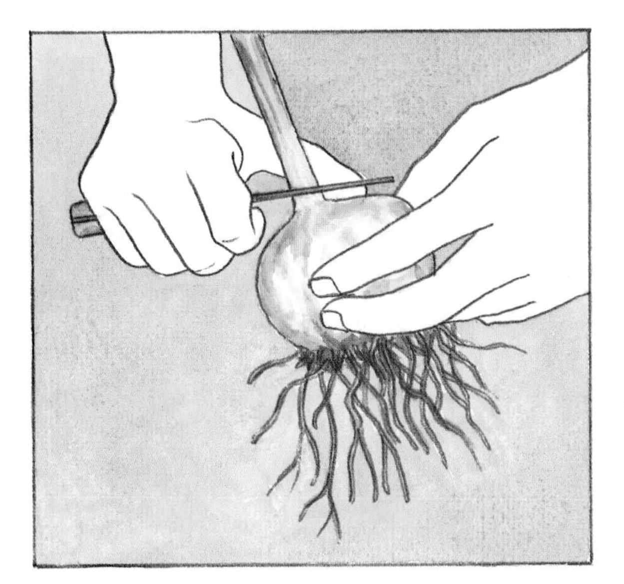

3 Cut off the corm's top growth and discard it. Discard the withered remains of the old corm, and cut the roots off the new one.

4 Rinse the corm and its cormels and let them dry in the air. Give them a dusting of fungicide by shaking them in a bag with some fungicide powder. Then place the corm and the cormels in a fresh paper bag partially filled with dry vermiculite. Store the bag for the winter in a cool, dark place. □

HELPING LILIES MULTIPLY BY STRIPPING THEIR SCALES

Although it sounds like a drastic procedure, "scaling" simply means reproducing a plant by taking apart the bulb and making the parts produce new little bulbs. It works with those plants, notably lilies and the ones called fritillaries, that have bulbs resembling artichokes—compact clusters of plump, pointed, overlapping leaves or scales. It is an easy way to get choice bulbs to produce numerous offspring, and at no cost whatsoever.

Scaling can be done to bulbs newbought from a nursery. Just remove a few outer leaves, breaking them off near the bottom of the bulb and including a bit of the basal plate—the area where roots grow. The newly purchased bulbs can still be planted, and will reproduce normal, full-sized stalks and flowers. Or scaling can be done to established bulbs by digging them from the ground, then plucking off four to six healthy leaves *(below and opposite)*. Again, the parent bulbs, once replanted, will continue to flourish.

The rest of the scaling process is equally uncomplicated. If you place the scales in a flat full of a propagating medium such as vermiculite, they will give birth to new bulbs that, when large enough, can be moved to a protected bed *(pages 66-67)*. Or they can be transplanted to a sunny spot outdoors and insulated with a thick cover of mulch.

The ideal time to begin the process is after the plants have flowered, usually midsummer. The parent bulbs should be full of growing energy then, and their offspring can be planted in their final outdoor beds early enough to become established before winter comes. Scaling's one drawback is that the new bulblets will not be mature enough to produce flowers for three years or so.

Living up to their name, regal lilies dominate a garden plot with their tall stems—up to 5 feet—and their theatrical white blossoms, streaked with purplish red and having yellow centers. These choice bulbs are easy to multiply by the scaling method, a single bulb yielding many small offspring.

1 Begin scaling an established plant by carefully digging its bulb—here a lily—from the ground with a garden fork. Cut off the top growth and discard it. Work the soil from the bulb with your fingers.

2 Remove several of the outer scales, choosing ones that seem thick and healthy. Make sure each one has a piece of its basal plate—the root area, where the new bulblets will grow. As soon as you take off the scales, replant the parent bulb at its former depth —quickly, so it does not dry out. Try to avoid harming the bulb's roots.

3 Rinse the separated scales in tap water, air-dry them on a sheet of newspaper, then shake them in a bag with some fungicide powder. Fill a flat with moist vermiculite. Plant each scale so that it is about half-submerged in the soil, pointed end up and basal plate down. Put the flat in a plastic bag with a couple of holes punched in it for ventilation. Place the covered flat in a bright, warm area about 70° F.

4 After about six weeks, when the scales have turned brown and begun to shrivel, remove the plastic and check to see whether roots have formed by tugging gently on the scales. When resistance signals good root development, gently pull up the scales *(left)* and examine them. New bulblets about ¼ to ½ inch in size should also have formed. If so, remove the bulblets from the scales and plant as shown on pages 66-67. □

SLICING A TUNICATE BULB TO BEGET MANY FROM ONE

Daffodils, tulips, squill and several similar plants can be made to reproduce by a simple process of slicing up their bulbs and planting the pieces, as shown at right. These are the plants whose bulbs are called "tunicate"; they are smooth, neat structures that rather resemble onions. Like onions, they consist of fleshy scales laminated in concentric rings and having a papery outer coating (the tunic). Trying to propagate them by peeling the layers, though, does not work; the scales have no way to root and grow. But slicing the bulbs from top to bottom does work. Planted in vermiculite, the vertical sections will produce tiny new bulblets—providing each section includes part of what is called the basal plate, the gnarled area on the bottom of the bulb where roots form.

The right season to propagate these tunicate bulbs is late summer or early fall—August or September. The bulbs are then dormant but their tissues contain a summer's worth of stored food energy, which helps produce the new bulbs. The only potential difficulty is getting the bulbs dug up efficiently. Most tunicate bulbs are spring bloomers. By fall their foliage has died back and disappeared, leaving little indication where the bulbs are located beneath the soil. So it is important—and this is true for other bulbs as well—to put some markers in the bed when planting, to pinpoint the exact spots for future digging.

When the bulbs have been dug up, they should be sliced with a sharp knife, its blade sterilized in a solution of 1 part bleach to 9 parts water. The entire process, including planting the sliced sections, need take only a minute or two per bulb, a small investment of time to multiply a stock of tulips or daffodils four times over or even more.

Dramatic-looking with their bright blooms and long, leafless stems, a row of belladonna lilies grows profusely by a plain slat fence. These plants, like tulips, grow from tunicate bulbs, which are easily cut up for propagation, but they flourish only in the warmth of climatic zones 9 and 10.

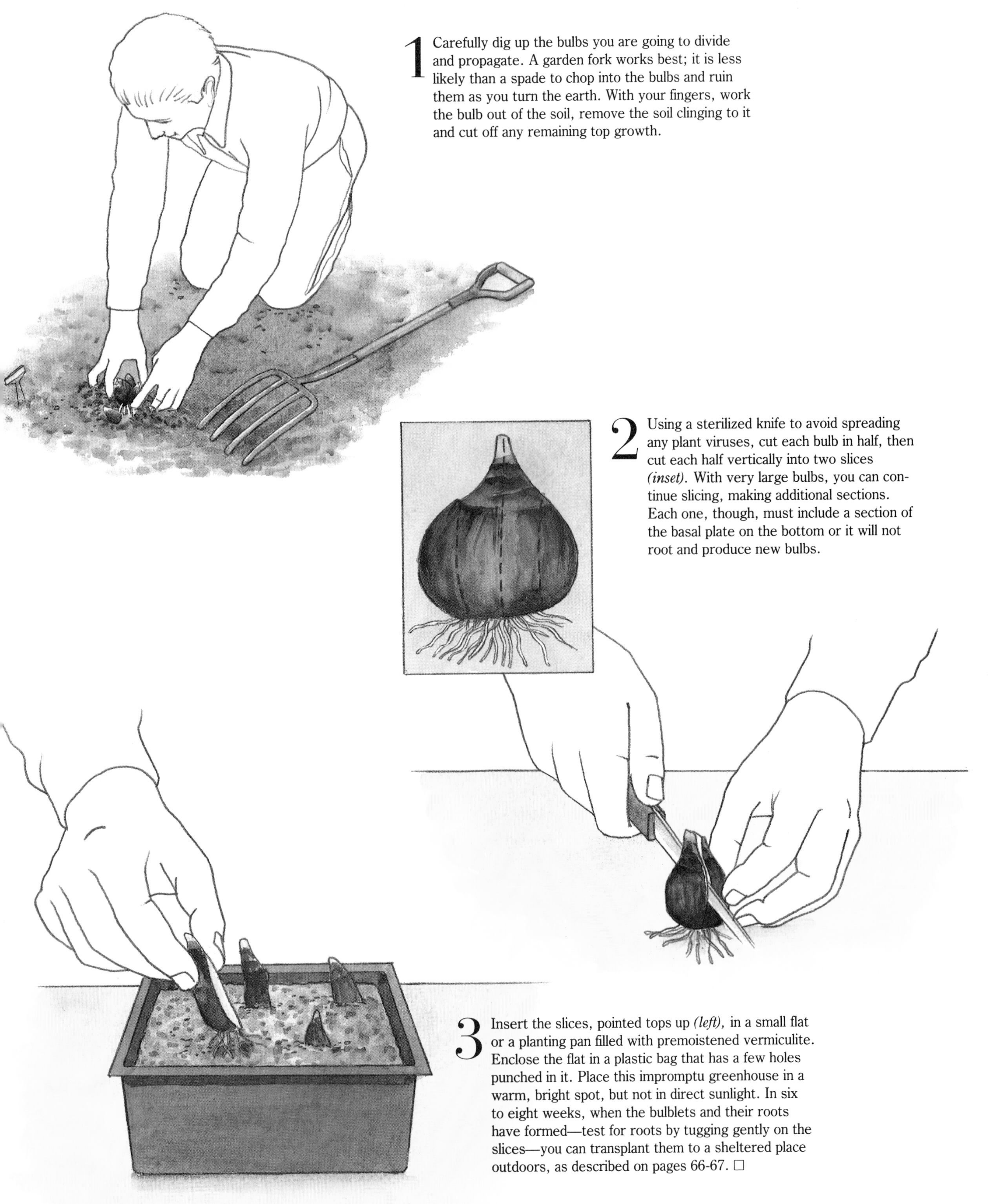

1 Carefully dig up the bulbs you are going to divide and propagate. A garden fork works best; it is less likely than a spade to chop into the bulbs and ruin them as you turn the earth. With your fingers, work the bulb out of the soil, remove the soil clinging to it and cut off any remaining top growth.

2 Using a sterilized knife to avoid spreading any plant viruses, cut each bulb in half, then cut each half vertically into two slices *(inset)*. With very large bulbs, you can continue slicing, making additional sections. Each one, though, must include a section of the basal plate on the bottom or it will not root and produce new bulbs.

3 Insert the slices, pointed tops up *(left)*, in a small flat or a planting pan filled with premoistened vermiculite. Enclose the flat in a plastic bag that has a few holes punched in it. Place this impromptu greenhouse in a warm, bright spot, but not in direct sunlight. In six to eight weeks, when the bulblets and their roots have formed—test for roots by tugging gently on the slices—you can transplant them to a sheltered place outdoors, as described on pages 66-67. □

SCORING AND SCOOPING: TWO MORE WAYS TO PROPAGATE

Two of the choicest of the tunicate, or onionlike, bulbs— colorful, fragrant hyacinths and squill—are best propagated by techniques descriptively known as scoring and scooping. Either method can be used; both involve cutting the bottom portions of large, healthy bulbs with a small, sharp knife *(opposite, top)*. The purpose is to destroy the basal plate's main shoot, or growing point. Oddly, with this gone, the bulbs will engender numerous new bulblets along the exposed interior scales. A single good-sized hyacinth bulb, carefully scooped and then incubated, can produce as many as 60 offspring—which makes this a wonderfully economical way to acquire enough bulbs for a big, glorious, spring-blooming hyacinth bed. The only drawback is that the bulblets need to mature for three years or so before they can produce flowers.

Nursery-bought bulbs can be scored or scooped; in fact, it is a good idea when buying bulbs to set aside two or three for propagation purposes. Or mature bulbs can be dug from the garden in summer when their foliage has died back. After the cutting has been done, the bulbs should be dusted with fungicide and placed in dry vermiculite or other fine planting medium for a few weeks until protective calluses form over the cuts; the medium must be dry, or the callus will not form. Then the bulbs should be incubated further in a planting tray for six to eight weeks in a dark area at about 85° F, and the air should be humid.

After about three months, the bulblets should have formed inside the parent bulbs and be ready for planting in a nursery bed set aside for the purpose. From then on, they can be nurtured in the same fashion as the bulblets discussed on pages 66-67.

Large, snowy hyacinth blossoms, cupped by their own spiky foliage, stand out handsomely against a background of deep green ivy. A dozen or more hyacinths like these can be propagated by either scoring or scooping a single mother bulb, which will produce clusters of new bulblets.

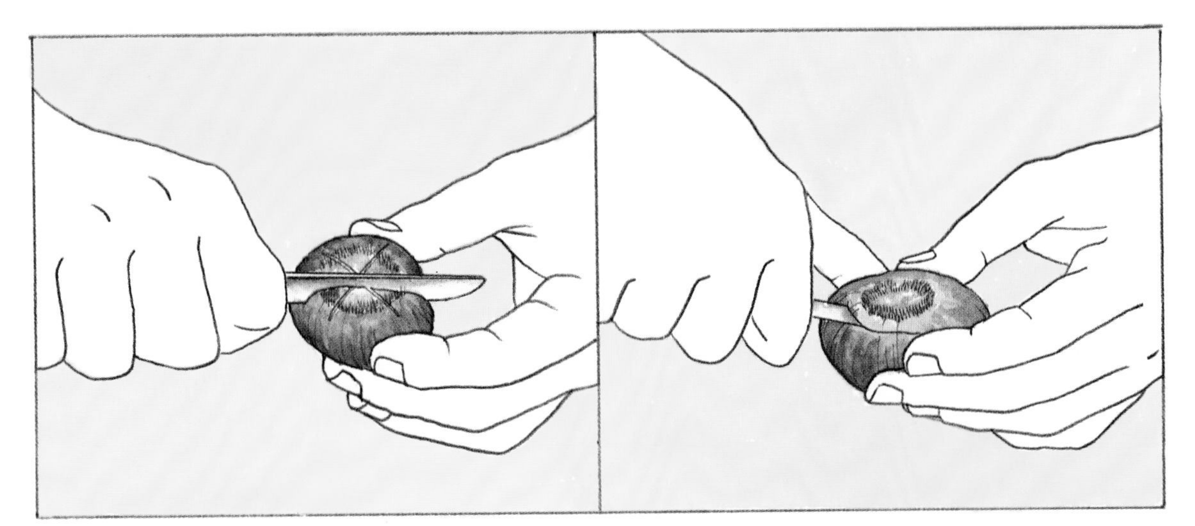

1 To score a hyacinth, make three ½-inch-deep intersecting cuts across the basal plate *(above, left)*. Scooping, which produces more bulblets, entails slicing out the entire plate *(above, right)*.

2 Place the scored or scooped bulb on a rack and keep it at room temperature for a day while it dries and the scored bulb splits open. Wearing gloves, dust the bulb with a fungicide; place it, bottom down, in a tray of dry vermiculite *(left)* and keep it at 65° to 70° F for about two weeks. Then raise the temperature to 85° and provide some humidity by lightly misting the tray.

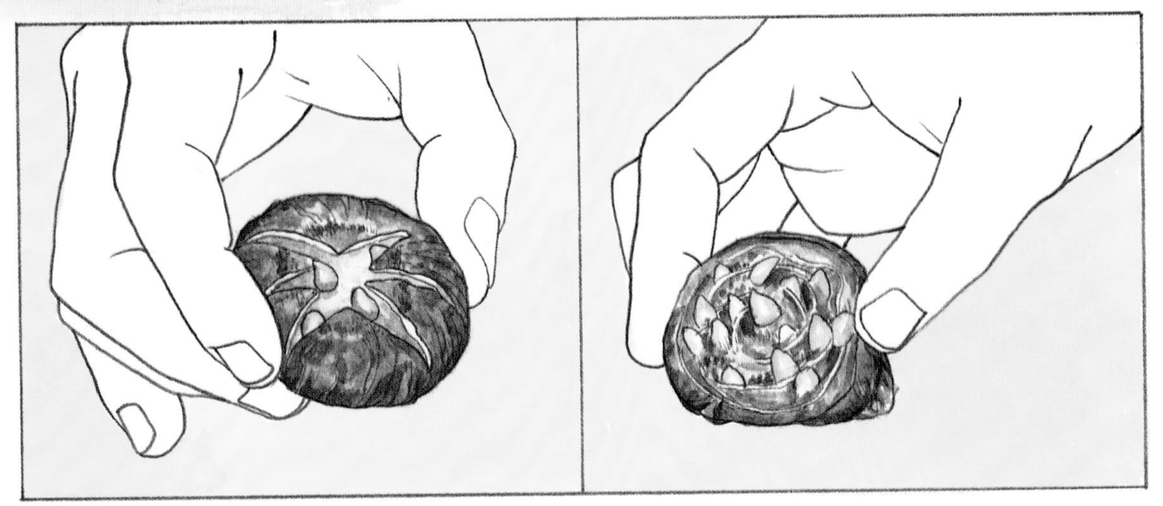

3 In six to eight weeks, examine the parent bulb to see whether bulblets have formed along the scored edges or inside the scooped interior. When the new little bulbs are ¼ to ½ inch in size, pick them off and plant them as described on pages 66-67. □

4

WORKING IN TANDEM WITH NATURE

Partly because they bloom for such a short time, and even more because the vital parts of their structures are underground, bulbs are less vulnerable than most plants to the usual garden pests and diseases. Their worst enemies are likely to be animals, especially those that burrow. Voles and gophers consider many types of bulbs to be great delicacies, but so do chipmunks and squirrels. A subterranean barrier of chicken wire can sometimes protect bulbs from the burrowing animals, but the only way to deal with determined squirrels and chipmunks may be to plant bulbs they find distasteful—daffodils and ornamental onions.

For the other pests and diseases that affect bulbs, there are standard remedies, and these are described on pages 84-85. Also on the following pages are other quick references: a zone map, which is useful for calculating which bulbs will grow in your area, and a monthly checklist of maintenance chores. For bulbs, the most critical of these chores is probably timing the planting.

Finally, a special section on tips and techniques introduces some special tools, gives advice on dealing with the problem of fading foliage, and proposes using bulbs as subjects for rock gardening and hydroponic gardening. Grown in water in a glass vase or a carafe, bulbs—especially the many-blossomed hyacinth—put on a display of root growth that is a short lesson in botany.

THE ZONE MAP AND PLANTING

Bulbs, like all plants, have varied needs and constraints. Some like it hot; some, cold. Some cannot survive low winter temperatures; others must have winter cold in order to bloom the following spring. A successful display of colorful bulbs depends on your selection of the right bulbs for the climate in your area.

The map at right, compiled by the U.S. Department of Agriculture, divides the United States and Canada into 10 climatic zones based on minimum winter temperatures. Zone 1 is the coldest. Zone 10 is the warmest and is usually frost-free. Once you determine the zone you live in, you can consult the Dictionary of Bulbs *(pages 88-137)* to find which bulbs grow best in your area.

The zonal range for each bulb indicates its ideal climate, but a bulb can be grown in a zone beyond the ideal with some help from the gardener. If you live in the zone just below the lowest recommended zone for a particular bulb, you may succeed with the bulb if you plant it in a sheltered location in well-drained soil and protect it during winter with a heavy layer of mulch. If your garden is located in a very cold area, two or more zones below a bulb's recommended range, you can still enjoy the bulb's blossoms with a little extra labor. You can plant the bulb in spring after danger of frost has passed, then dig it up in fall and store it indoors in a cool location over the winter.

If your garden is in a zone that is warmer than the highest recommended zone for a bulb, you can plant the bulb if you supply it with the needed winter chilling period via your refrigerator *(page 87)*. Check with local nurseries or your county agricultural extension service to determine if refrigeration is recommended for a specific bulb in your area.

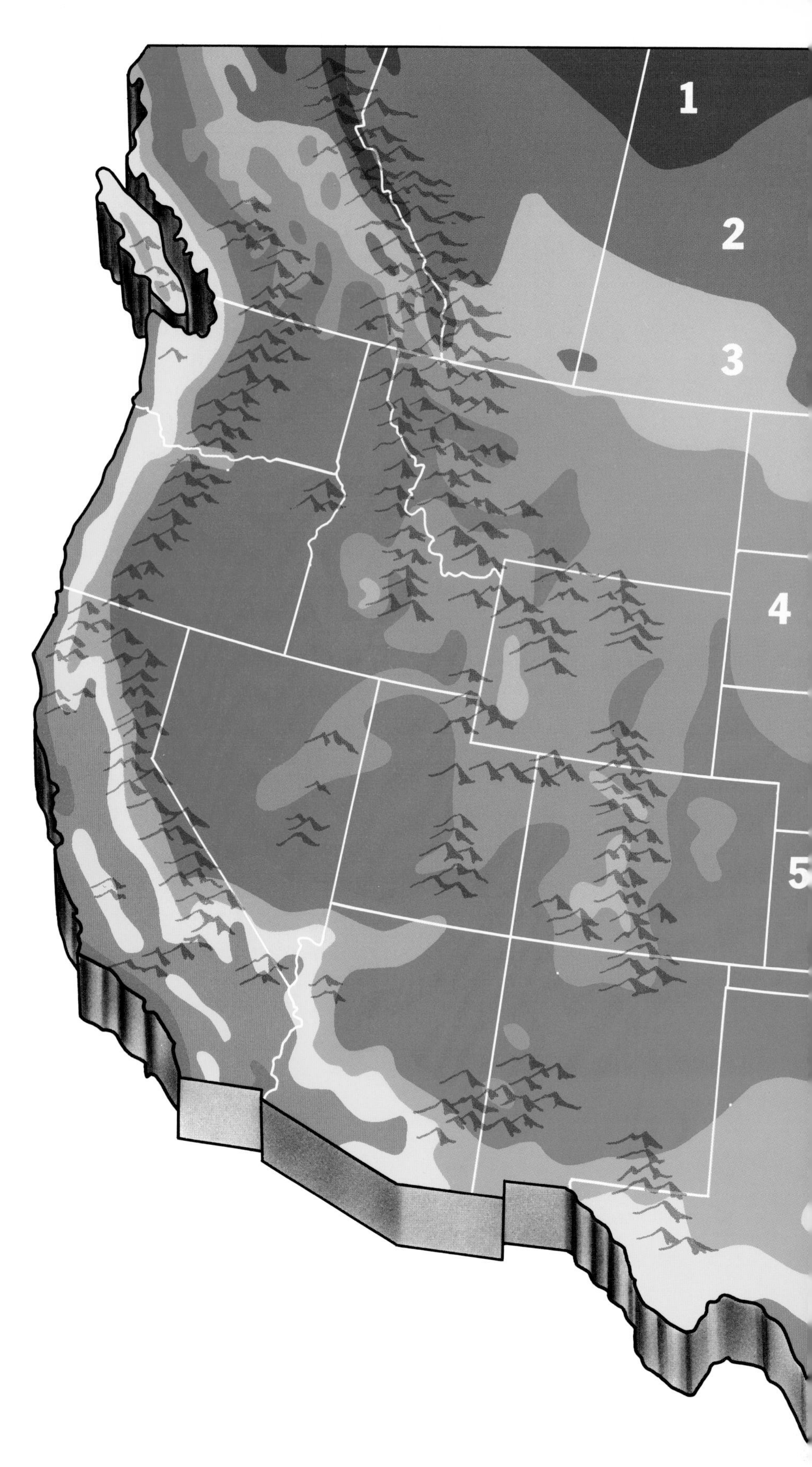

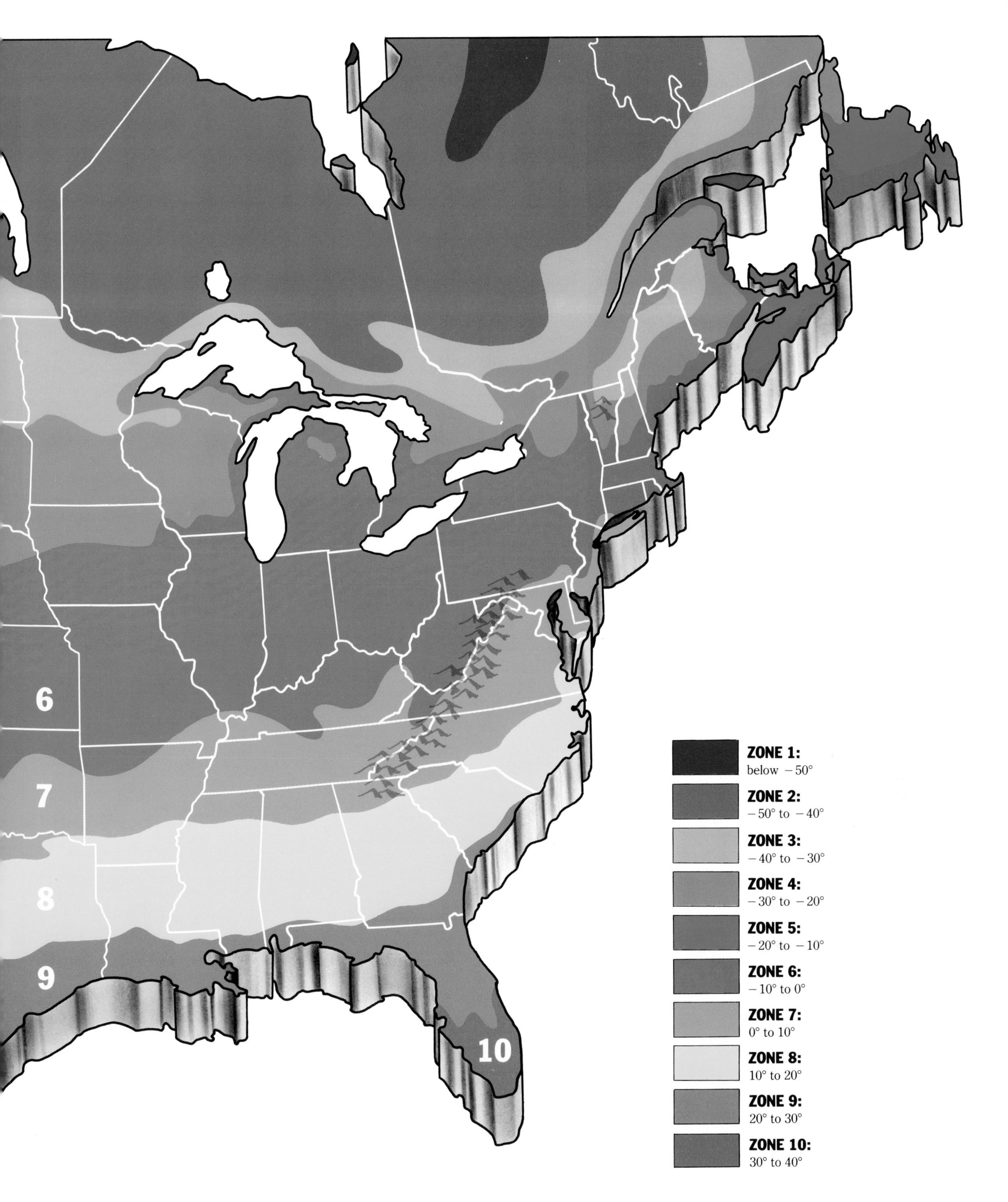
6
7
8
9
10
ZONE 1:
below −50°
ZONE 2:
−50° to −40°
ZONE 3:
−40° to −30°
ZONE 4:
−30° to −20°
ZONE 5:
−20° to −10°
ZONE 6:
−10° to 0°
ZONE 7:
0° to 10°
ZONE 8:
10° to 20°
ZONE 9:
20° to 30°
ZONE 10:
30° to 40°

A CHECKLIST FOR MAINTENANCE MONTH BY MONTH

	ZONE 1	ZONE 2	ZONE 3	ZONE 4	ZONE 5
JANUARY/FEBRUARY	• Check mulch; add if necessary • Order summer-flowering bulbs • Pot tender bulbs for indoor spring bloom • Discontinue chilling hardy bulbs and place them in a well-lit area to force foliage and flowers • Start tuberous begonia seeds indoors	• Check mulch; add if necessary • Order summer-flowering bulbs • Pot tender bulbs for indoor spring bloom • Discontinue chilling hardy bulbs and place them in a well-lit area to force foliage and flowers • Start tuberous begonia seeds indoors	• Check mulch; add if necessary • Order summer-flowering bulbs • Pot tender bulbs for indoor spring bloom • Discontinue chilling hardy bulbs and place them in a well-lit area to force foliage and flowers • Start tuberous begonia seeds indoors	• Check mulch; add if necessary • Order summer-flowering bulbs • Pot tender bulbs for indoor spring bloom • Discontinue chilling hardy bulbs and place them in a well-lit area to force foliage and flowers • Start tuberous begonia seeds indoors	• Check mulch; add if necessary • Order summer-flowering bulbs • Pot tender bulbs for indoor spring bloom • Discontinue chilling hardy bulbs and place them in a well-lit area to force foliage and flowers • Start tuberous begonia seeds indoors
MARCH/APRIL	• Remove mulch from new growth and flowers • Fertilize spring-flowering bulbs • Start tuberous begonias from tubers indoors • Start cannas from rhizomes indoors • Start dahlias from seeds or from tuberous roots indoors • Start tuberoses from tubers indoors • Prepare beds for planting	• Remove mulch from new growth and flowers • Fertilize spring-flowering bulbs • Start tuberous begonias from tubers indoors • Start cannas from rhizomes indoors • Start dahlias from seeds or from tuberous roots indoors • Start tuberoses from tubers indoors • Prepare beds for planting	• Start tuberous begonias from tubers indoors • Start cannas from rhizomes indoors • Start dahlias from seeds or from tuberous roots indoors • Start tuberoses from tubers indoors • Plant summer-flowering bulbs after frost • Remove faded flowers • Remove yellowed foliage • Transplant and divide spring-flowering bulbs • Apply mulch for summer • Water as necessary	• Start tuberous begonias from tubers indoors • Start cannas from rhizomes indoors • Start dahlias from seeds or from tuberous roots indoors • Start tuberoses from tubers indoors • Continue to plant summer-flowering bulbs • Remove faded flowers • Remove yellowed foliage • Transplant and divide spring-flowering bulbs • Apply mulch for summer • Water as necessary	• Continue to plant summer-flowering bulbs • Remove faded flowers • Remove yellowed foliage • Transplant and divide spring-flowering bulbs • Apply mulch for summer • Water as necessary
MAY/JUNE	• Prepare beds for planting • Plant summer-flowering bulbs after frost • Remove faded flowers • Remove yellowed foliage • Transplant and divide spring-flowering bulbs • Apply mulch for summer • Water as necessary	• Prepare beds for planting • Plant summer-flowering bulbs after frost • Remove faded flowers • Remove yellowed foliage • Transplant and divide spring-flowering bulbs • Apply mulch for summer • Water as necessary	• Prepare beds for planting • Plant summer-flowering bulbs after frost • Remove faded flowers • Remove yellowed foliage • Transplant and divide spring-flowering bulbs • Dig and store bulbs that cannot tolerate wet soil in summer • Apply mulch for summer • Water as necessary	• Prepare beds for planting • Plant summer-flowering bulbs after frost • Remove faded flowers • Remove yellowed foliage • Transplant and divide spring-flowering bulbs • Dig and store bulbs that cannot tolerate wet soil in summer • Apply mulch for summer • Water as necessary	• Prepare beds for planting • Plant summer-flowering bulbs after frost • Remove faded flowers • Remove yellowed foliage • Transplant and divide spring-flowering bulbs • Dig and store bulbs that cannot tolerate wet soil in summer • Apply mulch for summer • Water as necessary

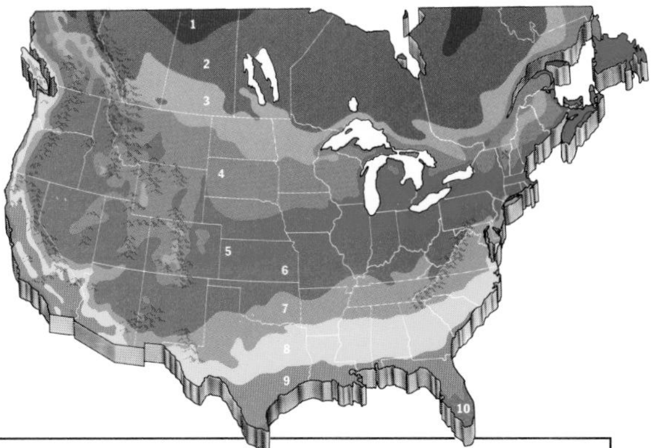

	ZONE 6	ZONE 7	ZONE 8	ZONE 9	ZONE 10
JANUARY/FEBRUARY	• Check mulch; add if necessary • Order summer-flowering bulbs • Pot tender bulbs for indoor spring bloom • Discontinue chilling hardy bulbs and place them in a well-lit area to force foliage and flowers • Start tuberous begonia seeds indoors	• Check mulch; add if necessary • Order summer-flowering bulbs • Pot tender bulbs for indoor spring bloom • Discontinue chilling hardy bulbs and place them in a well-lit area to force foliage and flowers • Start tuberous begonia seeds indoors	• Remove mulch from new growth and flowers • Fertilize spring-flowering bulbs • Order summer-flowering bulbs • Pot tender bulbs for indoor spring bloom • Discontinue chilling hardy bulbs and place them in a well-lit area to force foliage and flowers • Start tuberous begonia seeds indoors • Prepare beds for planting	• Order summer-flowering bulbs • Pot tender bulbs for indoor spring bloom • Discontinue chilling hardy bulbs and place them in a well-lit area to force foliage and flowers • Start tuberous begonia seeds indoors • Prepare beds for planting • Plant refrigerated bulbs outdoors • Plant summer-flowering bulbs after frost • Fertilize spring-flowering bulbs • Water as necessary	• Order summer-flowering bulbs • Pot tender bulbs for indoor spring bloom • Discontinue chilling hardy bulbs and place them in a well-lit area to force foliage and flowers • Prepare beds for planting • Plant refrigerated bulbs outdoors • Plant summer-flowering bulbs • Fertilize spring-flowering bulbs • Water as necessary
MARCH/APRIL	• Remove mulch from new growth and flowers • Fertilize spring-flowering bulbs • Start tuberous begonias from tubers indoors • Start cannas from rhizomes indoors • Start dahlias from seeds or from tuberous roots indoors • Start tuberoses from tubers indoors	• Remove mulch from new growth and flowers • Fertilize spring-flowering bulbs • Start tuberous begonias from tubers indoors • Start cannas from rhizomes indoors • Start dahlias from seeds or from tuberous roots indoors • Start tuberoses from tubers indoors	• Remove mulch from new growth and flowers • Fertilize spring-flowering bulbs • Start tuberous begonias from tubers indoors • Start cannas from rhizomes indoors • Start dahlias from seeds or from tuberous roots indoors • Start tuberoses from tubers indoors	• Remove mulch from new growth and flowers • Fertilize spring-flowering bulbs • Start tuberous begonias from tubers indoors • Start cannas from rhizomes indoors • Start dahlias from seeds or from tuberous roots indoors • Start tuberoses from tubers indoors	• Remove mulch from new growth and flowers • Fertilize spring-flowering bulbs • Start tuberous begonias from tubers indoors • Start cannas from rhizomes indoors • Start dahlias from seeds or from tuberous roots indoors • Start tuberoses from tubers indoors
MAY/JUNE	• Plant summer-flowering bulbs after frost • Remove faded flowers • Remove yellowed foliage • Transplant and divide spring-flowering bulbs • Dig and store bulbs that cannot tolerate wet soil in summer • Apply mulch for summer • Water as necessary	• Plant summer-flowering bulbs after frost • Remove faded flowers • Remove yellowed foliage • Transplant and divide spring-flowering bulbs • Dig and store bulbs that cannot tolerate wet soil in summer • Apply mulch for summer • Water as necessary	• Continue to plant summer-flowering bulbs • Remove faded flowers • Remove yellowed foliage • Dig and store bulbs that cannot tolerate wet soil in summer • Apply mulch for summer • Water as necessary	• Continue to plant summer-flowering bulbs • Remove faded flowers • Remove yellowed foliage • Dig and store bulbs that cannot tolerate wet soil in summer • Apply mulch for summer • Water as necessary	• Continue to plant summer-flowering bulbs • Remove faded flowers • Remove yellowed foliage • Dig and store bulbs that cannot tolerate wet soil in summer • Apply mulch for summer • Water as necessary

	ZONE 1	ZONE 2	ZONE 3	ZONE 4	ZONE 5
JULY/AUGUST	• Order spring-flowering bulbs • Prune side branches of dahlias to produce large flowers • Stake tall plants • Plant fall-flowering bulbs • Water as necessary	• Order spring-flowering bulbs • Prune side branches of dahlias to produce large flowers • Stake tall plants • Plant fall-flowering bulbs • Water as necessary	• Order spring-flowering bulbs • Prune side branches of dahlias to produce large flowers • Stake tall plants • Plant fall-flowering bulbs • Water as necessary	• Order spring-flowering bulbs • Prune side branches of dahlias to produce large flowers • Stake tall plants • Plant fall-flowering bulbs • Water as necessary	• Order spring-flowering bulbs • Prune side branches of dahlias to produce large flowers • Stake tall plants • Plant fall-flowering bulbs • Water as necessary
SEPTEMBER/OCTOBER	• Prepare beds for planting • Plant spring-flowering bulbs • Dig and store tender bulbs • Take stem cuttings from achimenes, tuberous begonias and dahlias for propagation • Fertilize hardy summer-flowering and other established bulbs • Apply mulch for winter • Water if necessary • Pot hardy bulbs for forcing and begin chilling them	• Prepare beds for planting • Plant spring-flowering bulbs • Dig and store tender bulbs • Take stem cuttings from achimenes, tuberous begonias and dahlias for propagation • Fertilize hardy summer-flowering and other established bulbs • Apply mulch for winter • Water if necessary • Pot hardy bulbs for forcing and begin chilling them	• Prepare beds for planting • Plant spring-flowering bulbs • Dig and store tender bulbs • Take stem cuttings from achimenes, tuberous begonias and dahlias for propagation • Fertilize hardy summer-flowering and other established bulbs • Apply mulch for winter • Water if necessary • Pot hardy bulbs for forcing and begin chilling them	• Prepare beds for planting • Plant spring-flowering bulbs • Dig and store tender bulbs • Take stem cuttings from achimenes, tuberous begonias and dahlias for propagation • Fertilize hardy summer-flowering and other established bulbs • Apply mulch for winter • Water if necessary • Pot hardy bulbs for forcing and begin chilling them	• Prepare beds for planting • Plant spring-flowering bulbs • Dig and store tender bulbs • Take stem cuttings from achimenes, tuberous begonias and dahlias for propagation • Fertilize hardy summer-flowering and other established bulbs • Apply mulch for winter • Water if necessary • Pot hardy bulbs for forcing and begin chilling them
NOVEMBER/DECEMBER	• Check mulch; add if necessary • Pot tender bulbs for indoor winter bloom	• Check mulch; add if necessary • Pot tender bulbs for indoor winter bloom	• Check mulch; add if necessary • Pot tender bulbs for indoor winter bloom	• Check mulch; add if necessary • Pot tender bulbs for indoor winter bloom	• Check mulch; add if necessary • Pot tender bulbs for indoor winter bloom

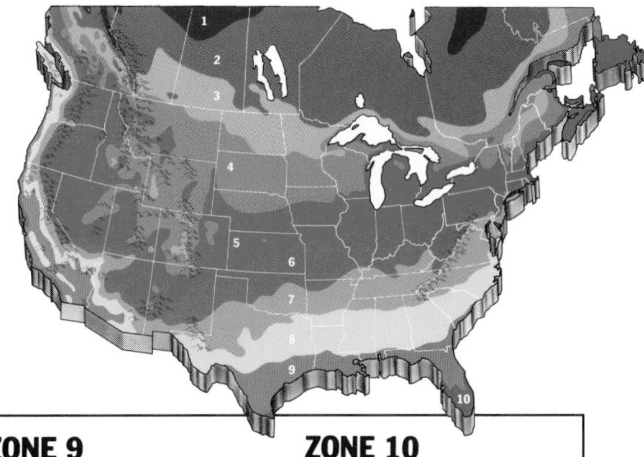

	ZONE 6	ZONE 7	ZONE 8	ZONE 9	ZONE 10
JULY/AUGUST	• Order spring-flowering bulbs • Prune side branches of dahlias to produce large flowers • Stake tall plants • Plant fall-flowering bulbs • Water as necessary	• Order spring-flowering bulbs • Prune side branches of dahlias to produce large flowers • Stake tall plants • Plant fall-flowering bulbs • Water as necessary	• Order spring-flowering bulbs • Prune side branches of dahlias to produce large flowers • Stake tall plants • Plant fall-flowering bulbs • Water as necessary	• Order spring-flowering bulbs • Prune side branches of dahlias to produce large flowers • Stake tall plants • Plant fall-flowering bulbs • Water as necessary	• Order spring-flowering bulbs • Stake tall plants • Plant fall-flowering bulbs • Water as necessary
SEPTEMBER/OCTOBER	• Prepare beds for planting • Plant spring-flowering bulbs • Dig and store tender bulbs • Take stem cuttings from achimenes, tuberous begonias and dahlias for propagation • Fertilize hardy summer-flowering and other established bulbs • Apply mulch for winter • Water if necessary • Pot hardy bulbs for forcing and begin chilling them	• Prepare beds for planting • Plant spring-flowering bulbs • Dig and store tender bulbs • Take stem cuttings from achimenes, tuberous begonias and dahlias for propagation • Fertilize hardy summer-flowering and other established bulbs • Water if necessary • Pot hardy bulbs for forcing and begin chilling them	• Prepare beds for planting • Plant spring-flowering bulbs • Dig and store tender bulbs • Take stem cuttings from achimenes, tuberous begonias and dahlias for propagation • Fertilize hardy summer-flowering and other established bulbs • Water if necessary • Pot hardy bulbs for forcing and begin chilling them	• Prepare beds for planting • Dig and store tender bulbs • Take stem cuttings from achimenes, tuberous begonias and dahlias for propagation • Fertilize hardy summer-flowering and other established bulbs • Water if necessary • Pot hardy bulbs for forcing and begin chilling them	• Prepare beds for planting • Dig and store tender bulbs • Take stem cuttings from achimenes, tuberous begonias and dahlias for propagation • Fertilize hardy summer-flowering and other established bulbs • Water if necessary • Pot hardy bulbs for forcing and begin chilling them
NOVEMBER/DECEMBER	• Continue to plant spring-flowering bulbs • Continue to dig and store tender bulbs • Apply mulch for winter • Pot tender bulbs for indoor winter bloom	• Continue to plant spring-flowering bulbs • Continue to dig and store tender bulbs • Apply mulch for winter • Pot tender bulbs for indoor winter bloom	• Continue to plant spring-flowering bulbs • Continue to dig and store tender bulbs • Apply mulch for winter • Pot tender bulbs for indoor winter bloom	• Plant spring-flowering bulbs • Continue to dig and store tender bulbs • Pot tender bulbs for indoor winter bloom • Water if necessary • Refrigerate hardy bulbs that require a chilling period	• Plant spring-flowering bulbs • Continue to dig and store tender bulbs • Pot tender bulbs for indoor winter bloom • Water if necessary • Refrigerate hardy bulbs that require a chilling period

WHAT TO DO WHEN THINGS GO WRONG

PROBLEM	CAUSE	SOLUTION
Bulbs fail to grow or they have been dug out of the ground and eaten. If bulbs have grown, the flowers and stems have been chewed off or eaten.	Chipmunks, field mice, gophers, voles and squirrels. Field mice, gophers and voles make underground tunnels to reach bulbs; chipmunks and squirrels dig them out of the ground and may eat the foliage and flowers.	Before planting bulbs, dig a bed or a trench and line the bottom and the sides with chicken wire. Or plant bulbs the animals do not eat, such as ornamental onion and daffodils.
Leaves develop silvery white or brown streaks and flecks, and leaf tips turn brown. Eventually, leaves wither and die. Flower buds turn brown and may not open; if they do open, they are streaked and distorted. White and pastel-colored flowers are especially susceptible.	Thrips, nearly microscopic insects that suck sap from the flowers and leaves.	Remove and discard infested buds, flowers and foliage. Apply a systemic insecticide two or three times, seven to 10 days apart.
Large, jagged holes appear in established leaves. New leaves may disappear entirely. Shiny silver trails appear on plants and on the ground.	Snails and slugs, which are brown shell-less snails up to 3 inches long. They feed at night.	Shallow saucers of beer and inverted grapefruit halves set around plants will trap snails and slugs. Snail and slug bait is also available; it should be applied at dusk, and may need to be reapplied after plants have been watered and after a rainfall.
Leaves curl or are distorted in shape, and the plant is stunted. Flowers may be streaked and malformed. A clear, sticky substance appears on the foliage.	Aphids, which are green, yellow, black or brown insects ⅛ inch long. Aphids appear in clusters on buds and leaves and at the base of the plant, where they feed on sap. They also carry and spread diseases.	Aphids can be knocked off plants with a strong stream of water. If the infestation is severe, spray with an insecticidal soap or an insecticide approved by government agencies for use on bulbs.
Leaves and stems lose their color. The entire plant collapses and dies.	Wireworms, which are brown worms with segmented bodies ¾ inch long. They are the larvae of click beetles. They bore into bulbs and up the stems of plants.	Apply an insecticide to the plants and the surrounding soil. To prevent infestation, apply an insecticide to the soil and to the bulbs before planting them.
Small, rounded or oblong holes appear in leaves and may also appear in flowers. Eventually, the leaf surface between veins disappears.	Beetles, including Asiatic garden, blister, cucumber, Japanese and rose chafer beetles. They are from ¼ to ¾ inch long and have hard shells.	Beetles can be picked off plants by hand. If the adult population is large, apply an insecticide. To control beetles in the larval stage, use a grub-proofing insecticide. The larvae of Japanese beetles can be controlled with milky spore, a bacterium fatal to beetles but harmless to plants and other animals.

PROBLEM	CAUSE	SOLUTION
Leaves become speckled, then turn dry and lose their color. The plant is stunted. Eventually, a fine white webbing appears on the plant.	Spider mites, nearly microscopic red, black, yellow or green pests that suck the sap from foliage.	Spray the undersides of the leaves with a strong stream of water every three days. If symptoms persist, apply a miticide three times, three days apart.
Plants wilt and foliage loses its color. Bulbs are soft and spongy.	Bulb mites, tiny white pests that feed on bulbs. Colonies of mites may be contained within the bulb, or they may be visible on an exterior portion of the bulb. Bulb mites transmit diseases such as bulb rot to healthy bulbs.	There are no chemical cures for bulb mites. Discard infested bulbs. To prevent infestation, apply an insecticide to bulbs you have stored before planting them.
Leaves curl, split and are covered with yellow or brown blotches. In severe cases, plants cease to grow. Small knotty growths appear on the roots.	Nematodes, microscopic worms that feed on both foliage and bulbs.	Dig up and discard infested plants. Do not plant bulbs in an area that is infested with nematodes. Consult your local extension service for soil testing information. Soil treatment by a professional fumigator may be necessary.
Leaves, stems and flower buds are covered with a white powder. Foliage and buds are distorted in shape. The plant may be stunted.	Powdery mildew, a fungus disease that is most severe when nights are cool and days are warm. Mildew spreads rapidly among crowded bulbs.	Mildew can be both eradicated and prevented with a fungicide applied once every 10 days when nights are cool and days are warm. Allow adequate space between bulbs when planting them.
Yellow, red, brown, gray or black spots appear on the leaves. Eventually, the spots merge and the entire leaf turns yellow and dies.	Leaf spot, a fungus disease that is most severe in warm, humid weather.	Prune and discard infected leaves. To prevent leaf spot from spreading, apply a fungicide every seven to 10 days.
Leaves turn red or yellow, wilt and die. Growth is stunted. Flowers may not develop. Bulbs are either soft and mushy, or hard and dried out. They may be covered with sunken lesions. White, pink, gray or black mold may form on the bulb or on the stem near the soil line. Roots are dark and slimy.	Root rot and bulb rot, fungus and bacterial diseases that may occur either while the bulb is in the ground or during storage.	Discard all infected bulbs and the surrounding soil. Be careful not to damage bulbs when digging or handling them; damaged bulbs are highly susceptible to disease. To prevent root or bulb rot, dust bulbs with a powdered fungicide or soak them in a fungicide solution before storage and again before replanting.
Fuzzy gray or brown mold appears on buds, flowers and foliage. Leaves develop brown or gray spots and eventually turn yellow and die. Flowers may not open. Bulbs have dark, sunken areas and are covered with a brown growth. Tulips are especially susceptible.	Botrytis blight, also called gray mold, a fungus disease most prevalent in cool, wet weather.	Remove and discard infected leaves and flowers. Apply a fungicide every seven to 10 days during cool, wet weather. Before planting them, dust bulbs with a powdered fungicide or soak them in a fungicide solution. Do not overcrowd plantings.
Leaves become mottled with yellow and eventually turn completely yellow. Leaves curl or are misshapen. Flowers are smaller than normal and may be streaked or spotted with yellow, blue or green. The plant ceases to grow. Lilies are especially susceptible.	Virus diseases, including mosaic, yellows and ring spot viruses.	There are no chemical controls for viruses. Remove and discard infected bulbs. Disinfect gardening tools with rubbing alcohol after working on infected plants. To help prevent virus, control aphids *(opposite),* which spread virus diseases. Plant virus-resistant species of lilies.

TIPS AND TECHNIQUES

ORNAMENTAL ONIONS AS CUT FLOWERS

The dozen or so ornamental onions of the genus *Allium* commonly grown outdoors can also be enjoyed indoors, as cut flowers. They have striking, unusual blooms in globelike clusters that resemble star bursts of yellow, red, purple, pink and white. They can be displayed alone or used in mixed-flower arrangements. The only drawback is that some of them smell like edible onions. But deodorizing them is simple. Just place freshly cut ornamental onion stems in a separate container of water and let them soak for several minutes. The odor will dissipate, and the onions can then be combined in any arrangement of your choice.

MASS PLANTING MADE EASY

The common spade and trowel are adequate for planting a few handfuls of bulbs, but when you are planting a great many, some special tools can save you time and effort. One is a bulb planter, a cylindrical tool that is particularly useful if you are planting in a lawn or in a bed that already contains other plants. It is available in a hand-held model *(below)* and in models that include a side bar for pushing the planter into the ground by foot and handlebars for pulling the planter out of the ground. Both types create bulb-sized planting holes by removing plugs of soil from the ground. Another useful device (provided your soil is free of rocks) is a drill bit that can be attached to a workshop drill and used as an auger for making planting holes.

TEMPORARY BULB STORAGE

If instead of interplanting you want to replace your flower bed altogether when spring bulbs have finished blooming, you can lift the bulbs from the ground—with their foliage still intact—and temporarily put them in a holding trench. The trench should be in a sunny spot so that the leaves can take in sunlight and go on manufacturing food for next season. It should be 6 inches wide, 6 inches deep and long enough to hold all the bulbs side by side at 6-inch intervals.

Set the bulbs in the bottom of the trench with their leaves draped over the top edges to one side or the other. Next, refill the trench so that the bulbs are covered with soil. Leave the foliage uncovered and exposed to sunlight.

After six to eight weeks, when the foliage turns brown, lift the bulbs from the trench, remove the foliage and store the bulbs in a cool, dark, well-ventilated spot until you are ready to plant them again in the fall.

BULBS ON THE ROCKS

Large rocks are useful in a bulb garden. With their different shapes, sizes and colors, they provide interesting backgrounds for foliage and blooms. They also supply protective microhabitats in which bulb plants can prosper because—even in winter's chilly temperatures—they absorb and store heat from sunlight by day and then slowly release the heat at night. The release of heat can modify night temperatures just enough to prevent root damage caused by rapid changes in soil temperatures. If they have large surfaces slanting toward bulb plants, they can deliver extra moisture; as rain strikes the surfaces, it flows in the direction of the plants, instead of away from them.

Planting among rocks does not require any special procedures, and almost any bulb that is small enough to nestle in the nooks and crannies between rocks will do. For bright color and length of show, a carpet of Greek anemones meandering among rock outcroppings is superb. For early-spring color, use glory-of-the-snow, winter aconite, violet-scented iris or Siberian squill. And if you are looking for a low-growing daffodil for your rock garden, try 'Little Gem' or 'Xit'.

BULBS AND OTHER FLOWERS IN A SINGLE PLANTING

Bulbs are usually planted so close together that planting other flowers among them is tedious. It's also risky; the bulbs can be nicked or bruised by a spade or trowel. If you want spring annuals and perennials to follow the bulb show, the easiest way to get them is to seed the annuals and perennials in the fall, at the same time that you plant the bulbs. First plant the bulbs, then level the soil surface and broadcast the seed where you want the plants to grow next year.

Not all seeds can be sown outdoors in the fall and survive the winter, but the list of those that can is large enough. In the southern reaches of the country, where temperatures do not drop below 20° F, try flax, gilia, love-in-a-mist and wallflower. If you live in a northern zone, try beard-tongue, coneflower, forget-me-not and foxglove.

THE BIG CHILL

If you live in an area where winters are mild, you can still enjoy the bulbs that require a winter chill. Most hardy bulbs need at least 13 weeks of temperatures below 48° F but above freezing. You can create this chilling period indoors if you are willing to give space in your refrigerator to the cause.

Simply place bulbs on a tray or a cookie sheet, set the tray on a refrigerator shelf and leave it there for 13 weeks (or 13 weeks minus the number of weeks it does turn cold outdoors). To determine when refrigeration should begin, just count back 13 weeks from the time you want to plant the bulbs you chill.

After they have been refrigerated, plant the bulbs directly in the soil. They will bloom four to six weeks after chilling.

GROWING BULBS HYDROPONICALLY

A good way to give children the fun of seeing roots develop—and a painless lesson in botany—is to grow bulbs hydroponically: that is, in nothing but water. Hyacinths, paperwhite narcissus and some tulips can be grown and displayed in transparent containers of water. Each container should have a neck narrow enough to hold the bulb firmly just above the water's surface. Some containers, called hyacinth glasses *(above),* are especially made for hydroponic forcing. Bud vases and some flower vases work nicely, as do wine carafes and even some salad dressing and vinegar containers. If you use a recycled container, just make sure that it is absolutely clean.

Fill the container with water to the level where the bottom of the bulb will rest, and then set the bulb snugly into place. Add water as it evaporates, gently lifting the bulb from the neck, if necessary.

5

DICTIONARY OF BULBS

There is virtually no garden that lacks a place for one kind of bulb or another, so wide-ranging is this group of plants in size and season of bloom, in cultural requirements, form, color and impact. Woodland gardens shelter the fleeting fragility of spring beauties such as the little dog-tooth violet; a sunny border can glow with the flashy tropical brilliance of cannas all summer long. Fall brings its own burst of bloom, and where winters are mild or graced by warm spells, bulbs are a mainstay in any landscape.

Although the 96 genera of plants described in this dictionary are commonly called bulbs, they actually form a horticultural alliance of five different groups, each possessing a distinctive belowground structure. The structure may be that of a true bulb, a corm, a tuber, a tuberous root or a rhizome. They are anatomically unlike one another, but the structures serve a common function: to hold a large store of food that tides a plant over a long period of dormancy.

As a group, bulbs possess a special toughness that endears them to gardeners interested in beautiful effect with a minimum of labor. Given a location that fulfills their cultural needs, bulbs are among the most self-sufficient of plants. The gardener need not even (indeed, must resist the impulse to) cut back foliage after flowers fade, since the plant is still manufacturing food. Sprawling leaves can be braided together or tied into neat bundles. Easier still is to place bulbs where other plants, such as emerging perennials, will obscure the bulbs' leaves when they wither. Once they have turned yellow, it is safe to cut them.

One note of caution: some species have been so extensively collected in their native habitats that they are in danger of extinction. The dictionary indicates those species that are threatened. Do not purchase bulbs of these species unless the merchant states unequivocally that they have been propagated at a nursery and not collected in the wild.

ACHIMENES LONGIFLORA 'BLAUER PLANET'

ACIDANTHERA BICOLOR

AGAPANTHUS ORIENTALIS

Achimenes (a-KIM-e-neez)

Monkey-faced pansy, orchid pansy

A genus of species distributed throughout the American tropics. They are in the gesneriad family and are related to African violets and gloxinias. Plants have fibrous roots with scaly rhizomes and are 1 to 2 feet tall. The blooms are trumpet-shaped with flaring lobes and flat, pansy- or impatiens-like faces. Grow achimenes outdoors in beds or baskets as annuals, indoors as potted plants. Zone 10.

Selected species and varieties. *A. longiflora* has large, red-purple, white-throated flowers that are 1½ inches long and 1½ inches wide. Leaves are hairy and up to 3 inches long and 1½ inches wide. 'Blauer Planet' is more compact than the species. It has 1½- to 2-inch blue-purple flowers with white throats.

Growing conditions. Grow achimenes in bright light but out of direct sun and in rich, well-drained soil to which organic matter and coarse sand or vermiculite have been added. Keep soil evenly moist after plants begin to grow. Plant the rhizomes in pots or baskets in early spring for summer bloom, three or four rhizomes per 6-inch pot. Place the rhizomes horizontally, ½ to 1 inch below the surface. Rhizomes can also be started in flats filled with moist peat moss and moved to pots or beds when growth is 3 inches high. Achimenes can also be grown from stem cuttings. Plants perform best when temperatures remain above 60° F at night and not above 80° F during the day. In fall, gradually withhold water and dry the plants out. Store the rhizomes in a cool, dry place over winter. In spring, resume watering and repot if necessary.

Acidanthera (a-si-DAN-ther-a)

Peacock orchid

Tender, summer-blooming plants native to tropical and South Africa. Flowers are graceful and delicate-looking, somewhat resembling butterflies or orchids. They are borne in loose spikes and open in succession. Foliage is sword-shaped. Plants arise from corms. Effective when grown in clumps of 10 or more. Plant where the fragrance of the flowers can be appreciated. Zones 7-10.

Selected species and varieties. *A. bicolor* (sometimes listed as *A. murielai*) bears spikes with three or more white flowers with chocolate brown centers. Plants are 2 to 3 feet tall. Blooms are 3 inches across and very fragrant, and make excellent cut flowers.

Growing conditions. Plant peacock orchids in full sun in a location protected from high winds. Space corms about 6 inches apart at a depth of 3 to 4 inches. Enrich the soil with compost and fertilize with 5-10-5 when the plants emerge and again one month later. North of Zone 7, start peacock orchids indoors and move them to the garden after danger of frost has passed. They can be difficult to transplant, so start the plants in peat pots that can go directly into the ground or grow them in tubs. North of Zone 7, peacock orchids should be dug after the first hard frost. Shake off excess soil and allow them to dry for several days in a cool, dry place out of direct sun. Cut back the tops of the plants, discard the remains of the previous season's corms and separate the cormels. Store the corms and cormels in dry peat moss or vermiculite at a temperature of 55° to 60° F. Peacock orchids require a long growing season to bloom. Propagate plants from the small cormels that are borne around old corms. Small corms take up to two seasons to bloom.

Adder's tongue see *Erythronium*

African lily see *Agapanthus*

Agapanthus (ag-a-PAN-thus)

Amaryllis-family members from South Africa with thick rhizomes and fleshy roots. Strap-shaped or linear leaves are borne at the base of the stems and may be deciduous or evergreen. Flowers are tubular and borne in umbels on leafless stalks. They come in blue, purplish blue or white. Zones 9 and 10.

Selected species and varieties. *A. africanus,* African lily, blue lily-of-the-Nile, bears blue, 1½-inch blooms in striking clusters of 12 to 30 flowers. Stalks are 10 to 20 inches tall; flowers are generally carried above the foliage. 'Albus' is a white-flowered cultivar; 'Peter Pan' is a free-blooming dwarf type, with foliage 8 to 12 inches in height and blue blooms reaching 18 inches. *A. campanulatus* bears upward-pointing, bell-shaped white or blue blooms and has deciduous foliage. *A. orientalis* (also listed as *A. praecox)* is an evergreen species reaching 3 feet in height. Flowers are blue, funnel-shaped and borne in 40- to 100-bloom umbels.

Growing conditions. Agapanthuses are grown outdoors year round in Zones 9 and 10. North of these zones, they are grown in greenhouses in tubs or large pots and moved outdoors during the summer. Plants will grow in full sun or light shade. Pot-grown plants require regular applications of fertilizer during the growing season. Keep soil evenly moist during the growing season; dry off gradually in fall for winter rest. Divide plants only when overcrowding causes reduced flowering.

Alkali grass see *Zigadenus*

Allium (AL-ee-um)

Onion

A large genus best known for its edible members: chives, onions, garlic and leeks. Leaves are usually grasslike or cylindrical and hollow. Like the vegetables to which they are related, ornamental onions arise from rhizomes or bulbs and are onion-scented when bruised. Small flowers are borne in few- to many-flowered umbels on leafless stems. Blooms appear in spring and summer and are yellow, white, pink, red, violet and blue. Excellent for beds and borders; smaller species are fine for the rock garden. All make excellent cut flowers, and also can be used for dried arrangements. Zones 2-10.

Selected species and varieties. *A. aflatunense* bears 4-inch globes of rose-purple flowers on 2½- to 5-foot stalks. Flowers appear in spring. Zones 5-10. *A. caeruleum* (also listed as *A. azureum),* blue globe onion, carries deep blue flowers in 2-inch clusters atop 2- to 4-foot stems that appear in late spring. Zones 4-10. *A. cernuum,* nodding onion, wild onion, is a 2-foot plant with rose to purple or white flowers borne in nodding, loose heads of 30 to 40 flowers. Blooms appear in summer. Zones 3-10. *A. christophii,* stars-of-Persia, is a 3-foot plant bearing lacy-looking, 8- to 12-inch umbels of star-shaped flowers that are lilac and have a metallic sheen. Blooms appear in late spring. Zones 4-10. *A. elatum* produces many-flowered umbels of violet flowers atop 2- to 3½-foot plants. Zones 6-10. *A. flavum,* yellow onion, is a summer-blooming plant with bell-shaped, yellow flowers borne in loose umbels on 2-foot plants. Zones 4-10. *A. giganteum,* giant onion, produces 4- to 5-inch, ball-shaped umbels of flowers carried on leafless 4-foot stems. Lilac flowers appear in early midsummer. Zones 5-10.

A. karataviense, Turkestan onion, bears wide, strap-shaped, blue-green foliage and many-flowered, 4-inch umbels of whitish pink flowers atop 6- to 10-inch plants. Blooms in late spring. Zones 4-10. *A. moly,* lily leek, golden garlic, bears 3-inch clusters of yellow, star-shaped flowers in June. Zones 4-10. *A. narcissiflorum* bears handsome, nodding umbels of bell-shaped, rose-pink flowers in summer on 4- to 10-inch plants. Zones 5-9. *A. neapolitanum,* daffodil garlic, Naples onion, is a spring-blooming, 1½-foot plant with fragrant, white, starlike flowers borne in 2- to 3-inch umbels. 'Grandiflorum' is a large-flowered cultivar. Zones 6-9. *A. oreophilum* bears loose, 4-inch clusters of purplish pink flowers in late spring on 4- to 8-inch plants. 'Zanenburg' has pink flowers. Zones 4-9. *A. pulchellum* produces loose umbels of tiny, drooping, bell-shaped flowers on 1½- to 2-foot plants. Blooms are pink, rose-purple or yellowish and appear in summer. 'Alba' is a white-flowered form. Zones 6-9.

A. roseum, rosy onion, produces ½-inch, rose-white flowers in 3-inch umbels that appear in June on 2-foot plants. Rosy onion often bears bulbils at the top of the flower stalk in fall. Zones 5-9. *A. schoenoprasum,* chive, is a 12-inch plant with tubular, aromatic leaves. It is widely used as an herb. Flowers appear in spring, are rose-pink and are borne in dense, 1-inch, many-flowered umbels. Zones 4-9. *A. senescens* has slightly curved or twisted green leaves on 4- to 8-inch plants. Flowers are rose-pink and borne in small, many-flowered umbels in late summer. *S. senescens glaucum* has flat, curved, gray-green leaves. Zones 4-9. *A. sphaerocephalum,* ballhead onion, produces dense, ball-shaped, 2-inch umbels of reddish purple flowers in midsummer. Plants reach 2 to 3 feet. Zones 4-9. *A. stellatum,* prairie onion, is an 18-inch plant that bears pink flowers in fall. Zones 5-9. *A. tanguticum,* Tangut

ALLIUM AFLATUNENSE

ALLIUM KARATAVIENSE

ALLIUM MOLY

AMARYLLIS BELLADONNA

AMIANTHIUM MUSCITOXICUM

ANEMONE BLANDA 'BLUE STAR'

onion, bears 3-inch umbels of light blue flowers on 3-foot stalks. Zones 6-9. *A. tuberosum,* Chinese chive, Chinese garlic, is an edible, 1½-foot plant producing small, fragrant, white flowers in summer. Zones 5-9.

Growing conditions. Plant ornamental onions in full sun at a depth of two to three times the diameter of the bulbs. Space plants 6 to 18 inches apart, depending on the height of the species. Bulbs can be planted in spring or fall. Ornamental onions will grow in any good garden soil. Bulbs multiply easily. Clumps may be left undisturbed in the garden for years, requiring division only when crowding reduces flower production. Many ornamental onions can be propagated by bulbils produced in the flower clusters or the small bulbs that appear around the larger bulbs underground.

Alp lily see *Lloydia*

Amaryllis (am-a-RIL-is)

A one-species South African genus that once contained many species now classified as *Hippeastrum.* Flowers are funnel-shaped and appear in clusters on stems that are solid. *(Hippeastrum* bears its flowers on hollow stems.) The bulbs produce strap-shaped leaves after the flowers have begun to fade. Amaryllis can be grown in beds and borders in frost-free areas and in greenhouses where not hardy. Zones 9 and 10.

Selected species and varieties. *A. belladonna,* belladonna lily, naked lady, bears fragrant, rose, pink or white blooms that are 3½ inches across. Flowers appear atop naked 18-inch stalks; foliage appears after the flowers.

Growing conditions. Grow belladonna lilies outdoors in a sunny site with deeply prepared, rich, well-drained soil. Plant the bulbs in spring or early summer, before the leaves develop, at a depth of 4 to 6 inches. Do not disturb the bulbs unless absolutely necessary. Pot-grown plants should be set with the neck of the bulb at the soil surface. Keep the soil moist but not wet.

Amaryllis see also *Hippeastrum*
Amazon lily see *Eucharis*
Amberbell see *Erythronium*

Amianthium
(am-ee-AN-thee-um)

A small North American genus of plants with long, narrow leaves. Flowers are borne in dense spikes. Leaves, flowers, bulbs and rhizomes are all very poisonous. Zones 5-10.

Selected species and varieties. *A. muscitoxicum,* fly-poison, crow-poison, is a 3-foot species bearing fluffy spikes of ½-inch white flowers in summer.

Growing conditions. Grow fly-poison in a location with full sun and moist, well-drained, acid soil. Do not plant in areas where grazing animals or curious children might consume it.

Anemone
(a-NEM-o-nee or a-ne-MO-nee)
Windflower, lily-of-the-field

A large genus, belonging to the buttercup family, that contains many popular perennials, some of which grow from tubers. Fernlike leaves are divided or composed of two or more leaflets. Flowers may be daisylike or poppylike and double or single, but have petal-like sepals, not true petals. Clustered stamens at the center of the flowers are also often showy. Blossoms are usually borne singly on stems that rise above the foliage. They close at night and during cloudy weather. Anemones are fine for beds and borders as well as rock gardens. Zones 3-10.

Selected species and varieties. *A. apennina,* Apennine anemone, bears erect, 9-inch flower stalks topped by solitary, 1½-inch flowers that are daisylike and sky blue or white. Leaves are hairy on the undersides. Zones 6-9. *A. blanda,* Greek anemone, resembles Apennine anemone but does not have any hair on its foliage. Flowers are daisylike and deep blue. Plants are 2 to 8 inches tall. Collection in the wild has endangered the species; purchase from reputable dealers that sell only propagated tubers. 'Blue Star' bears violet-blue flowers on 3-inch stems; 'Pink Star' has pink blooms on 6- to 10-inch stems; 'White Splendor' has white flowers on 6-inch stems. Zones 6-9. *A. coronaria,* poppy anemone, bears 1½- to 2½-inch flowers on 6- to 18-inch stalks. Flowers are red, lavender, blue or white, and may be single or double. 'St. Brigid' and 'De Caen' are cultivars that have especially showy flowers. Zones 6-10. *A.* × *fulgens,* scarlet windflower, flame anemone, bears brilliant red 2- to 2½-inch flowers with black stamens. Plants are 10 to 12 inches tall. Zones 5-9. *A. nemorosa,* European wood anemone, is an 8-inch, spring-blooming species with 1-inch, white, rose or purplish flowers. Zones 3-9. *A. palmata,* Mediterranean anemone, is a 9-inch species with yellow 2-inch flowers that appear in spring. Zones 8 and 9.

Growing conditions. The tubers of these anemones look like bark chips and it is often difficult to tell which end is up. Soak them overnight in warm water and put them in the ground on their sides. Anemones prefer humus-rich soil and a site shaded from midday sun. Where they are hardy they are planted in the fall and mulched over winter. To grow them where they are not hardy, plant them outdoors in early spring; dig them in fall and store the roots in dry sand or peat moss indoors over winter.

Angel's-fishing-rod
see *Dierama*

Angel's tears see *Narcissus*

Arisaema (ar-i-SEE-ma)

Jack-in-the-pulpit, Indian turnip

A genus of nearly 200 tuberous herbs grown for their lush, spear-shaped leaves, which are three-lobed. The flowers, which are tiny and insignificant, are borne on a fleshy spike called a spadix, commonly referred to as the Jack. The spadix is surrounded by a showy spathe, or pulpit, that is cuplike at the bottom but expands into a flap or lid that shelters the spadix. The spathe is green or white and may be marked with purple. Ripened fruit is often red and showy. Arisaemas are fine plants for a shady wildflower garden. Zones 4-9.

Selected species and varieties. *A. dracontium,* green dragon, dragonroot, bears a single leaf that is divided into seven to 19 segments. Plants reach 3 feet in height. The flowering stalk is shorter than the leafstalk. The spathe is slender and surrounds the spadix, which has a tail-like tip that reaches 2 to 4 inches in length. Zones 4-9. *A. sikokianum* has a spathe that is maroon-striped on the outside; the spadix and the inside of the spathe are ivory-white. The foliage is marked with cream. Zones 5-9. *A. thunbergii* has foliage variegated with red or purple. The spathe is striped with purplish brown and the spadix has an 8- to 12-inch, threadlike tip. Zones 8 and 9. *A. triphyllum,* Jack-in-the-pulpit, Indian turnip, bears two leaves, each with three leaflets. Plants reach 2 feet in height. The spathe is striped with purple or maroon inside and is greenish on the outside. It bears brilliant red berries in spikes in early fall. Zones 4-9.

Growing conditions. Plant arisaemas in dappled to full shade in a location with rich, well-drained soil that has plenty of organic matter. They require a regular supply of moisture during the growing season. Plant the tubers in fall and place them deep enough to accommodate the roots, which arise from the top of the tuber. Propagate by division or by seed sown outdoors in fall.

Arum (AY-rum or AR-um)

A small genus of tuberous plants with showy, arrow-shaped leaves. The flowers are insignificant and borne on a fleshy spadix that is surrounded by a green or petal-like spathe. The clusters of bright red berries are also showy and appear in the fall before new foliage grows. Arums are fine plants for woodland and rock gardens. Zones 5-9.

Selected species and varieties. *A. italicum,* Italian arum, bears arrow-shaped leaves that may be green or marked with white or cream. Plants are dormant in the summer; foliage appears in fall and lasts through the winter. The cultivar 'Marmoratum' has leaves marked with yellow to whitish green. 'Pictum', black calla, has narrow leaves marked with cream and gray.

Growing conditions. Arums are best grown in light shade. They require deep, rich soil that remains moist throughout the time the leaves are above ground. Plant the tubers deep enough to accommodate the roots, which arise from the top of the tubers.

Atamasco lily see *Zephyranthes*
Atlantic camass see *Camassia*
Autumn crocus see *Colchicum*
Avalanche lily see *Erythronium*

ANEMONE CORONARIA 'DE CAEN'

ARISAEMA SIKOKIANUM

ARUM ITALICUM

ARUM ITALICUM

BEGONIA GRANDIS

BEGONIA × TUBERHYBRIDA

BRIMEURA AMETHYSTINA

Aztec lily see *Sprekelia*

Ballhead onion see *Allium*

Barbados lily see *Hippeastrum*

Basket flower see *Hymenocallis*

Begonia (be-GO-nee-a)

A genus of succulent tropical and subtropical plants that are grown for their ornamental foliage or showy blossoms. Flowers may be pink, red, yellow or white, and have a succulent or fleshy texture. Male and female flowers are borne on the same plant.

Selected species and varieties. *B. grandis* (also listed as *B. evansiana),* hardy begonia, Evans begonia, bears pink flowers on 2-foot plants. Leaves are dark green on top and maroon underneath. Hardy in Zones 7-9, but with mulching and a protected location hardy as far north as Zone 5. *B.* × *tuberhybrida,* tuberous begonia, is a group of hybrids developed by crossing several different species from the Andes in South America. Flowers are brilliant red, pink, orange, yellow or white and may be marked with contrasting colors. The cultivars have been classified into divisions according to flower form and plant habit. Groups include rosebud, or rose-flowered, which have large, double flowers with raised, roselike centers. Camellia-flowered tuberous begonias bear double, camellia-like blooms up to 6 inches across. Carnation-flowered cultivars produce double flowers that are ruffled like carnations. Hanging basket begonias have pendent stems and blooms that are best displayed from baskets or flower boxes. Blooms may be single or double. Picotee begonias bear large, usually double, flowers that have petal edges outlined with a contrasting color —white with a red edge, for example. Non-Stop series hybrids produce double flowers on compact plants.

Growing conditions. Grow *B. grandis* outdoors in a shady location with moist, rich soil high in organic matter. Mulch plants in winter. *B. grandis* can be propagated from seeds, cuttings or bulbils. Tuberous begonias perform best in areas with cool, moist summers; for best results, day temperatures should remain below 80° F and night temperatures should be below 60° F. Start tubers indoors in February or March in a shallow container with adequate drainage filled with 2 inches of peat or sphagnum moss. Place the tubers concave side up and lightly cover with peat or sphagnum moss. Place the container in a warm (60°-70° F), bright place. Sprinkle the surface of the medium lightly with water when it dries out. When growth begins, water more often. Carefully move the tubers to pots, planters or beds when the shoots are about 4 inches tall. Plant tubers 1 inch below the surface. Soil mixture should be rich and perfectly drained: ⅔ peat moss and ⅓ sand is ideal. Pots should be at least 6 inches wide and 6 inches deep; planters 8 inches wide by 6 inches deep to provide adequate room for roots. Do not set plants outside until danger of frost has passed. Place plants in light shade or a location with early-morning or late-afternoon sun only. Water in the morning, and to prevent mildew, avoid sprinkling foliage and flowers. Soil should be moist but allowed to dry slightly between waterings. Plants that are kept too wet or too dry will drop their flower buds. Stake plants to keep them from breaking; place the stake 3 inches from the tuber and tie the stems with yarn or rags; string will cut the fleshy stems. Fertilize every other week with a balanced fertilizer. Remove fallen petals and leaves, to avoid rot. Allow frost to kill the foliage in fall, then dig the tubers and set them indoors in a cool, dry place.

Belladonna lily see *Amaryllis*

Bell-flowered squill see *Endymion*

Bermuda buttercup see *Oxalis*

Black calla see *Arum*

Blazing star see *Tritonia*

Blond lilian see *Erythronium*

Blood lily see *Haemanthus*

Blue dicks see *Dichelostemma*

Blue globe onion see *Allium*

Blue lily-of-the-Nile see *Agapanthus*

Brimeura (bry-MEW-ra)

A small genus of plants once classified in the genus *Hyacinthus.* Plants bear four to eight narrow leaves that arise from a bulb. Flowers are bell-shaped and blue, rose or white in color. Brimeuras are fine subjects for a rock garden. Zones 6-10.

Selected species and varieties. *B. amethystina* (formerly *Hyacinthus amethystinus* and *Scilla amethystina)* bears 8-inch leaves and loose spikes of small, bell-shaped flowers. Flowers are light blue. 'Alba' is a white form.

Growing conditions. Grow brimeuras in full sun or light shade in a location with deep, rich soil that is somewhat sandy. Plant bulbs in fall at a depth of 3 inches and space plants 3 to 4 inches apart. Mulch for winter protection. Brimeuras can be propagated by division.

Brodiaea (bro-DI-ee-a)

Triplet lily

Triplet lilies are cormous plants with grasslike leaves and funnel-shaped flowers borne singly or in loose umbels. In western states, they make fine additions to native plant gardens, naturalized areas and perennial borders. Zones 7-10.

Selected species and varieties. *B. californica* is a 2½-foot California native with 1- to 1¾-inch, lilac, violet or sometimes pink flowers. Blooms are borne in umbels of up to 12 flowers. Zones 8-10. *B. coronaria,* harvest brodiaea, bears 1½-inch, violet-purple flowers on 12- to 18-inch plants. Zones 8-10.

Growing conditions. Plant triplet lily corms outdoors in fall in full sun and well-drained, sandy or gritty soil. Plant the corms at a depth of 3 to 5 inches and space them 2 to 3 inches apart. These plants are easy to grow in California and other areas where summers are dry. They cannot tolerate excessive moisture after they go dormant in summer; in areas where summers are wet, dig the corms after the foliage dies down and store them in a dry place over the summer. Replant in fall.

Brodiaea see also *Ipheion*

Bugle lily see *Watsonia*

Bulbocodium

(bul-bo-KO-dee-um)

Meadow saffron

A very small genus of spring-flowering, crocuslike plants that grow from corms. Flowers are trumpet-shaped and violet- or rose-purple. They generally appear before the foliage. Excellent for rock gardens. Zones 5-10.

Selected species and varieties. *B. vernum,* spring meadow saffron, is a 4- to 6-inch plant bearing one to three, large, rose-violet flowers close to the ground.

Growing conditions. Grow meadow saffrons in a location with full sun or lightly dappled shade. Plant corms in late summer or early fall at a depth of 3 inches. Space plants 3 to 4 inches apart. Dig and divide plants every two or three years in early summer as soon as the foliage has died down completely. Plants prefer a well-drained soil to which organic matter and sand or grit has been added.

Buttercup see *Ranunculus*

Butterfly iris see *Moraea*

Butterfly tulip see *Calochortus*

Caladium (ka-LAY-dee-um)

A genus of tropical plants in the arum family grown for their showy leaves. Flowers are borne on a spadix surrounded by a sometimes showy spathe. Caladiums make fine additions to shady beds and borders. Where they are not hardy, they are often dug and stored indoors in winter or grown as annuals. Zone 10.

Selected species and varieties. *C. × hortulanum,* fancy-leaved caladium, is grown for its large, arrow- or heart-shaped leaves that are variegated or shaded with pink, deep rose, maroon, green and white. Plants range from 8 to 36 inches in height; leaves range from 6 to 24 inches in length. The flowers are not very ornamental and are often removed to prevent the plants from setting seed. Many cultivars are available. 'Candidum' is a 2-foot plant with white leaves and green veins. 'Little Miss Muffit' reaches 8 to 12 inches and has leaves marked with maroon. 'Pink Beauty' bears green-edged leaves with pink centers and deep pink veins. 'Postman Joyner' has deep red leaves with green margins.

Growing conditions. Plant caladiums outdoors in a shady location with rich soil at a depth of about 1

BRODIAEA CORONARIA

BULBOCODIUM VERNUM

CALADIUM × HORTULANUM 'POSTMAN JOYNER'

CALOCHORTUS NUTTALLII

CAMASSIA LEICHTLINII 'PLENA'

CAMASSIA QUAMASH

inch. North of Zone 10, grow them in containers or as annuals for the shade. Start plants indoors in late winter in the pots or tubs in which they are to grow or in peat pots. Plant tubers at a depth of 2 to 3 inches. Caladiums prefer day temperatures above 70° F, so do not move plants to the garden until late spring. Keep caladiums evenly moist throughout the growing season. At the end of the season allow the plant to dry out. Dig the tubers and store them indoors in a cool, dry place over winter.

Caladium see also *Colocasia*

Calla lily see *Zantedeschia*

Calochortus (kal-o-KOR-tus)
Mariposa lily, globe tulip, butterfly tulip

Mariposa lilies are bulbous plants native to western North America. They have grassy, somewhat fleshy leaves and yellow, white, orange, red, lavender, purple or sometimes brownish flowers. Blooms are borne singly or in small clusters. Each flower has three petals and three showy, petal-like sepals and often exhibits a showy "beard" inside. Zones 3-10.

Selected species and varieties. *C. gunnisonii,* mariposa lily, sego lily, is an erect, 1½-foot plant with white, bell-shaped, 1¾-inch flowers that are streaked with purple and have showy yellow beards. Flowers appear in late spring. Zones 4-10. *C. luteus,* yellow mariposa, produces 1½- to 2-inch flowers that are bright yellow or orange and striped with brown at the base. The flowers are borne in late spring on 1- to 2½-foot plants. Zones 5-10. *C. nuttallii,* sego lily, bears bell-shaped, 2- to 3-inch flowers that are white marked with purple. Flowers are borne in late summer on 1½-foot plants. *C. nuttallii aureus* bears lemon yellow flowers. Zones 5-10.

Growing conditions. Mariposa lilies are easy to grow in the western United States, where they are native. Plant corms 2 inches deep in a location with infertile, well-drained, sandy soil that is slightly acidic. Keep plants dry in summer after the foliage dies down. They cannot tolerate the damp soil or the winter freezing and thawing of northeastern winters; so plant corms in pots and keep them in a cold frame for the winter. Move them to the garden for flowering and lift them when the foliage dies down in early summer. Store the corms over summer in a dry place and replant in fall. Do not fertilize. Mariposa lilies tend to be short-lived in cultivation and can be treated as annuals.

Camass see *Camassia*

Camassia (ka-MAS-ee-a)
Camass, camas

Camassias are spring-blooming North American natives that grow from bulbs. They have grasslike, somewhat succulent leaves and star-like white, blue or violet-blue flowers. Flowers are carried in tall, lacy-looking spikes and appear in late spring. Zones 5-9.

Selected species and varieties. *C. cusickii,* Cusick camass, bears 20-inch leaves that are only ¾ to 1½ inches wide. Flowers are borne in 3-foot spikes and are pale blue to violet-blue. *C. leichtlinii,* Leichtlin camass, is a 4-foot plant with 2-foot leaves and spikes of light blue or creamy white, 1-inch flowers. 'Plena' is a multiple-petaled form. *C. quamash* (formerly *C. esculenta),* common quamash or camosh, bears spikes of white, light blue or blue-violet flowers on 1- to 2-foot plants. *C. scilloides,* wild hyacinth, Atlantic camass, indigo squill, is a 2½-foot plant bearing spikes of white, blue or violet-blue flowers.

Growing conditions. Plant camassias in fall in a rich, moist soil that is well drained. Add sand to the soil mixture to improve drainage. Space bulbs 6 to 8 inches apart and plant at a depth of 4 inches. Do not allow the soil to dry out during the growing season. Leave the plants undisturbed unless they become overcrowded and flowering declines.

Camosh see *Camassia*

Canna (KAN-a)
Indian shot, canna

A heat-loving, tropical genus of large, showy plants that have been widely hybridized. The plants are 4 to

8 feet tall, arise from thick rhizomes and have broad, 18- to 25-inch-long leaves. Flowers reach 4 inches in diameter and are borne in terminal clusters. They consist of small greenish petals and showy, petal-like sterile stamens. Cannas are fine for beds or borders and are often grown as annuals where they are not hardy. Zones 7-10.

Selected species and varieties. *C. flaccida,* golden canna, is native to marshes in the eastern United States. Plants are 5 feet in height and bear showy spikes of yellow flowers. *C.* × *generalis,* common garden canna, is a group of large-flowered hybrids with flowers that come in red, yellow, cream, orange and pink, and may also be marked with contrasting colors. Height ranges from 2 feet for dwarf cultivars to 8 feet for full-sized cultivars. 'Challenger' has salmon-colored flowers and green foliage. 'City of Portland' is a rose-pink-flowered selection. The Pfitzer series cultivars, which come in apricot, red, yellow and pink, are dwarf plants generally under 2½ feet tall. Zones 9 and 10. *C. indica,* Indian shot, is a 4-foot plant with bright red flowers that have orange lips spotted with red. Zones 9 and 10. *C.* × *orchiodes,* orchid-flowered canna, produces very large yellow or red flowers that are marked with contrasting colors. Zones 9 and 10. *C. warscewiczii* bears purplish or brownish purple foliage on 5-foot plants. Flowers are red. Zones 9 and 10.

Growing conditions. Plant cannas in a sunny location in a bed that has rich, well-drained soil with plenty of organic matter. To improve drainage, mound the bed so the center is 4 to 6 inches above the edge. Cannas will not tolerate poor, dry or rocky soil. Provide plenty of water during the growing season. Cannas are heat-loving plants and most cannot tolerate frost. In Zones 9 and 10, grow them outdoors year round. North of Zone 9, start rootstocks indoors four weeks before plants are to be moved outside, which should be done after all danger of frost has passed. Or, plant outdoors after the soil temperature has warmed to 60° or 70° F; place them several inches below the surface. In fall, once the tops have been killed by the first frost, dig the plants, cut the tops off, shake the soil off the roots and dry the plants in the sun for several hours. Store the roots in dry sand or vermiculite in a cool, dry place over winter. In spring, cut the stored rootstocks into sections, each with one or two buds, and replant.

Cape cowslip see *Lachenalia*

Cape tulip see *Homeria*

Catherine-wheel see *Haemanthus*

Checkered lily see *Fritillaria*

Chilean crocus see *Tecophilaea*

Chincherinchee see *Ornithogalum*

Chinese chive see *Allium*

Chinese garlic see *Allium*

Chionodoxa (ky-on-o-DOK-sa)

Glory-of-the-snow

A genus of early-flowering, bulbous plants with blue, white or pink flowers borne in terminal spikes. Leaves are long and narrow. Glory-of-the-snow is planted in rock gardens, under deeply rooted trees such as oaks and in wildflower gardens. Zones 4-9.

Selected species and varieties. *C. luciliae* is a 3- to 6-inch species with narrow foliage that bears spikes of four to six 1-inch flowers. Blooms are usually blue with a white center, but 'Alba' is a white-flowered cultivar. 'Gigantea' is a large-flowered selection. 'Pink Giant' bears pink, 1-inch flowers with white centers. Zones 4-9. *C. sardensis* is a 6-inch plant with slightly smaller blue flowers. Collection in the wild has endangered the species; purchase from reputable dealers that sell only propagated bulbs. Zones 4-9.

Growing conditions. Plant glory-of-the-snow in autumn in a location with rich, well-drained soil at a depth of 3 inches. It will grow in full sun or light shade and perform best if left undisturbed. Divide only if plants become overcrowded and flowering declines.

Chive see *Allium*

Claytonia (klay-TOH-nee-a)

Spring beauty

A small genus of fleshy-foliaged, spring-blooming plants related to the annual portulaca. The plants bear small clusters of pink or white flowers, and most arise from corms. Most spring beauties are native

CANNA × GENERALIS 'CHALLENGER'

CHIONODOXA LUCILIAE

CLAYTONIA VIRGINICA

CLIVIA MINIATA

COLCHICUM SPECIOSUM 'THE GIANT'

COLOCASIA ESCULENTA

American wildflowers and are fine subjects for wildflower and rock gardens. Zones 5-9.

Selected species and varieties. *C. caroliniana,* Carolina spring beauty, bears leaves that are broad in the middle, not grasslike. Zones 5-9. *C. lanceolata* is native to the Pacific Northwest. It bears 4-inch spikes of up to 15 flowers that are pink or white marked with pink. Some flowers are blotched with yellow. Zones 7-9. *C. megarhiza* is native to Washington state and bears dense spikes of white to dark pink flowers. Zones 6-8. *C. virginica,* Virginia spring beauty, closely resembles *C. caroliniana,* with loose spikes of two to 15 flowers that are pink or white marked with pink and borne atop 6- to 12-inch plants. The foliage is grasslike and narrow. Zones 5-9.

Growing conditions. Plant spring beauties in a location with rich, moist soil that is high in organic matter. They prefer a site with light shade. *C. megarhiza* is best grown only in areas with cool summers. Plants can be propagated by seed or by division.

Climbing lily see *Gloriosa*

Clivia (KLY-vee-a)
Kafir lily

A genus of evergreen perennials from South Africa with fleshy roots and fanlike clumps of dark green, leathery, strap-shaped leaves. Flowers, which are reddish yellow, orange or red, are funnel-shaped and carried in umbels on leafless stalks. Kafir lilies are grown as houseplants or as greenhouse plants in the North, in borders and in containers in the South. Zone 10.

Selected species and varieties. *C. miniata,* scarlet kafir lily, is a 2-foot plant bearing umbels of up to 20 trumpet-shaped flowers that are orange-red on the outside and yellowish inside. *C.* × *cyrtanthiflora* produces clusters of nodding, narrow, tube-shaped flowers that are red and yellow.

Growing conditions. Outdoors in Zone 10, grow kafir lilies in shady borders that have rich, well-drained soil and receive bright light but no direct sun. They bloom in winter or early spring. Clumps should remain undivided and undisturbed. North of Zone 10, plants can be grown indoors in winter and be brought out to a shady spot in summer. Fertilize in spring and propagate by division or from seed.

Cojomaria see *Paramongaia*

Colchicum (KOLE-chi-kum)
Meadow saffron, autumn crocus

Despite the common name autumn crocus, colchicum is not a true crocus but a member of the lily family. It produces foliage in spring and showy white, rosy purple or yellow flowers in fall after the foliage has died down. They make fine additions to a rock or wildflower garden and also can be planted under trees. Zones 4-10.

Selected species and varieties. *C. agrippinum* has two or three lilac-spotted flowers extending from a white tube and 4- to 6-inch-long foliage. *C. autumnale,* common autumn crocus, meadow saffron, bears one to four white to light purple flowers up to 4 inches long. 'Plenum' is double-flowered. *C. cilicium* bears foot-long leaves and up to 25 rose-purple, 3-inch flowers. *C. luteum* is a spring-blooming species bearing up to four yellow, 1½-inch flowers. *C. speciosum* produces long, narrow (12- to 16-inch by 3- to 4-inch) foliage in spring and showy, cup-shaped flowers in fall. Blooms are up to 4 inches across and 6 to 12 inches long and are rose to purple with white throats. Many hybrids are available, and these are often showier than the species. 'Autumn Queen' bears deep violet flowers. 'The Giant' produces pinkish mauve flowers with white bases. 'Violet Queen' has deep violet flowers. 'Waterlily' is a double-flowered plant with lilac-mauve flowers.

Growing conditions. Plant colchicums in late summer, as soon as possible after receiving the corms, or they will begin blooming before they are planted. Select a site with rich, well-drained soil and plant the corms at a depth of 2 to 3 inches. Allow the foliage to die back naturally; cutting the foliage back prematurely will prevent future bloom. Colchicum corms are poisonous.

Colocasia (ko-lo-KAY-see-a)
Elephant's ear

A small genus of large tropical plants in the arum family. One species is grown as an ornamental for its enormous foliage. The flowers are borne on a fleshy spadix surrounded by a leafy spathe. Zones 9 and 10.

Selected species and varieties. *C. esculenta* (also listed as *Caladium esculenta),* taro, dasheen, is cultivated in the tropics for its fleshy tubers, which to be edible must be thoroughly cooked. (In Hawaii the cooked dish is known as poi.) The leaves can also be cooked and eaten like spinach. The plants are 3 to 7 feet in height. Leaves are arrow-shaped, up to 2 feet in length and borne on 4- to 6-foot stems. The foliage may be green or marked with red-purple or bluish black.

Growing conditions. Grow elephant's ear in partial shade in a location with deep, moist, fertile soil. Select a site protected from high winds, which can damage the foliage. Plant the fleshy tubers at a depth of 6 inches and space them 3 to 6 feet apart. North of Zones 9 and 10, elephant's ear can be planted in late spring, when the soil is warm, and dug up when the tops are killed by the first frost. Dry the roots and store them in dry peat or sand in a cool, frost-free place over winter.

Corn flag see *Gladiolus*

Corn lily see *Ixia*

Corydalis (ko-RID-al-is)

A genus of shade-loving plants that bear handsome spikes of small, tube-shaped flowers, each of which has a single spur. Foliage is ferny and green or blue-green. Grown in shady borders and in rock gardens for their spring or early-summer flowers. Zones 5-10.

Selected species and varieties. *C. bulbosa,* fumewort, has a round tuber and bears clusters of 10 to 20 rosy lavender flowers in spring. Plants are 8 inches in height and die down in summer after flowering. Zones 6-10. *C. cava* resembles *C. bulbosa,* but it has larger tubers and the blossom spur is more sharply curved. Flowers are purple or white; 'Albaflora' is a white-flowered cultivar. *C. lutea,* yellow corydalis, is a 15-inch plant with short rhizomes and fibrous roots. It bears spikes of up to 16 golden yellow flowers. Foliage is very lacy and blue-green in color. It remains attractive throughout the summer.

Growing conditions. Plant corydalis in a location with light to deep shade and moist, somewhat sandy soil that is well drained and rich in organic matter. Plant yellow corydalis in early spring or early fall. Tuberous kinds are best moved immediately after the foliage dies down in summer. Mulch plants annually with leaf mold, compost or hardwood bark.

Crinum (KRY-num)

Crinum, crinum lily, spider lily

Crinums are tropical, lilylike plants grown for their showy white, pink or red flowers, which appear in spring or summer. Contrary to their common names, they are actually members of the amaryllis family. They have long, strap-shaped leaves that may be deciduous or evergreen. Flowers are trumpet-shaped and borne in umbels atop leafless stalks. Plants arise from bulbs. Crinums are planted alone as specimen plants and allowed to form large clumps, or grouped in borders or along pools or ponds. They can be grown in large tubs as well. Zones 7-10.

Selected species and varieties. *C. americanum,* southern swamp crinum, swamp lily, bears white flowers that are 3 inches across and 3 to 4 inches long. Leafless flower stalks, which appear before the foliage, carry up to six flowers and reach 1½ to 2 feet in height. Southern swamp crinum is native to wet places in the southern United States. Zones 9 and 10. *C. asiaticum,* poison bulb, produces a clump of 3- to 4-inch-wide leaves and umbels of 20 to 50 fragrant white flowers with greenish tubes. Zones 9 and 10. *C. bulbispermum,* Jamaica crinum, bears six- to 12-flowered umbels of white or pink flowers. Plants reach 3 feet in height and have long, narrow leaves. Zones 9 and 10. *C. moorei,* long-neck crinum, is a 2- to 4-foot plant that bears rose-red flowers up to 4 inches across. Zones 9 and 10. *C.* × *powellii* is the name given to crosses between *C. bulbispermum* and *C. moorei.* These plants bear clumps of leaves that are 3 to 4 feet long and 3 to 4 inches wide and produce umbels of about eight flowers. 'Album' is a white-flowered cultivar; 'Rosea' bears pink flowers. Zones 8-10.

Growing conditions. Crinums prefer rich, moist soil and light shade.

CORYDALIS LUTEA

CRINUM ASIATICUM

CRINUM × POWELLII 'ALBUM'

CROCOSMIA × CROCOSMIIFLORA 'EMBER GLOW'

CROCUS SATIVUS

Plant the bulbs 2 to 3 feet apart with the tips just beneath the surface of the soil. Leave in place, since digging and dividing can interrupt flowering. North of Zone 8, plant in a protected location and mulch heavily in winter. Or overwinter the bulbs indoors.

Crocosmia (kro-KOZ-mee-a)

Montebretia

A small genus of summer-blooming plants belonging to the iris family and native to South Africa. Plants arise from corms and bear 1-inch, funnel-shaped flowers that are yellow, orange or red. Foliage is flat and sword-shaped. Montebretias are planted in beds and borders, and make fine cut flowers. Zones 7-10.

Selected species and varieties. *C.* × *crocosmiiflora,* common montebretia, bears erect, 4-foot spikes of orange-yellow flowers that are somewhat star-shaped. 'Ember Glow' is 15 to 20 inches tall and has scarlet flowers. *C. masoniorum* is a 2- to 4-foot plant with spikes bearing many scarlet-orange flowers. Zones 7-10.

Growing conditions. Plant montebretias in spring in a location with full sun to light shade and rich, well-drained soil. They also need protection from high winds. Plant the corms 3 inches deep and 2 to 4 inches apart, and mulch the plants to retain moisture and to keep the roots cool. Water during dry spells and fertilize in midsummer. Where montebretias are not hardy, the corms should be dug after the first hard frost and stored after a few days' drying in sunlight. Shake off excess soil and allow them to dry for several days in a cool, dry place out of direct sun. Cut back the tops of the plants and discard the remains of the previous season's corms. Store in dry peat moss or vermiculite at a temperature of approximately 50° F.

Crocus (KRO-kus)

Crocuses are traditional harbingers of spring that bear grasslike leaves and cup-shaped, white, yellow, pink, lilac or deep purple flowers held close to the ground. The stigmas in the centers of the blooms are often showy. In some species, the leaves appear after the flowers; in others, with the flowers. All arise from corms and are generally 3 to 6 inches in height. There are autumn-flowering species in this genus, which is classified in the iris family. These true crocuses should not be confused with the so-called autumn crocuses, or *Colchicum* species, which are members of the lily family. Crocuses can be planted at the front of beds and borders, in woodland gardens, around the bases of deep-rooted trees such as oaks or in rock gardens. Zones 3-10.

Selected species and varieties. *C. ancyrensis* bears golden yellow, ¾-inch flowers in late winter. 'Golden Bunch' is a free-flowering cultivar with orange-yellow flowers. Zones 5-10. *C. biflorus,* Scotch crocus, bears 4-inch-long flowers that may be white or lilac and can be striped or veined with purplish blue. Flowers appear in early spring. Zones 5-10. *C. chrysanthus* bears 4-inch-long blooms that range from pale yellow to orange-yellow. The flowers are fragrant and appear in early spring. 'Advance' has pale yellow flowers striped with purple. 'Blue Pearl' bears pale blue flowers. 'Cream Beauty' has pale yellow blooms. Zones 4-9. *C. etruscus* bears 4-inch-long lilac flowers with yellow throats in early spring. Zones 3-9. *C. flavus* produces golden yellow flowers that range from 2½ to 7 inches in early spring. Zones 4-9. *C. goulimyi* is an autumn-blooming species that does well in Southern California. Blooms are star-shaped, deep pinkish purple and fragrant. Zones 8-10.

C. imperati, early crocus, bears 2½- to 5½-inch flowers that are buff-colored or yellow with purple stripes on the outside and purple inside. Flowers are fragrant and appear in very early spring. *C. korolkowii,* celandine crocus, bears orange-yellow blooms in spring. Zones 6-9. *C. kotschyanus* is a fall-blooming species that produces rosy lilac, 2-inch-long flowers that are spotted inside with orange. *C. kotschyanus leucopharynx* is bluish lavender with a creamy white throat. Zones 5-9. *C. laevigatus* bears very fragrant white flowers with orange-yellow throats in autumn or winter. 'Fontenayi' bears buff-colored blooms that are rose-lilac on the outside. *C. longiflorus* has lavender to purple blossoms with purple throats and blooms in fall. Zone 5. *C. medius* is an autumn-blooming species with lilac to purple blooms that are 4 to 10 inches in length. Zones 6-10. *C. niveus* is a robust autumn-flowering species bearing white flowers with golden orange throats. Zones 5-8.

C. ochroleucus produces pale cream flowers that are orange on the inside in fall. Zones 5-9. *C. pulchellus* has autumn-borne blooms that are lavender to lilac with orange throats. Zones 6-9. *C. sativus,* saffron crocus, bears large, fragrant purple or white blooms in fall. The orange-red stigmas and styles, when dried, are the source of the herb saffron. Zones 6-10. *C. sieberi,* Sieber crocus, has 1½-inch-long lilac flowers in late winter or early spring. Zones 7-10. *C. speciosus* is a very showy fall-blooming species with violet-blue flowers and bright orange stigmas. Zones 5-10. *C. tomasinianus* has lilac to purple flowers with white throats. Flowers 2½ to 5½ inches long appear in early spring. 'Whitewell Purple' has reddish purple flowers. *C. vernus,* common crocus, Dutch crocus, has been the most commonly grown species in the United States for many years. It bears flowers that are lilac or white and are often striped with purple and blooms in early spring. Cultivars include 'Haarlem Gem', which has lilac-blue flowers; 'Striped Beauty', which has lilac flowers with white stripes; and 'Yellow Mammouth', which bears large golden yellow blooms. Zones 4-10. *C. versicolor,* cloth-of-silver crocus, has spring-borne flowers that are purple on the outside and yellow or white on the inside. Zones 5-9.

Growing conditions. Grow crocuses in a location that has full sun at least during the season the foliage is apparent (spring or fall). Crocuses require good drainage and perform best in well-drained sandy or gritty soil. They will not grow well in wet clay soil. For best results, prepare the soil to a depth of about 6 inches. Plant corms with the bases 3 to 4 inches below the surface. Crocuses do not need dividing and can be left undisturbed for many years. Feed annually in spring with a balanced garden fertilizer. The foliage must be allowed to mature and yellow naturally if the plants are to produce corms and blooms for the following year: do not mow it or cut it back. Crocuses planted in a lawn or any other location where they must compete with plants other than shallow-rooted annuals will need to be replaced every few years. Gophers, voles and squirrels all eat the corms. Crocuses require varying periods of cold temperatures to bloom, and gardeners in Zones 9 and 10 should experiment with small quantities of bulbs to determine which bloom most reliably in their area.

Crown imperial see *Fritillaria*
Crow-poison see *Amianthium*

Cuban lily see *Scilla*
Cusick camass see *Camassia*

Cyclamen

(SIK-la-men or SY-kla-men)
Florist's cyclamen, hardy cyclamen, Persian violet

Best known for the popular florist's cyclamen, this genus also contains several hardy perennials that bloom in spring or fall and produce both attractive foliage and flowers. The leaves are round or heart-shaped, dark green in color and patterned with silver or cream; flowers are borne on leafless stalks and have reflexed petals resembling shooting stars. Blooms are white, rose, pink or red. The flowers of florist's cyclamen appear with the foliage; the diminutive hardy cyclamen often bears its flowers before the foliage appears. Cyclamen makes a fine addition to woodland and rock gardens and can also be planted under deeply rooted trees such as oaks. Collection in the wild has endangered most species in the genus; purchase from reputable dealers that sell only propagated corms or seeds. Zones 5-10.

Selected species and varieties. *C. africanum* bears pale to rose-pink flowers and large glossy green leaves. Zone 10. *C.* × *atkinsii* is a late-winter- or early-spring-blooming hybrid that has nearly round leaves marked with white. Plants are 3 to 6 inches tall, and the 1-inch flowers are white to pale pink marked with red. Zones 7-10. *C. balearicum* bears nearly round 3½-inch leaves that are blue-gray marked with silver above and maroon underneath. Flowers are ¾ inch across, white with pink veins and borne in spring. Zones 9 and 10. *C. cilicium,* Sicily cyclamen, is a 3-inch plant that produces roundish leaves that are marbled with silver above and deep red beneath. Flowers appear in fall and are rose-pink to white with a red blotch at the base. Zones 7-10. *C. coum,* Atkins cyclamen, bears plain green or marbled leaves that are reddish purple beneath. Flowers are borne from winter to early spring on 4-inch plants and are pink or pink marked with white. Zones 7-10. *C. graecum* bears dark green leaves marbled with gray-green above and dark violet-purple beneath. The flowers, which appear in fall, are 1 inch long and pale pink with magenta streaks. Zones 8-10. *C. hederifolium* (sometimes listed as *C. neopolitanum),* Neapolitan cycla-

CROCUS TOMASINIANUS

CROCUS VERNUS 'STRIPED BEAUTY'

CYCLAMEN PERSICUM

DAHLIA 'KEEWATIN PIONEER'

DAHLIA 'BROOKSIDE SNOWBALL'

DAHLIA 'BORDER PRINCESS'

men, produces rose-pink to white flowers with a red blotch at the base in late summer or fall. Foliage is marbled with silver above and gray-green or deep red beneath. Plants reach 4 inches in height. Zones 5-10. *C. persicum,* florist's cyclamen, common cyclamen, is a tender, 6- to 12-inch plant with showy deep green leaves marbled with silver. Flowers are double or single, 2 inches in length, and may be pink, salmon, rose, lilac, white or bicolored. Florist's cyclamen is an early-spring bloomer when grown outdoors; a winter bloomer when grown indoors. Zones 9 and 10. *C. repandum* produces 1¼-inch flowers that are red, pink or white, and foliage that may be marbled or plain above and is purplish red beneath. Flowers appear in spring. Zones 6-10.

Growing conditions. Grow hardy cyclamen in a protected location with light shade and deep, well-drained soil that is well tilled and has been amended with organic matter and sand. Mulch the plants for protection and leave them undisturbed. All cyclamens are dormant during part of the year, usually throughout the summer months, so be sure to mark the plantings to avoid damaging them by careless digging. Florist's cyclamen can be planted outdoors in shaded, frost-free areas as a winter or spring bedding plant.

Daffodil see *Narcissus*
Daffodil garlic see *Allium*

Dahlia (DAL-ya)

Although commonly grown as annuals, dahlias actually are tender, tuberous-rooted perennials that can be saved and grown year after year. Plants range in size from 1 to 6 feet in height, and flowers range from 2 to 10 inches across. Dahlias are members of the daisy family and bear flower heads made up of showy ray florets, or "petals," surrounding tightly packed, buttonlike centers. Blooms may be single or double, and come in many flower forms. Colors range from white to rose, red, orange, yellow and purple, and blooms may be bicolored. Zones 9 and 10.

Selected species and varieties. All of the dahlias grown today are of hybrid origin, most descending from crosses between *D. pinnata* and *D. coccinea.* So many different flower forms have been developed that dahlias have been classified into groups according to the type of bloom by the American Dahlia Society. Single dahlias bear daisylike blooms that have an open center and a single row of ray florets. They may be one color or two-toned. Anemone-flowered dahlias have open centers with one or more rows of ray florets and tubular disc florets that give a pincushion effect. 'Fable' is an anemone-flowered cultivar. Cactus-flowered dahlias are fully double blooms with ray florets that either curve in toward the center of the flower or out toward its base. 'Keewatin Pioneer' is a cactus-flowered cultivar with red and yellow 4- to 6-inch flowers. There are two types of so-called decorative dahlias: formal and informal. Both have fully double blooms, but formal decoratives have broad ray florets that are regularly arranged, pointed or rounded on the tips, and curved in toward the center of the flower and out at the base. Informal decoratives have ray florets that are long and twisted and irregularly arranged. Mignon dahlias bear single flowers and are under 18 inches in height.

Other forms include ball dahlias, which have ball-shaped blooms; pompom dahlias, with ball-shaped blooms that are under 2 inches; collarette dahlias, which have single, daisylike blooms with a collar of contrasting color around the central disc; and peony dahlias, which have open centers and three to five rows of ray florets. 'Brookside Snowball' is a ball dahlia with 4- to 4½-inch white flowers.

There are also cultivars available that are not classified by flower form. 'Border Princess' grows 12 to 14 inches high and comes in various colors. 'Rigoletto' has single or double flowers in several colors.

Gardeners looking for compact-growing plants should be aware that the term "miniature dahlias" is used for plants that have flowers less than 4 inches across regardless of the size of the plant. Selections listed as "dwarf dahlias" are shorter than standard-size dahlias, but different dwarf selections may range from under 1 to 3 feet in height.

Growing conditions. Grow dahlias in full sun or light shade in a location with light, rich, well-drained soil. Dahlias should be planted outdoors after all danger of frost has passed. Space plants 8 to 24 inches apart, depending on their ultimate height, and feed with 5-10-5 fertilizer at planting and repeat monthly during the growing season. Mulch and water heavily; never let the soil dry out completely. Most dahlias require staking. For best results, place stakes in the ground before planting, and as the plants grow tie the stems to the stake with rags or yarn. To store dahlias over winter north of Zone 9, dig the tuberous roots after the tops of the plants have been blackened by frost, shake off the excess soil and dry them in the sun for several hours. Remove the tops of the plants and store the roots in a cool, dry place over winter. Check them periodically to make sure they do not dry out. Plants that begin to grow are receiving too much heat or light. Most dahlia cultivars are propagated by cuttings or division. To divide dahlias, cut the stored roots into sections in spring before planting. Make sure that each root section has a bud. Dahlias can also be started from seed, but the colors and forms will not breed true.

Dasheen see *Colocasia*
Death camas see *Zigadenus*
Desert candle see *Eremurus*

Dichelostemma
(dik-e-lo-STEM-a)
Firecracker plant, blue dicks

A small genus of amaryllis-family members native to the western United States. They arise from corms, have long, narrow leaves and bear umbels of small, bell-shaped flowers. Dichelostemmas make fine additions to native plant gardens, naturalized areas and perennial borders in the western states. In the East, they can be grown in rock gardens, where improved drainage provides a better chance for survival. Zones 5-10.

Selected species and varieties. *D. multiflorum* (sometimes listed as *Brodiaea grandiflorum* or *B. multiflorum),* wild hyacinth, is a 2½-foot plant that bears umbels of ¾-inch violet-purple flowers. *D. pulchellum* (sometimes listed as *B. capitata* or *B. pulchellum),* blue dicks, wild hyacinth, is a 2-foot plant with clusters of violet or white flowers.

Growing conditions. Plant dichelostemmas outdoors in fall in a location with full sun and well-drained sandy or gritty soil. Plant the corms at a depth of 3 to 5 inches and space them 2 to 3 inches apart. These plants are easy to grow in California but are intolerant of wet eastern summers. In the East, keep the plants evenly moist while the foliage and blooms are apparent in spring and early summer. After the foliage dies down, dig the corms and store them in a dry place over the summer. Replant in fall.

Dierama (dee-a-RAH-ma)
Wandflower

Dieramas are cormous iris-family members native to South Africa. They bear long, narrow, rigid leaves and showy curving spikes of funnel-shaped flowers. Use them in borders or near water. Zones 9 and 10.

Selected species and varieties. *D. pendulum,* grassy-bell, angel's-fishing-rods, is a 5-foot, summer-blooming plant with leaves mostly at the base of the stems. Flowers are 1 inch long, borne in thin, drooping spikes, white to lavender. *D. pulcherrimum* bears drooping spikes of violet-purple flowers that are about 1½ inches long.

Growing conditions. Plant wandflowers in fall in a location with full sun and rich, moist, well-drained, sandy soil. Space corms 3 inches apart and plant them 3 inches deep. Plants may be lifted and divided every few years, but they can be difficult to transplant. North of Zone 9, wandflowers are grown in pots in greenhouses.

Dog-tooth violet see *Erythronium*
Dragonroot see *Arisaema*
Elephant's ear see *Colocasia*

Endymion (en-DIM-ee-on)
Wood hyacinth

A genus of bulbous, spring-blooming plants with spikes of nodding, bell-shaped flowers that are blue, pink or white. Foliage is narrow and grass-like. Wood hyacinths, which are also

DAHLIA 'RIGOLETTO'

DICHELOSTEMMA PULCHELLUM

DIERAMA PULCHERRIMUM

ENDYMION HISPANICUS

ERANTHIS HYEMALIS

EREMURUS STENOPHYLLUS

listed as *Hyacinthoides* and *Scilla,* are used in woodland gardens and in borders and make excellent cut flowers. Zones 5-9.

Selected species and varieties. *E. hispanicus* (also listed as *Hyacinthoides hispanicus, Scilla campanulata* and *S. hispanicus),* Spanish bluebell, bell-flowered squill, bears strap-shaped leaves that are 1 foot long and 1½ inches wide. Plants reach about 20 inches and produce 10- to 30-flowered spikes of bell-shaped, ¾-inch flowers that come in blue, rose-purple, white and pink. 'Alba Maxima' has white flowers. 'Blue Queen' and 'Excelsior' produce profuse quantities of blue flowers; 'Rosabella' has pink flowers. *E. italicus* (also listed as *Hyacinthoides italicus* and *Scilla italica),* Italian squill, is a 1-foot plant with 8-inch leaves that are ½ inch wide. The flowers are fragrant, pale blue in color and ¼ inch long. They are borne in three- to 30-flowered spikes. *E. non-scriptus* (also listed as *Hyacinthoides non-scriptus* and *Scilla non-scriptus),* English bluebell, harebell, produces four- to 16-flowered spikes of ½-inch, bell-shaped flowers atop 1½-foot plants. Flowers are usually blue, but pink- and white-flowered forms are also available. Zones 6-9.

Growing conditions. Grow wood hyacinths in medium to heavy shade, such as under deciduous trees, in humus-rich soil that is moist. Plant the bulbs in fall 3 inches deep and 6 inches apart. Do not dig or divide the plants unless absolutely necessary. They will multiply by offsets and self-seeding.

English bluebell see *Endymion*

Eranthis (e-RAN-this)

Winter aconite

Winter aconites are early-spring-blooming members of the buttercup family that arise from tuberous roots. The foliage is deeply divided and borne at the base of the plant, with the exception of one dissected leaf that is carried just below the flower. Flowers are borne one per stem and consist of showy sepals (usually yellow, occasionally white) surrounding small, nectar-producing petals. Winter aconites make fine additions to woodland and rock gardens and also can be used for naturalizing. Zones 4-9.

Selected species and varieties. *E. hyemalis* is an upright, 3- to 8-inch species with brilliant yellow flowers. Collection in the wild has endangered the species; purchase from reputable dealers that sell only propagated tuberous roots.

Growing conditions. Winter aconites require rich, well-drained soil that remains moist during the summer months. The tuberous roots should be in the ground when growth begins in early fall, so plant in late summer or early fall. Soak the tubers overnight in water before planting, and select a location with full sun or light shade. Plant at a depth of 3 inches and space plants 3 to 4 inches apart. Mulch to preserve soil moisture. Plants will die down in middle to late spring and can be overplanted with shallow-rooted annuals or perennials. Mark the plantings to avoid inadvertently digging them up, and do not divide them.

Eremurus (er-e-MEW-rus)

Desert candle, king's spear, foxtail lily

Desert candles are lily-family members with thick, brittle roots and narrow, sword-shaped leaves borne as a tuft or rosette at the base of the plant. The flowers are borne in long, dense spikes above the foliage and may be white, yellow, pink, orange or brown. They can be used at the back of borders, but their flower spikes show to best advantage when planted in front of a dark background such as evergreens. Zones 3-9.

Selected species and varieties. *E. himalaicus* bears dense, 2- to 3-foot spikes of white flowers that are 4 inches thick above 1½-foot leaves. Zones 4-8. *E.* × *isabellinus* is an 8-foot hybrid with white, pink, pale yellow, orange or copper-yellow spikes of flowers. Shelford Hybrids (sometimes listed as *E.* × *shelfordii)* bear red, pink, yellow, orange and white blooms on 3- to 4-foot plants. Zones 5-8. Pastel Hybrids are 3-foot plants with spikes of pink, orange or pale yellow flowers. Zones 5-8. *E. robustus* grows 7 feet tall and bears 3-foot spikes of flowers in early summer. Buds are pink and flowers are whitish pink. Zones 7-9. *E. stenophyllus* grows 2 to 3 feet tall and has golden yellow flowers.

Growing conditions. Plant desert candles in full sun in a location with rich, well-drained soil. Prepare the soil to a depth of 1½ to 2 feet, and spread the brittle roots on 1 to 2 inches of coarse sand to improve drainage before covering to a depth of 4 to 6 inches. Do not divide or move desert candles unless absolutely necessary. They need protection from wind because of their tall flower spikes. In the North, mound several inches of sawdust, mulch or peat moss over the plants after the ground has frozen in fall to protect the shoots, which emerge in early spring, from frost. If shoots emerge from the mulch before danger of frost has passed, cover the plants nightly with cardboard boxes or other protective structures. Remove the mounds when frost no longer threatens.

Erythronium

(er-i-THRO-nee-um)
Dog-tooth violet, trout lily, adder's-tongue, fawn lily

A lily-family member that arises from corms and ranges in height from 8 to 12 inches. Each plant bears two leaves at the base, and foliage may be mottled or solid green. Flowers are white, yellow, pink, rose or purple, and may be borne one or several per stem. Blooms, which appear in early spring, are nodding and lilylike with petals that are reflexed, or curve backward toward the base of the stem. Most species are native to North America and are excellent for wildflower and rock gardens. Collection in the wild has endangered most species in the genus; purchase from reputable dealers that sell only propagated corms. Zones 2-9.

Selected species and varieties. *E. albidum,* white dog-tooth violet, blond lilian, bears green, 6-inch leaves and 1- to 2-inch flowers. Flowers are pinkish white and borne one per stem. Zones 5-9. *E. americanum,* trout lily, amberbell, has 6-inch leaves that are mottled with brown and white. Flowers are solitary, yellow, 2 inches long and often spotted at the base. Zones 4-9. *E. californicum,* California fawn lily, has heavily mottled leaves and white to cream-colored, 1½-inch flowers borne one to three per stem. Zones 6-9. *E. citrinum* bears white to pale lemon yellow, 1½-inch flowers, one to several per stem. Zones 6-9. *E. dens-canis,* dog-tooth violet, is a 6- to 12-inch species with leaves mottled in reddish brown and white. Flowers are solitary, 1 inch long and come in rose, purple or white. Zones 4-9. *E. grandiflorum,* avalanche lily, is a 1- to 2-foot plant with plain green leaves and bright yellow, 1- to 2-inch flowers borne one to several per stem. Zones 6-9. *E. hendersonii* bears pale pinkish purple, 1½-inch flowers above mottled leaves. Zones 6-9. *E. montanum,* alpine fawn lily, has plain green leaves and white, 1½-inch flowers marked with orange inside the base. Zones 6-9. *E.* × 'Pagoda' is a cross between *E. tuolumnense* and *E. revolutum.* It bears yellow blooms with a brown ring at the center atop slightly mottled foliage. Zones 4-9. *E. revolutum,* coast fawn lily, is a 16-inch species with mottled foliage and lavender-white to purple, 1¾-inch flowers. The cultivar 'White Beauty' bears white, 2- to 3-inch flowers on 7-inch stems. Zones 6-9. *E. tuolumnense* has bright green foliage and yellow, 1¼-inch flowers. Zones 4-9.

Growing conditions. Grow dog-tooth violets in a location with light shade, such as under deciduous trees, and moist soil that is rich in organic matter and near neutral in pH. The soil must not dry out during the growing season. Plant corms in fall 2 to 3 inches deep and 4 to 5 inches apart. Corms must not dry out while above ground and should be planted as soon as possible; pack them in damp sand or peat if they can't be planted immediately. Some western species do not adapt well to eastern gardens. The following species are best suited for the East: *E. americanum, E. californicum, E. dens-canis, E. hendersonii, E. revolutum,* and *E. tuolumnense.*

Eucharis (YEW-ka-ris)

A small genus of Central and South American members of the amaryllis family that arise from bulbs. They bear large, broad, evergreen leaves and showy umbels of large, white flowers that somewhat resemble short-trumpeted daffodils. They are usually grown as indoor plants, but can be grown outdoors in frost-free areas. Zone 10.

Selected species and varieties. *E. grandiflora,* Amazon lily, Eucharist lily, bears glossy, dark green leaves that are 1 foot long and 6 inches wide. Flowers are waxy white and borne in four- to eight-flowered umbels atop 20-inch stalks.

ERYTHRONIUM REVOLUTUM 'WHITE BEAUTY'

EUCHARIS GRANDIFLORA

EUCOMIS AUTUMNALIS

FERRARIA CRISPA

FREESIA × HYBRIDA

Growing conditions. Amazon lilies require warm temperatures, high humidity and bright light but no direct sun. Plant them outdoors in frost-free areas or indoors in large pots or tubs in rich, well-drained soil. Keep the soil moist and leave the plants undisturbed for as long as possible.

Eucharist lily see *Eucharis*

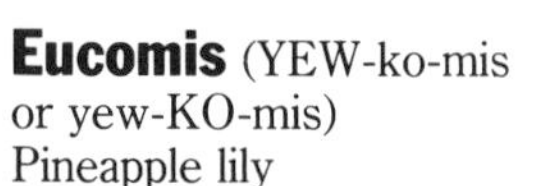

Eucomis (YEW-ko-mis or yew-KO-mis)

Pineapple lily

Pineapple lilies are summer-blooming lily-family members native to South Africa. They arise from bulbs and bear a rosette of leaves topped by a spike of greenish white, starlike flowers. The flower spikes are topped by a cluster of 10 to 30 leaflike bracts. Use pineapple lilies in flower borders in Zones 7-10, or in pots or tubs in the North. They make fine cut flowers. Zones 7-10.

Selected species and varieties. *E. autumnalis* is a 1- to 2-foot species with strap-shaped leaves having wavy margins and dense spikes of ¾-inch flowers. *E. bicolor* reaches 2 feet and bears spikes of greenish flowers edged in purple. Zones 8-10. *E. comosa,* pineapple flower, bears narrow, 2-foot-long leaves and dense spikes of ½-inch, greenish white flowers atop 2-foot plants.

Growing conditions. Grow pineapple lilies in a location with full sun or light shade. They should be planted in fall at a depth of 3 to 4 inches and will grow in most well-drained soils. The soil should be evenly moist when the leaves are above ground, but can be allowed to dry out after plants die down. Plants do not need dividing and can be left undisturbed for years.

European wood anemone see *Anemone*

Fairy lily see *Zephyranthes*

False garlic see *Nothoscordum*

Fawn lily see *Erythronium*

Ferraria (fer-RA-ree-a)

A small genus of plants belonging to the iris family and native to South Africa. Plants arise from corms and have sword-shaped leaves. The flowers appear in late spring or summer, are ill smelling and last only a day. Zones 9 and 10.

Selected species and varieties. *F. crispa* is an 18-inch plant with 3- to 4-inch, purplish brown to greenish brown flowers. Blooms have a sickly sweet smell. Each opens for only a day, but plants remain in flower for a month or more.

Growing conditions. Grow ferrarias in full sun in a location protected from wind and in rich, well-drained, deeply prepared soil. Plant corms from early spring to midsummer, 3 to 4 inches deep, depending on the size of the corm, and space them 6 to 9 inches apart. Enrich the soil with compost and fertilize with 5-10-5 when the plants emerge and again a month later. Plants need at least a 90-day growing season before the first frost in order to flower. In Zones 9 and 10, corms can be left in the ground over winter. In the North, dig the corms before the first hard frost, shake off excess soil and let them dry for several days in a cool, dry place out of direct sun. Cut back the tops of the plants and discard the remains of the previous season's corms. Store in dry peat moss or vermiculite at a temperature of 55° to 60° F. Propagate plants from the small cormels borne around old corms. Small corms take up to two seasons to bloom.

Firecracker plant see *Dichelostemma*

Fly-poison see *Amianthium*

Foxtail lily see *Eremurus*

Freesia (FREE-zha)

Freesias are extremely fragrant plants native to South Africa. They arise from tapered corms and bear narrow, sword-shaped leaves and spikes of funnel-shaped flowers that may be white, yellow, pink or purple. Freesias are generally grown as greenhouse plants or as annuals, except in the Deep South and Southern California. They make excellent cut flowers. Zones 9 and 10.

Selected species and varieties. *F.* × *hybrida* is a group of 1½- to

2-foot hybrids with single or double, 2-inch flowers that come in white or yellow but may be veined or shaded with pink, purple or orange. Many cultivars are available. 'Ballerina' has large, pure white flowers. *F. refracta* is an 8- to 18-inch species with very fragrant, greenish white flowers that are 1 inch long.

Growing conditions. In frost-free areas, plant freesias in the fall at a depth of 2 to 3 inches. They require full sun and rich, well-drained soil, and do best where temperatures are cool (45° to 55° F) at night. In the North, they can be grown in pots in a greenhouse or in sunny windows.

Fritillaria (fri-ti-LAIR-ee-a)
Fritillary

Fritillarias are spring-flowering, bulbous plants in the lily family. The flowers are nodding, funnel- to bell-shaped, and may be borne singly or in loose spikes or clusters. Blooms may be solid-colored or checkered. Most fritillarias are best used in rock gardens because they are intolerant of wet soil, especially in winter. A few species, such as *F. imperialis,* can be planted in borders. Zones 3-9.

Selected species and varieties. *F. dasyphylla* is a very rare 4- to 6-inch species bearing one or two bell-shaped, ¾-inch flowers that are wine-purple in color. Zones 5-9. *F. imperialis,* crown imperial, is a showy, 2- to 4-foot plant that is very popular despite its skunklike odor. The leaves are borne on the bottom two-thirds of the stem. The flowers are 2 inches long, bell-shaped, borne in a downward-pointing cluster at the top of the stem, and are orangish red, yellow or purplish. A number of cultivars are available. 'Lutea Maxima' bears large yellow flowers; 'Orange Brilliant', orange; and 'Rubra Maxima', large red flowers. Collection in the wild has endangered the species; purchase from reputable dealers that sell only propagated bulbs. Zones 5-9. *F. lanceolata,* checker lily, mission bells, bears one to four 1½-inch flowers that are purple mottled with greenish yellow. Plants reach 2 feet in height. Zones 6-9.

F. meleagris, guinea-hen flower, checkered lily, bears solitary, bell-shaped blooms that are 1½ inches long and have a checkered white and purplish or maroon pattern. Plants are 1 to 1½ feet tall. 'Alba' is a white-flowered form. Zones 3-9. *F. pallidiflora* bears bluish green foliage and 1½-inch, bell-shaped flowers that are yellowish white on the outside and dotted with purple inside. Zones 5-9. *F. persica* is a 3-foot plant that bears 10 to 30 bell-shaped, ¾-inch flowers that are violet-blue in color. 'Adiyama' bears 1-inch flowers that are plum-colored. Zones 5-9, but plants require protection from late frosts in the North. Collection in the wild has endangered the species; purchase from reputable dealers that sell only propagated bulbs. *F. pudica,* yellow fritillary, yellow bell, is a 9-inch species with grasslike leaves. It bears one to three yellow or orange bell-shaped flowers that are ¾ inch long. Zones 4-9.

F. pyrenaica produces one or two 1½-inch flowers that are dark purple spotted with green and checkered with reddish purple. Plants reach 1½ feet in height. Zones 5-8. *F. verticillata* bears 1¼-inch flowers atop 2-foot plants. Blooms are cup-shaped, and white or yellow marked with green on the outside and purplish inside. Zones 6-9.

Growing conditions. Fritillarias will grow in full sun or light shade and prefer a location with rich, well-drained soil. Plant bulbs at a depth of 4 to 6 inches as soon as they are available in the fall. They dry out quickly, so plant them as soon as possible. Most fritillarias from the western United States will not tolerate wet eastern winters. The best species for the East are *F. imperialis* and *F. pudica,* although in the East the latter requires full sun and extremely well drained soil that has little humus. Do not cultivate around the plants and leave them undisturbed for as long as possible. Divide only if plants become so crowded that flowering ceases.

Fritillary see *Fritillaria*
Fumewort see *Corydalis*

Galanthus (ga-LAN-thus)
Snowdrop

Snowdrops are members of the amaryllis family that bloom in late winter or very early spring. They are small, bulbous plants that have two or three grasslike leaves and nodding, waxy white flowers borne one per stem. Each bloom consists of six petal-like segments; there are three large outer segments that are white and three inner ones that are marked with green and appear tubular.

FRITILLARIA MELEAGRIS

FRITILLARIA PERSICA

GALANTHUS NIVALIS

GALTONIA CANDICANS

GLADIOLUS BYZANTINUS

GLADIOLUS × COLVILLEI

Snowdrops are grown in rock gardens and naturalized under deciduous trees and shrubs. Collection in the wild has endangered most species in the genus; purchase from reputable dealers that sell only propagated bulbs. Zones 3-10.

Selected species and varieties. *G. byzantinus* has 5½-inch leaves and nodding, ½- to 1-inch flowers. Zones 5-9. *G. elwesii,* giant snowdrop, bears leaves that are 1 inch wide and 4 inches long. Its blooms are 1¼ to 2 inches long. Zones 5-9. *G. nivalis,* common snowdrop, bears 4-inch leaves that are ¼ inch wide. It has 1-inch-long flowers. 'Flore Pleno' bears double flowers; 'Magnet' is a large-flowered form; 'Sam Arnott' is large-flowered but also has fragrant flowers. Zones 4-9. *G. reginae-olgae* is a fall-blooming species from Greece. Zones 5-10.

Growing conditions. Grow snowdrops in a location that has full sun or light shade, at least during the spring, when the foliage is apparent, and moist, rich, well-drained soil. Plant bulbs in late summer or early fall at a depth of 3 inches. Space plants 3 inches apart. They do not need dividing and if left undisturbed will form large colonies. The foliage must be allowed to mature and yellow naturally if the plants are to produce blooms the following year: do not mow it or cut it back.

Galtonia (gal-TOH-nee-a)

A small genus of summer-blooming South African plants in the lily family. They have fleshy, strap-shaped leaves and bear tall spikes of nodding, whitish flowers that are fragrant and bell-shaped. Galtonias can be used in beds and in borders. Zones 6-10.

Selected species and varieties. *G. candicans,* summer hyacinth, produces 2- to 4-foot spikes of fragrant, white, 2-inch flowers that open from late summer to early fall.

Growing conditions. Grow summer hyacinth in full sun in a location with deeply prepared soil that is rich in organic matter and well drained. Plant bulbs in spring at a depth of 6 inches. Summer hyacinths can be grown outdoors year round in Zones 6-10, but mulch heavily each fall in the North. North of Zone 6, lift the bulbs each fall. After lifting, dry the plants for several hours in the sun, remove excess soil and the tops of the plants, and store the bulbs in a cool (40° to 45° F), dry place over winter. Replant in spring.

Giant onion see *Allium*

Gladiolus (gla-dee-O-lus)

Corn flag, sword lily

A genus of showy, summer-blooming members of the iris family, most of which are native to South Africa. They arise from corms and have long, narrow, sword-shaped leaves. Flowers are borne in few- to many-flowered spikes covered with leaflike bracts. Individual blooms are flaring or trumpet-shaped. Gladioli are grown in beds and borders. In areas where they are not hardy, they can be dug and overwintered indoors. Zones 5-10.

Selected species and varieties. *G. byzantinus* is a 3-foot plant with many-flowered spikes of pinkish purple flowers that may be striped with white. White- and scarlet-flowered forms are also available. *G. carneus,* snowpink gladiolus, has pale pink or cream-white flowers with red central blotches. The 2-foot plants produce four to eight 2- to 3-inch flowers per spike. Zones 9 and 10. *G.* × *colvillei,* Colville gladiolus, is a fairly hardy species with red flowers that have a yellow central blotch. 'The Bride' is a pure-white-flowered cultivar. *G.* × *grandavensis,* breeders' gladiolus, is a sturdy plant with red or reddish yellow, 2- to 3-inch flowers that can be streaked with red or yellow. Zones 9 and 10. *G.* × *hortulanus,* common gladiolus, garden gladiolus, is the name given the many garden cultivars of gladiolus that breeders have produced. Plants generally reach 3 feet and produce showy spikes of funnel-shaped, 3- to 4-inch flowers in many colors, including yellow, orange, red, maroon, pink, rose and white. Flowers are often marked or blotched with contrasting colors. Zones 9 and 10. Many cultivars are available. *G. illyricus* bears loose spikes of crimson-purple, 1½-inch flowers on 1- to 3-foot plants. Zones 9 and 10. *G. segetum,* cornflag, produces spikes of pinkish purple flowers that are 1½-inch across atop 1½- to 2-foot plants. Zones 7-10. *G. tristis,* eveningflower gladiolus, is a 2-foot plant with white or yellowish white flowers that are very fragrant and open in the evening. Zones 7-10.

Growing conditions. Grow gladiolus in full sun, in deeply prepared soil that is rich and well drained. Dig a trench for planting that is 2 inches deeper than the recommended planting depth. Apply a balanced fertilizer such as 5-10-10 and cover it with 2 inches of soil. Plant small corms (under 1 inch) at a depth of 3 to 4 inches; larger corms 6 to 8 inches. When planting, cover the corms with several inches of soil and fill in the trench as the plants grow. Space corms 3 to 6 inches apart. Side-dress plants with fertilizer when they emerge and again when flowers start to show color. Stake gladioli to protect them from high winds. To prolong the blooming season, corms can be started at 10- to 14-day intervals from early spring to midsummer up until 90 days before the first killing frost. Dig the corms six weeks after blooming, when the foliage begins to brown. Or, in areas where the plants are hardy, the corms can be left in the ground over winter. Where the corms are not hardy, dig the last crop of corms before the first hard frost. Shake off excess soil and cut back the tops of the plants. Allow the corms to dry out of direct sun, discard the remains of the previous season's corms and dust the corms with fungicide before storing in a cool (40° F), dry place for the winter. In the warmest parts of Zones 9 and 10, corms benefit from three months of cold storage in the refrigerator. Propagate plants from the small cormels borne around old corms. The cormels take up to two seasons to bloom.

Globe tulip see *Calochortus*

Gloriosa (glor-ee-O-sa)

Gloriosa lily, climbing lily

Lily-family member with tuberous roots. It has weakly climbing vines whose leaves often end with tendril-like tips. The flowers are showy, have wide-spreading, reflexed petals and somewhat resemble shooting stars. Blooms are yellow to red or purple in color. Gloriosa lilies are grown in greenhouses or as summer annuals in the North. Zone 10.

Selected species and varieties. *G. rothschildiana* is an 8-foot vine with 5- to 7-inch leaves. The petals are 3 inches long and have edges that are usually smooth but sometimes wavy. They are red with yellow near the center of the flower and around the margin. Blooms face downward and have showy stamens. *G. superba* is a 12-foot vine with 4- to 6-inch leaves. The petals are yellow at the center and red at the tips when the flowers first open; they turn dark red with age. Each petal is narrow and 2 to 3 inches long; petal margins are very wavy or twisted.

Growing conditions. Grow gloriosa lilies in rich, well-drained soil in a site where the tops of the plants can be in full sun but where the roots are shaded by nearby, shallow-rooted plants. In Zone 10, they can be planted in borders or along fences and left undisturbed for years. Gloriosa lilies can be grown as annuals in areas where the growing season is long. Plant the tubers outdoors after all danger of frost has passed and the soil has warmed. They can also be started in tubs in a greenhouse and moved outside in midspring. Plant the tubers at a depth of 5 to 6 inches, but place them horizontally at a slight angle, with the growing end pointing up. Water sparingly until the plants begin to grow. Carefully dig the tubers after the first fall frost, shake off the excess soil, and store them in dry peat moss or sand through the winter at a temperature of 50° F.

Glory-of-the-snow see *Chionodoxa*

Golden canna see *Camassia*

Golden garlic see *Allium*

Good-luck plant see *Oxalis*

Grace garlic see *Nothoscordum*

Grape hyacinth see *Muscari*

Grassy-bell see *Dierama*

Green dragon see *Arisaema*

Guernsey lily see *Nerine*

Guinea-hen flower see *Fritillaria*

Habranthus (ha-BRAN-thus)

A genus of amaryllis-family members with narrow, grassy leaves and funnel-shaped, pink, yellow or red flowers. Blooms appear in summer, and usually are borne one per stem. These plants, which arise from bulbs, make fine additions to rock gardens and flower borders. Zones 9 and 10.

GLORIOSA ROTHSCHILDIANA

HABRANTHUS ANDERSONII

HAEMANTHUS MULTIFLORUS

HERMODACTYLUS TUBEROSUS

Selected species and varieties. *H. andersonii* (formerly *Zephyranthes andersonii)* is a 6-inch species with 1½-inch flowers that are yellow streaked with red on the outside, but often appear pinkish. *H. brachyandrus* (formerly designated *Hippeastrum brachyandrum)* produces 12-inch flowering stalks, each of which carries a single, 3-inch flower that is dark red at the base fading to pink at the tips of the petals. Zone 10. *H. tubispathus* (formerly designated *Hippeastrum robustus* and *Zephyranthes robusta)* is a 9-inch species with rose-red, 3-inch flowers.

Growing conditions. *Habranthus* species should be grown in a warm, sunny site with deep, rich, well-drained soil. The bulbs multiply by offsets and will self-sow in locations with favorable conditions. North of Zone 9, they can be grown in cool greenhouses.

Haemanthus (he-MAN-thus)

Blood lily

A genus of African natives that belong to the amaryllis family and have red, pink or white flowers with showy yellow stamens. The flowers, which appear in late summer or in autumn, are borne in dense heads (somewhat resembling shaving brushes) or in many-flowered umbels. Showy berries follow the flowers. The bulbs are large and stained with red, and the foliage is thick and leathery. In areas where they are hardy, blood lilies can be planted in rock gardens or borders. In North America they are most commonly grown in pots in greenhouses and moved outdoors in summer. Zones 9 and 10.

Selected species and varieties. *H. albiflos,* white blood lily, is a 1-foot species with thick, fleshy leaves that are 8 inches long and 4 inches wide. Flower heads are 2 inches across and white in color with showy yellow stamens. *H. coccineus,* scarlet blood lily, has 10-inch-long leaves that are 8 inches across and bears its 3-inch flower heads on 10-inch stalks. Individual blooms are bright red and 1 inch long. *H. katharinae,* Catherine-wheel, Katharine blood lily, produces nearly spherical, 9-inch umbels of bright red to salmon-pink blooms. Plants are 1 to 1½ feet tall. *H. multiflorus,* salmon blood lily, produces dense, 3- to 6-inch heads of scarlet flowers atop 1½-foot plants.

Growing conditions. Blood lilies will bloom most profusely if they are grown in pots. Start them indoors in winter or early spring with the tips of the bulbs at the surface of the soil. They require rich, well-drained, porous soil and night temperatures not above 50° F. Water sparingly until leaves appear. After danger of frost has passed, move plants outdoors to a location that has bright light but that is shaded from direct sun. Keep the soil evenly moist when plants are actively growing, and feed monthly with a balanced fertilizer.

Most blood lilies have a definite dormant season during which all of their foliage dies completely. (Catherine-wheel is evergreen if plants are kept warm and are watered through the year.) When the old foliage begins to show signs of dying, gradually reduce watering. Store the plants in pots in a cool, dry place through the winter. Repot only when necessary, since blood lilies' roots should not be disturbed. Remove some of the old soil at the top of the pot and replace it with fresh soil.

Harebell see *Endymion*

Harlequin flower see *Sparaxis*

Hermodactylus

(her-mo-DAK-ti-lus)

A one-species genus in the iris family that has tuberous roots and a clump-forming habit. The leaves are blue-green in color, grassy and evergreen. The flowers resemble irises, with three outer petal-like sepals called falls and three inner, upright petals called standards. Zones 6-9.

Selected species and varieties. *H. tuberosus,* snake's head iris, has fragrant, 2-inch-long flowers with deep, plum purple falls that obscure the short, pea green standards. Plants are 9 inches tall.

Growing conditions. Snake's head iris requires a location with rich, very well drained soil and full sun. Plant the tubers in early fall or early spring. Leave plants undisturbed for years unless they become crowded and flowering ceases. Snake's head iris also can be grown indoors in pots in cool greenhouses.

Hippeastrum (hip-ee-AS-trum)
Amaryllis, Barbados lily

A genus of tender, tropical bulbs formerly classified as *Amaryllis.* Plants produce two- to four-flowered umbels of trumpet-shaped blossoms. The leaves are strap-shaped and generally appear after the flowers fade. Zone 10.

Selected species and varieties. Although there are some 75 species in the *Hippeastrum* genus, most amaryllises cultivated today are hybrids with complex, largely unknown parentage. Hybrids come in white, pink, salmon, orange and red, and may be marked with contrasting colors. Flowers are enormous, 6 to 9 inches across, and are carried atop 20-inch stems. Many cultivars are available. 'Apple Blossom' has white blooms striped with pale pink. 'Cinderella' has red blooms striped with white. 'Christmas Gifts' and 'White Christmas' have pure white blooms. 'Ludwig's Goliath' bears 10-inch flowers that are bright scarlet.

Growing conditions. Amaryllises can be grown outdoors in the warmest parts of Zone 10, where they prefer a sunny site with rich, sandy, well-drained soil. When grown outdoors, flowers appear in spring. Indoors, plant bulbs in pots in late fall or winter for late-winter bloom. Allow for a 1-inch space between the bulb and the edge of the pot, and plant the bulbs with the upper half above the soil surface. Use a rich, sandy potting soil to which bone meal has been added. Keep plants barely moist and in a warm, dark place until growth begins. Move plants to a bright spot out of direct sun for flowering. Remove the stalks after flowering, feed twice a month with a weak fertilizer and keep watering until fall, when the leaves will begin to yellow. Store plants dry and repot in late fall or early winter.

Hippeastrum see also *Habranthus*

Homeria (ho-MEER-ee-a)
Cape tulip

A genus of iris-family members from South Africa that arise from corms and bear sword-shaped leaves. Cape tulips produce clusters of funnel-shaped flowers that have spreading, petal-like segments. Zones 9 and 10.

Selected species and varieties. *H. breyniana* is a 1½-foot plant that bears very fragrant, 1½-inch-long flowers that are salmon-pink or yellow. The cultivar 'Aurantiaca' has flowers that are yellow at the base. *H. ochroleuca* reaches 2½ feet in height and bears 2- to 2½-inch flowers that are ill smelling and come in salmon-pink or shades of yellow.

Growing conditions. Plant Cape tulips in fall in a location with full sun and rich, moist, well-drained, sandy soil. Space corms 3 inches apart and plant them 3 inches deep. The plants may be lifted and divided every few years, but they can be difficult to transplant. North of Zones 9 and 10, Cape tulips are grown in pots in greenhouses.

Hyacinth see *Hyacinthus*
Hyacinth-of-Peru see *Scilla*
Hyacinthoides see *Endymion*

Hyacinthus (hy-a-SIN-thus)
Hyacinth

A one-species genus in the lily family with colorful, heavily scented spikes of flowers that appear in spring. Leaves are strap-shaped, and the bulbs often have purplish coverings. Hyacinths are grown in beds and borders and can also be forced indoors. Zones 6-9.

Selected species and varieties. *H. orientalis,* common hyacinth, Dutch hyacinth, garden hyacinth, bears dense spikes of very fragrant flowers. The individual flowers are bell-shaped and blue, pink or white. Blooms are carried in stiff, football-shaped spikes. Many cultivars are available: 'L'Innocence' is white; 'Pink Pearl' is pink; 'Vanguard' is lilac-colored.

Growing conditions. Grow hyacinths in full sun in a location with rich, well-drained soil. Plant bulbs in fall at a depth of 6 to 8 inches. Mulch heavily, especially in the North, to protect the shoots that emerge in early spring. Fertilize monthly during the growing season. Large, newly planted bulbs will produce extra-large flower clusters the first season after planting, smaller clusters thereafter.

Hyacinthus see also *Brimeura*

HIPPEASTRUM 'WHITE CHRISTMAS'

HOMERIA BREYNIANA

HYACINTHUS ORIENTALIS 'VANGUARD'

HYMENOCALLIS CARIBAEA

HYPOXIS HIRSUTA

IPHEION UNIFLORUM 'WISLEY BLUE'

Hymenocallis (hy-men-o-KAL-is)
Spider lily, basket flower,
Peruvian daffodil

Spider lilies belong to a small genus of plants in the amaryllis family. They have thick, strap-shaped leaves that may be evergreen or deciduous. The white or yellow flowers, borne in umbels atop stout stalks, are fragrant and somewhat resemble daffodils. They have a central, funnel-shaped cup that is surrounded by six petal-like lobes or segments, which are attached at the base of the bloom. The lobes are narrow and curve out around the trumpetlike base. They also have long, spidery stamens. Spider lilies are grown in beds and borders. Zones 5-10.

Selected species and varieties. *H. caribaea* is an evergreen species with narrow, foot-long leaves and eight- to 10-flowered clusters of fragrant white flowers that have 2½-inch-long, funnel-shaped bases and narrow, 4-inch lobes. *H. caroliniana,* inland spider lily, is a marsh-dwelling, 3-foot plant with three- to nine-flowered umbels of fragrant white blooms. Flowers have narrow, 4-inch lobes and 1½-inch, funnel-shaped bases. *H.* × *festalis* is a 2-foot-tall hybrid with white flowers that have large, funnel-shaped cups and narrow, gracefully curling lobes. *H. narcissiflora,* basket flower, Peruvian daffodil, is a 2-foot-tall plant with two- to five-flowered clusters of fringed, 2-inch trumpets surrounded by curving lobes. Zones 7-10. *H.* × 'Sulfur Queen' is a hybrid cultivar resembling *H. narcissiflora,* which is one of its parents, with yellow flowers. Zones 7-10.

Growing conditions. Plant spider lilies in rich, fertile soil that is well drained but remains moist throughout the growing season. Deciduous species should remain dry during dormancy. Spider lilies will tolerate full sun or light shade. In areas where they are hardy, these plants can be left in the ground throughout the year. Where they are not hardy, plant them indoors in large pots and move the pots outdoors after all danger of frost has passed. Or plant them outdoors in spring and dig the bulbs in fall before the first frost. Leave the roots attached to the bulbs and dry them upside down so that any water runs away from the plants. Bulbs can be packed in nearly dry peat or stored in open trays at a temperature of 55° to 60° F. Tub-grown plants are set with the tip of the bulb 1 inch below the surface; bulbs planted in the ground should be set at a depth of 3 to 4 inches.

Hypoxis (hy-POK-sis)
Star grass

A genus of plants with short, cormlike rhizomes, grasslike leaves and one- to several-flowered spikes of flowers. Blooms are white or yellow and star-shaped. Star grasses can be used in wildflower gardens and in borders. Zones 4-10.

Selected species and varieties. *H. hirsuta,* common star grass, has narrow, grasslike leaves and sparsely flowered clusters of bright yellow, starlike flowers that appear in June.

Growing conditions. Grow common star grass in full sun or light shade in a location with dry soil. It is a fine subject for naturalizing, and can be propagated by division.

Indian shot see *Canna*
Indian turnip see *Arisaema*
Indigo squill see *Camassia*

Ipheion (i-FEE-on)

A small genus of bulbous plants in the amaryllis family that are native to South America. Plants have narrow, grasslike leaves that have an onionlike odor when bruised. Flowers are solitary, funnel-shaped and borne on leafless stalks. Zones 6-10.

Selected species and varieties. *I. uniflorum* (formerly *Brodiaea uniflora, Leucocoryne uniflora* and *Milla uniflora),* spring starflower, has ⅜-inch-wide leaves and 6- to 8-inch stalks topped by star-shaped, 1½-inch flowers that are whitish blue or blue. 'Wisley Blue' is fragrant and has light blue flowers with white centers. Zones 6-9.

Growing conditions. Spring starflower requires full sun and rich, extremely well drained, somewhat sandy soil. Plant the bulbs in late summer or early fall, 3 inches deep and 3 inches apart. Leave the plants undisturbed for as long as possible. Divide only if flowering ceases. Plants flower in spring, and the foliage disappears after flowering only to reappear in fall and persist through winter. In the northern zones, spring starflowers benefit from a light winter covering of cut evergreen branches.

Iris (I-ris)

A large genus for which the iris family is named containing perennials that arise from stout rhizomes, as well as species grown from bulbs *(below)*. Leaves are narrow and grasslike. The flowers are composed of six petal-like segments: the three outer ones, called falls, are generally reflexed, or point outward; the three inner ones, called standards, point upward and are usually smaller than the falls. Bulbous irises are used in rock gardens and in borders, and can be overplanted with small, shallow-rooted annuals. They also can be forced indoors in pots. Zones 5-10.

Selected species and varieties. *I. danfordiae* is a small species with solitary flowers borne in early spring on 2- to 4-inch stems. The leaves lengthen to 1 foot after the plants have bloomed. Flowers are 1 inch long and have falls that are yellow spotted with olive green; standards are reduced to erect, bristlelike structures. *I. histrio* produces solitary, 3-inch-wide blooms in early spring on 6- to 8-inch stems. Flowers are blue; falls have a yellow stripe with white in the center. Leaves are 8 inches long at flowering time and lengthen to 1 foot. *I. histrioides,* another spring bloomer, bears blue, 3-inch-wide flowers on 4- to 9-inch stalks. Falls are marked with yellow and blue. Leaves lengthen to 1½ feet after flowering. 'Major' is a bright blue-flowered cultivar.

I. reticulata, violet-scented iris, produces fragrant, 3½-inch, violet-purple blooms with falls that have yellow crests. Flowers are stemless when they bloom in early spring; the stems and leaves lengthen as the plant matures. 'Cantab' is a cultivar with pale blue flowers; 'Harmony' has purple flowers with yellow-and-white-marked falls; 'Violet Beauty' has deep purple blooms. *I. xiphioides,* English iris, bears 1½-foot-long leaves and two to three 3-inch-long flowers in late spring or early summer. Blooms are deep purplish blue with wedge-shaped falls marked in yellow.

I. xiphium, Spanish iris, is a 2-foot species with 4-inch flowers that have fiddle-shaped falls marked with orange or yellow. Blooms are borne in late spring and are purplish blue in color. Because *I. xiphium* is one of the parents of the hybrid Dutch irises, Dutch irises are usually included with Spanish irises. The cultivar 'Angel's Wings' has white standards and yellow falls. 'Blue Ribbon' has lavender-blue flowers with a bright yellow stripe on each fall. 'Golden Harvest' is bright yellow. 'White Excelsior' is pure white with falls marked in bright yellow.

Growing conditions. Grow bulbous iris in a location that has full sun at least during the season the foliage is apparent. The plants require good drainage and perform best in well-drained sandy or gritty soil. They will not grow well in wet clay soil. For best results, prepare the soil to a depth of about 6 inches. Plant the bulbs in fall 3 to 4 inches deep and 3 to 5 inches apart. Feed annually after flowering with a balanced garden fertilizer such as 5-10-10. The foliage must be allowed to mature and ripen naturally if the plants are to bloom the following year: do not mow it or cut it back. In the North, Spanish and Dutch iris need protection from cold. Plant them in a sheltered, south- or west-facing site and mulch with salt hay or with cut evergreen branches.

Spanish and Dutch iris require dry conditions in summer; bulbs can be left in the ground after the foliage dies, or they can be dug, dried for several hours in the sun, stored in open boxes during the summer and replanted in fall. English iris, which prefers cool, moist soil and is best left in the ground over winter, is somewhat more persistent in gardens than Spanish or Dutch iris. Violet-scented iris is long-lived in the North, provided it has well-drained soil and the foliage is not cut back and allowed to ripen.

Italian squill see *Endymion*

Ixia (IK-see-a)

Corn lily

A South African genus of tender, cormous plants in the iris family. The leaves are grasslike. The flowers, which are borne in few- to many-flowered spikes, have six petal-like

IRIS RETICULATA 'CANTAB'

IXIA MACULATA 'ROSE EMPRESS'

IXIOLIRION TATARICUM

LACHENALIA ALOIDES 'AUREA'

LAPEIROUSIA LAXA

segments and are star- or cup-shaped. Corn lilies bloom in late spring to summer and are used in beds and borders. They also can be forced in pots in cool greenhouses. Zones 7-10.

Selected species and varieties. *I. maculata* is a 1-foot-tall plant that bears yellow to white, 1-inch-long flowers with a purple to black central blotch. Blooms are borne in dense, many-flowered spikes. 'Rose Empress' has pink flowers. *I. viridiflora* produces many-flowered spikes of 1-inch blooms that are pale green with a black central blotch. Plants reach 20 inches in height.

Growing conditions. Grow corn lilies in a site with full sun and very well drained, rich soil. Plant corms in early to late fall at a depth of 3 to 4 inches and 1 to 1½ feet apart. Fertilize plantings with a balanced fertilizer annually in the fall. In the North, mulch to prevent the corms from freezing. Corn lilies also can be forced in greenhouses.

Ixiolirion (ik-si-o-LEER-ee-on)
Lily-of-the-Altai

A very small genus of plants belonging to the amaryllis family with small bulbs and narrow leaves. The flowers are funnel-shaped with six spreading lobes at the top and are borne in an umbel-like cluster atop leafy stalks. They are useful in rock gardens and in borders, make fine cut flowers and can be forced in cold frames in pots for spring bloom. Zones 7-10.

Selected species and varieties. *I. tataricum,* Siberian lily, Tartar lily, bears 1½-inch lilac flowers in four- to six-flowered clusters. Zones 7-10.

Growing conditions. Siberian lilies require full sun and rich, very well drained, porous soil, since they will not tolerate "wet feet." Plant the bulbs in fall at a depth of 4 inches and 3 to 4 inches apart. Keep the soil evenly moist while the plants are actively growing. North of Zone 7, mulch plants heavily in fall, or dig the plants before the first hard frost, dry the bulbs in the sun for several hours, remove the remaining foliage and store in a cool, dry place over winter.

Jack-in-the-pulpit see *Arisaema*

Jacobean lily see *Sprekelia*

Japanese jacinth see *Scilla*

Jonquil see *Narcissus*

Kafir lily see *Clivia*

King's spear see *Eremurus*

Lachenalia (lak-e-NAY-lee-a)
Cape cowslip

A genus of bulbous, lily-family members from South Africa that bear spikes of colorful, nodding, bell-shaped flowers in white, yellow or red. Leaves are borne at the base of the plant and are often spotted. Cape cowslips are planted in rock gardens in the South and forced indoors in pots in the North. Zones 9 and 10.

Selected species and varieties. *L. aloides,* tricolor Cape cowslip, is a 1-foot species with strap-shaped, 1-inch-wide leaves that are often spotted. Flowers, which are borne in three- to 12-flowered spikes, are 1 inch long and yellow tipped with red. 'Aurea' has bright orange-yellow blooms. 'Luteola' has lemon yellow flowers. 'Pearsonii' has yellow-orange to reddish orange buds and flower bases. *L. bulbiferum,* nodding Cape cowslip, bears 1-foot-long leaves that are 2 inches wide and are sometimes spotted. It bears few- to many-flowered racemes of 1½-inch flowers that are yellow blending to red or red-purple at the tips. 'Superba' has orange-red flowers.

Growing conditions. Cape cowslips will grow in almost any soil as long as it is well drained, porous and fairly rich. Plant the bulbs in fall. They can also be potted and forced in a cool greenhouse for late-winter or early-spring bloom indoors.

Lady's sorrel see *Oxalis*

Lapeirousia (la-pay-ROO-see-a)

A genus of South African species in the iris family that arise from corms. Leaves are narrow and borne at the base of the plant. Flowers are small and tubular at the base, and spreading, somewhat star-shaped at the top. They are borne in few-flowered spikes that appear in late spring to summer. *Lapeirousia* species are used in beds and borders. They also can be forced in pots in cool greenhouses. Zones 7-10.

Selected species and varieties. *L. laxa* is a summer-blooming species with thin, sword-shaped, 6- to 10-inch leaves; flowers are six-petaled, dark pink with deep red blotches at the bases of the three lower petals.

Growing conditions. Grow lapeirousias in a site with full sun and rich, well-drained soil. Plant corms in early to late fall at a depth of 3 to 4 inches and 1 to 1½ feet apart. Fertilize plantings with a balanced fertilizer annually in the fall. In the North, mulch to prevent the corms from freezing.

Ledebouria (led-e-BOR-ee-a)

A small genus of lily-family members native mostly to South Africa that were once classified as *Scilla.* The plants arise from bulbs and often have leaves marked with green or red spots. The flowers are cup-shaped, borne in spikes, and come in whitish green, pink, dull red or green with purple. Zone 10.

Selected species and varieties. *L. socialis* bears 2- to 4-inch flower stalks and pale green flowers with white edges. Flowers appear in early spring and the foliage is marked with silver.

Growing conditions. Plant ledebourias on the surface of rich, well-drained soil in a sunny location. They prefer areas with dry summers. The bulbs grow on the surface of the soil. In areas where ledebouria is not hardy, it may be grown as a houseplant. To do so, leave the bulb partially exposed in the pot. Place it where it will have filtered light and cool night temperatures, 55° to 65° F.

Leichtlin camass see *Camassia*

Leucocoryne see *Ipheion*

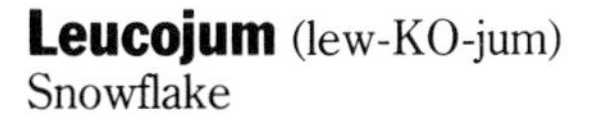

Leucojum (lew-KO-jum)
Snowflake

A very small genus of European natives in the amaryllis family that have small bulbs and narrow leaves. Flowers are nodding and bell-shaped, and borne alone or in umbels atop hollow stalks. Snowflakes are used in rock gardens, in borders and for naturalizing. Collection in the wild has endangered most species in the genus; purchase from reputable dealers that sell only propagated bulbs. Zones 4-10.

Selected species and varieties. *L. aestivum,* giant snowflake, summer snowflake, is a spring-blooming species that produces two- to eight-flowered spikes of white, cup-shaped flowers tipped with green. Blooms are borne on 9- to 12-inch stalks. 'Gravetye' is a large-flowered cultivar. *L. autumnale,* autumn snowflake, produces white flowers tinged with pink atop 6-inch stalks. The flowers and threadlike leaves are borne in early fall. Zones 6-10. *L. vernum,* spring snowflake, has white, ¾-inch flowers with green tips. Blooms are borne atop 6- to 12-inch stalks in early spring. *L. vernum carpathicum* has white petals tipped with yellow.

Growing conditions. Grow snowflakes in rich, well-drained soil in a location protected from hot sun. For best results, dig a generous quantity of organic matter such as compost or leaf mold into the soil at planting time. Keep plants evenly moist while they are actively growing. Plant bulbs in late summer or fall at a depth of 2 inches; space 3 inches apart. Leave plants undisturbed for as long as possible; divide only if necessary for propagation.

Lilium (LIL-ee-um)
Lily

The genus of the true lilies, from which so many plants in other genera have taken their common names. True lilies are very showy plants with trumpet- or bell-shaped flowers borne pointing up or down, and singly or in many-flowered clusters. Each has six petal-like segments called tepals that are usually the same color, and may be white, yellow, orange, red, maroon or purple. Tepals generally curve backward at the tips; species with reflexed petals have tepals that curve in a semicircle. Blooms have six stamens and are often spotted on the inside. The bulbs are scaly and the flowers are borne on erect, leafy stems.

LEDEBOURIA SOCIALIS

LEUCOJUM VERNUM

LILIUM CANADENSE

LILIUM CANDIDUM

LILIUM PHILADELPHICUM

LILIUM 'CONNECTICUT KING'

There are between 80 and 90 species of lilies and many more cultivars. In addition to true species lilies, which are listed below by botanical name, many hybrids have been developed. Hybrid lilies, which are generally easier to grow than the species, have been divided into groups according to the origin of the parent species. Within these groups the plants are further divided according to the form of the flowers.

Lilies make fine additions to borders, can be planted in clumps as specimen plants and also are used for naturalizing. Zones 4-10.

Selected species and varieties. *L. amabile,* Korean lily, is a 3-foot species with one- to six-flowered spikes of orange-red, 2-inch blooms with dark spots. Flowers have an unpleasant scent and appear in late spring. 'Luteum' has pure yellow flowers. *L. auratum,* gold-band lily, has lance-shaped leaves and flaring, fragrant, 6- to 12-inch flowers that are white with red spots and a gold stripe down the center of each tepal. Blooms appear in summer atop 3- to 9-foot plants in spikes of up to 35 flowers. Zones 5-10. *L. canadense,* Canada lily, meadow lily, is a summer-blooming, 5-foot-tall plant native to bogs and wet meadows in eastern North America. Blooms are bell-shaped and nodding with very reflexed tepals, 3 inches across, and yellow, orange or red in color. *L. canadense editorum* is native to drier sites than the species and bears red flowers. *L. candidum,* Madonna lily, Annunciation lily, is a 6-foot-tall plant bearing five to 20 fragrant, pure white blooms with yellow anthers in spring or early summer. Unlike most lilies, it dies down after blooming and develops new growth in the fall. Madonna lilies are susceptible to botrytis blight. Zones 5-10.

L. columbianum, Columbia lily, Oregon lily, is a summer-blooming, West Coast native reaching 5 feet and bearing few- to many-flowered spikes of nodding, 2-inch flowers. Blooms have very reflexed petals and are yellow to red with maroon spots. Zones 7-10. *L. concolor,* star lily, morning-star lily, is a scarlet-flowered species that reaches 3 to 4 feet in height. The cup-shaped blooms point upward and are 3½ inches wide and 2 inches long. Zones 5-10. *L. formosianum,* Formosa lily, is a late-summer- to early-autumn-blooming species with white, funnel-shaped blooms that are fragrant and marked with purple on the outside. It is very susceptible to virus diseases. Zones 6-10. *L. hansonii,* Hanson lily, Japanese Turk's-cap, is a 5-foot species with loose spikes of fragrant, nodding, 2½-inch-wide flowers. The blooms appear in late spring and are orange-yellow spotted with purplish brown. *L. henryi* bears spikes of 10 to 20 bright orange, nodding flowers in August. It tolerates virus diseases and is resistant to wilt. 'Citrinum' is a bright-yellow-flowered cultivar. Zones 5-10.

L. × *hollandicum,* candlestick lily, is a hybrid between *L. bulbiferum* and *L. maculatum* that bears 4-inch-wide, upward-pointing blooms on 2½-foot plants. Flowers are cup-shaped and yellow to red in color. Zones 5-10. *L. japonicum,* Japanese lily, is a 3-foot species with fragrant, funnel-shaped flowers that are 6 inches long and 6 inches wide. Blooms appear in summer, one to five per stalk, and are pale pink in color. Japanese lily is susceptible to virus diseases. Zones 6-10. *L. lancifolium* (also listed as *L. tigrinum),* tiger lily, produces 6-foot stems of one to 25 flowers in July. Blooms are nodding, 5 inches wide, and orange or red spotted with purple. Small, black bulbils are often borne in the leaf axils. 'Splendens' has larger, deep red flowers with prominent dark spots; it blooms in August. Tiger lilies are often infected with lily mosaic virus. It does not harm them but spreads easily to other bulbs, so tiger lilies should be planted in isolation from other lilies.

L. × *maculatum* (also listed as *L.* × *elegans),* is a hybrid with erect, cup-shaped flowers borne atop 2-foot plants. Blooms are borne in summer, are 4 inches wide and are yellow to deep red in color. Zones 5-10. *L. martagon,* Turk's-cap lily, Martagon lily, has drooping, ill-smelling flowers borne three to 50 per spike in late spring. Blooms are usually purple spotted with black, but may be white to pink. 'Album' has pure white flowers. Collection in the wild has endangered the species; purchase from reputable dealers that sell only propagated bulbs. *L. michiganense,* Michigan lily, is a 5-foot plant with nodding, 3-inch-wide flowers that have reflexed petals. Blooms are borne one to eight per plant and are orange-red spotted with maroon. Zones 5-10. *L. monadelphym,* Caucasian lily, bears many-flowered spikes of bell-shaped, fragrant flowers in late spring atop 5-foot plants. Blooms are 5 inches across and golden yellow, sometimes spotted with purple. *L. parryi,* lemon lily, has 4-inch, funnel-shaped blooms that are lemon yellow and may be spotted with maroon. Flowers are fragrant and borne atop 4- to 6-foot plants. Zones 7-10.

L. philadelphicum, wood lily, orange-cup lily, produces upward-pointing, cup-shaped blooms that are 4 inches long and orange-red with dark spots. Flowers are borne in late spring to summer atop 2- to 3-foot plants. Zones 5-10. *L. pyrenaicum,* yellow Turk's-cap lily, is a 4-foot species with unpleasantly scented 1½- to 2-inch flowers with reflexed petals. Blooms are sulfur yellow and appear in late spring. 'Rubrum' is an orange-red-flowered cultivar. Zones 5-10. *L. regale,* regal lily, royal lily, produces umbels of fragrant, 6-inch-long flowers purplish outside and white with a yellow throat inside. Blooms are borne in summer atop 6-foot plants. *L. speciosum,* Japanese lily, showy lily, is a late-summer- or early-fall-blooming species with fragrant flowers that have tepals so spreading the flowers appear flat. Blooms are white marked with red or pink. *L. speciosum* is susceptible to virus. Many cultivars are available. 'Rubrum' has deep pink and red flowers. 'White Glory' has white blooms. Zones 5-10. *L. superbum,* Turk's-cap lily, bears nodding, 3-inch-wide, yellow to orange-red blooms atop 5- to 8-foot-tall plants. Flowers are spotted with maroon and appear in summer.

L. × testacum, nankeen lily, bears up to 12 fragrant, nodding, 3-inch flowers that are apricot to yellow atop 6-foot plants. It is susceptible to botrytis blight and basal rot. *L. washingtonianum,* Washington lily, is a 3- to 6-foot species with white to greenish white flowers. Blooms are fragrant, funnel-shaped, up to 8 inches across and borne in summer. Zones 7-10.

American Hybrid Lilies are cultivars developed from native American species. The Bellingham cultivars, which are typical of this group, are 4- to 6-foot plants that produce nodding, 4- to 6-inch flowers with reflexed petals in pink, red, orange or yellow and spotted with reddish brown. Blooms are borne up to 20 per plant in summer.

Asiatic Hybrid Lilies are compact, 2- to 5-foot plants that bear many-flowered spikes of 4- to 6-inch flowers that may point up, out or down. Blooms may be red, pink, orange, yellow, lavender or white and appear in summer. 'Connecticut King' grows 3 to 4 feet tall and has upright lemon yellow flowers with gold throats. 'Connecticut Yankee' has nodding orange flowers with deeply reflexed petals. 'Enchantment' bears dark-spotted orange blooms that point upward. 'Melon Time' grows 3 feet tall and has upward-facing salmon to orange flowers. 'Rose Fire' has coppery rose blooms that are deep red at the center with gold flashes.

Aurelian Hybrid Lilies, which are sometimes called Trumpet or Olympic hybrids, have fragrant flowers up to 8 inches long that may be trumpet-shaped, bowl-shaped or even flat and are borne in summer. Blooms may be greenish or pure white, yellow, orange or pink, and are carried atop 3- to 8-foot plants. 'Black Dragon' is an Aurelian Hybrid with nodding, trumpet-shaped blooms that are purplish on the outside and white with a yellow throat on the inside. 'Golden Splendor' has rich golden yellow blooms. 'Pink Perfection' has nodding, deep rose-pink trumpets. Zones 4-7.

Oriental Hybrid Lilies were developed from crosses between *L. auratum, L. speciosum* and *L. japonicum,* among others. The flowers are fragrant, 3 to 10 inches wide and are the last of the lilies to flower, in late summer. They come in pure white or white with pink, yellow or red stripes. Plants are 2½ to 7 feet tall. 'Imperial Crimson' has flat-faced blooms that are white blushed with rose-pink edged in white. 'Imperial Gold' is white dotted with maroon and has a yellow stripe down the center of each tepal. 'Stargazer' has fragrant crimson flowers with white borders and dark spots. Unlike the blooms of most Oriental Hybrids, the flowers of 'Stargazer' face upward. Zones 5-10.

Growing conditions. Grow lilies in rich, well-tilled porous soil that is very well drained. They will grow in full sun or light shade, although flowers sometimes fade if they are exposed to hot sun. Plants prefer soil that remains moist and cool at all times. If possible, select a site where the bases of the plants will remain shaded; choose companion plants such as small rhododendrons or azaleas, tall ferns or other perennials that will not provide too much competition. Mulch also helps keep the soil moist and cool. Lilies also require staking and a location protected from strong wind.

Plant lilies in beds that are dug to a depth of at least 1 foot. Add generous quantities of organic matter such as compost, peat moss or humus. Lily bulbs, which are very fragile and must be handled with care, may have roots along the stem that arises on top of the bulb. Plant in fall or early spring, leaving all roots intact. Dust the bulbs with fungicide before planting to prevent rot. Set bulbs in the ground with the base of the bulb three times as deep as the bulb is high. (For exam-

LILIUM 'ROSE FIRE'

LILIUM 'PINK PERFECTION'

LILIUM 'IMPERIAL CRIMSON'

LLOYDIA SEROTINA

LYCORIS RADIATA

MORAEA RAMOSISSIMA

ple, a 3-inch-tall bulb should be planted with the base 9 inches below the soil surface.) Hybrids and cultivars of *L. candidum* are an exception to this rule; plant them in late summer or early fall only, with no more than 1 inch of soil over the tops of the bulbs.

Fertilize all lilies with a slow-release fertilizer or well-rotted manure when growth emerges in spring. Tall plants may require staking; be sure to keep stakes well away from the base of the plant to avoid damaging the bulbs. Lilies should not be dug or divided unless absolutely necessary. Many lilies are susceptible to virus diseases, which are transmitted by aphids from lily to lily and from other infected plants. There is no cure for infected plants, so it is important to control aphid populations and destroy any infected plants. Streaked, spotted or stunted foliage; dwarfed plants; or distorted, misshapen flowers are all indications of virus disease. Dig and discard all portions of any infected plants. Do not add infected plant material to the compost heap.

Lily see *Lilium*

Lily leek see *Allium*

Lily-of-the-Altai see *Ixiolirion*

Lily-of-the-field see *Anemone; Sternbergia*

Lloydia (LOY-dee-a)

Alp lily

A small, European genus in the lily family containing bulbous plants with grasslike leaves. Flowers are white, cup-shaped, and borne alone or in a spike. Alp lilies are suitable for rock gardens. Zones 5-9.

Selected species and varieties. *L. serotina* is a 6-inch plant that bears ½-inch, solitary flowers that are white with yellow centers and striped with purple.

Growing conditions. Grow Alp lily in full sun or partial shade in a location with well-drained soil that is rich in compost or other organic matter. Plant the bulbs in early fall at a depth of 2 inches. Alp lilies are native to mountainous areas and will not grow well in areas with hot, dry summers.

Lycoris (ly-KOR-is)

A genus of bulbous species in the amaryllis family that are native to China and Japan. Plants bear umbels of star-shaped flowers that are fragrant and have a short tube at the base. Blooms are white, yellow or pink, and generally appear when the plants are leafless. The leaves are strap-shaped and narrow and either die down before the flowers appear or arise after the flowers have faded. Lycoris can be planted in beds and borders, and can also be grown in tubs or large pots in areas where it is not hardy. Zones 5-10.

Selected species and varieties. *L. africana,* golden lycoris, golden spider lily, bears five- to eight-flowered clusters of 3-inch-long, golden yellow flowers in late summer or early fall. The petal-like lobes of the blooms are narrow and curl backward. Leaves and flower stalks are 1½ to 2 inches tall. Zone 10. *L. radiata,* spider lily, short-tube lycoris, bears dark pink to bright red flowers that are 1½ inches long. The petal-like lobes of each flower are narrow and curve backward, and together with the long stamens they give the blooms a spidery appearance. Zones 7-10. *L. sanguinea* bears bright red, 2-inch-long flowers in late summer. Zones 7-10. *L. squamigera,* magic lily, hardy amaryllis, is a 2-foot plant with trumpet-shaped, 3-inch-long flowers that appear in summer and are rose-lilac or pink.

Growing conditions. Plant lycoris in a location with sun and rich, well-drained soil. Plant the bulbs at a depth of 5 inches, and leave plants undisturbed as long as possible. Digging and dividing can prevent flowering for several years.

Magic lily see *Lycoris*

Mariposa lily see *Calochortus*

Meadow lily see *Lilium*

Meadow saffron see *Bulbocodium; Colchicum*

Milla see *Ipheion*

Mission bells see *Fritillaria*

Monkey-faced pansy see *Achimenes*

Montebretia see *Crocosmia*

Moraea (MOR-ee-a)

Butterfly iris, Natal lily

A genus of tropical or South African natives that arise from corms. The leaves are narrow and grasslike, and the flowers resemble iris, with three outer petal-like sepals that droop downward and three inner, upright petals. Zones 9 and 10.

Selected species and varieties. *M. ramosissima* is a spring-blooming species with narrow, 18-inch leaves and 2- to 3-foot-long stems that bear clusters of several fragrant, bright yellow flowers. Blossoms open for only one day.

Growing conditions. Grow butterfly iris in light shade in a location with moist but well-drained soil. In frost-free areas, plant corms in the fall at a depth of 2 to 3 inches. For best results they require cool temperatures (45° to 55° F) at night. In the North, they can be grown in pots in greenhouses.

Morningstar lily see *Lilium*

Muscari (mus-KAR-ee)
Grape hyacinth

A genus of spring-blooming, lily-family members with small bulbs and narrow leaves. Flowers are blue or white, may be musky or sweet-scented, and are urn-shaped or nearly spherical. The blooms are borne in dense spikes that in some species resemble clusters of grapes. Grape hyacinths can be used as edgings, in beds and borders, and are also fine for naturalizing. Zones 3-10.

Selected species and varieties. *M. armeniacum* is a 9-inch-tall species with narrow, foot-long leaves that appear in fall. The flowers, which appear in early spring, are 5⁄16 inch long, deep violet-blue with white tips and borne in dense spikes of 30 to 40 blooms. The cultivar 'Blue Spike' has double light blue flowers. 'Early Giant' bears fragrant, light blue blooms. 'White Beauty' has white flowers. Zones 5-10. *L. azureum* is an early-spring bloomer with 6-inch-long leaves and bright blue, 3⁄16-inch flowers. Blooms are fragrant and are borne in dense, 8-inch-tall spikes of 20 to 40 flowers. 'Album' is a white-flowered cultivar. Zones 4-10.

M. botryoides, common grape hyacinth, is a 1-foot species with dense spikes of tiny, fragrant, globe-shaped, 1⁄8-inch-long flowers that appear in very early spring. Flowers are blue, but 'Album' is a white-flowered cultivar. *M. comosum,* tassel hyacinth, is a 1- to 1½-foot plant with strap-shaped, 1-inch-wide leaves. The flowers are borne in spikes, with brownish green fertile flowers at the bottom of the spike and 20 to 30 sterile flowers that are purplish blue at the top. The cultivar 'Monstrosum', commonly called feather hyacinth, has sterile, violet-blue flowers cut into fine shreds. 'Plumosum', another feather hyacinth, has shredded reddish purple flowers. Zones 5-10. *M. latifolium* is a 1-foot plant that bears only one leaf and blooms in early spring. The flowers are ¼ inch long, blue in color and borne in a loose spike of 10 to 20 flowers. Zones 5-10. *M. neglectum* has very narrow leaves and dense clusters of 30 to 40 dark blue, fragrant flowers. Zones 5-10. *M. paradoxum,* Caucasus grape hyacinth, bears dense spikes of blue-black flowers on 9-inch-tall plants.

Growing conditions. Grow grape hyacinths in full sun or light shade in a location with deep, rich, well-drained soil that is somewhat sandy. Plant bulbs in fall 3 inches deep and 3 to 4 inches apart. Plants thrive if left undisturbed, and will multiply rapidly.

Naked lady see *Amaryllis*
Nap-at-noon see *Ornithogalum*
Naples onion see *Allium*

Narcissus (nar-SIS-sus)
Daffodil

Daffodils are among the best known of spring-flowering bulbs, and although there are only about 26 species in the genus, there are hundreds of hybrids with varying flower forms. Members of the amaryllis family, daffodils arise from bulbs and generally have flat, narrow leaves. The flowers are usually nodding and may be white, yellow or bicolored. They are borne alone or several per stem. The bloom consists of a corona, or crown, which is cup- or trumpet-shaped, stands in the center, and may be long and tubular or short and ringlike. The corona is surrounded by six petal-like segments that are referred to collectively as the perianth. Most daffodils bloom in spring, but some species bloom in fall. They are used in beds or borders, in rock gardens and for naturalizing. Zones 4-9.

Selected species and varieties. There are so many species and hybrid

MUSCARI ARMENIACUM

NARCISSUS 'CARLTON'

NARCISSUS 'THALIA'

NARCISSUS 'JACK SNIPE'

NARCISSUS 'GRAND SOLEIL D'OR'

daffodils that horticulturists classify them in divisions according to flower form and size or to the species from which they were developed. The divisions are further subdivided according to the color of the floral parts.

Division I. Trumpet Daffodils bear one bloom per stem, and flowers have trumpets, or coronas, that are at least as long as the perianth segments. Blooms appear in early to middle spring. 'Cantatrice' grows 16 inches tall and has white flowers.

'Foresight' has white perianth segments and golden yellow trumpets. 'Lunar Sea' grows 18 inches tall and blooms in midseason with a yellow perianth and white corona (the reverse of most daffodils). 'Mount Hood' grows 15 inches tall and has all-white flowers. 'Unsurpassable' bears golden yellow flowers with 5-inch-wide perianths atop 18-inch plants. Miniature cultivars are included in this class as well: 'Little Beauty' grows 6 inches tall and has white perianth segments and pale yellow trumpets. 'Little Gem' is 5 inches tall with yellow blooms. 'W. P. Milner' is a miniature that grows 5 inches tall and blooms in early to middle spring with all-white blossoms. Zones 4-8.

Division II. Large Cup Daffodils have one flower per stem, and bloom in early to middle spring. The corona is more than one-third the length of the perianth segments, but less than their total length. Plants generally are 16 to 18 inches tall, and the flowers are 3½ to 4½ inches wide. 'Carlton' has bright yellow blooms. 'Ceylon' grows 14 inches tall and blooms in early to middle spring; it has yellow perianth segments and a white corona. 'Daydream' grows 16 inches tall and blooms in middle to late spring. It has yellow and white perianth segments and a white corona. 'Ice Follies' has white perianth segments surrounding creamy yellow cups. 'Pink Charm' has white perianth segments and pink cups. Zones 4-8.

Division III. Small Cup Daffodils have coronas that are less than one-third the length of the perianth segments. They bear one flower per stem and bloom in early spring. Plants generally are 14 to 16 inches tall and flowers are 2 to 3 inches wide. 'Birma' grows 16 inches tall and blooms early; it has yellow perianth segments and a red corona. It naturalizes easily. 'Blarney' has white perianth segments and small salmon-orange cups edged with yellow. 'Verger' grows 18 inches tall, blooms in midseason with white perianth segments and a red corona, and naturalizes easily. Among miniatures, 'Segovia' grows 6 inches tall and blooms in midseason with white perianth segments and a yellow corona; 'Xit' grows to 10 inches and has 2-inch, all-white flowers. Zones 4-8.

Division IV. Double Daffodils do not look like typical daffodils; there is usually no defined corona but instead a cluster of petaloids at the center, and there may be more than one bloom per stem. Plants range from 14 to 18 inches tall, and blooms are from 1 to 3 inches across. 'Acropolis' grows 18 inches tall, usually blooms late in the season, and is white with red and white petaloids. 'Cheerfulness' bears clusters of double white flowers that are fragrant. 'Tahiti' grows 16 inches tall and usually blooms late in the season; it is yellow with red petaloids. 'White Marvel' has pure white, double blooms on 14-inch plants. 'Pencrebar' is a miniature that grows to 10 inches and has 2-inch, all-yellow flowers. Zones 4-8.

Division V. Triandrus Hybrid Daffodils are hybrids and cultivars developed from *N. triandrus.* Flowers generally are smaller than those in the first four divisions, and are fragrant and nodding, and borne one or more per stem. Blooms of Triandrus Hybrids appear in middle to late spring, at the end of the daffodil season. 'Liberty Bells' bears two- to four-flowered clusters of dark lemon yellow blooms atop 12-inch stems. Blooms are nodding and have long trumpets. 'Petrel' grows 12 inches tall, usually blooms late, and has an abundance of flowers that are all-white and fragrant. 'Thalia' is a late-flowering cultivar with fragrant, pure white flowers borne in two- to four-flowered clusters atop 16-inch stems. There are also miniature Triandrus Hybrids: 'Hawera' is an 8-inch plant with yellow, 1-inch-long flowers. Zones 4-8.

Division VI. Cyclamineus Hybrid Daffodils are hybrids and cultivars of *N. cyclamineus.* Plants bloom in early spring and are 6 to 10 inches tall. Flowers are ½ to 2 inches wide and have reflexed perianth segments. 'Dove Wings' has creamy white perianth segments and canary yellow coronas. 'February Gold' has pure yellow blooms. 'February Silver' has cream-colored trumpets and white perianth segments. 'Jack Snipe' has white flowers with lemon yellow trumpets. 'Jet Fire' grows 12 inches tall, blooms from early to middle spring and is yellow with a red corona. Among miniatures, 'Jumblie' grows 6 inches tall, blooms from early to middle spring and is yellow with an orange corona; 'Quince' grows 5 inches tall, blooms in midseason and is all yellow. 'Tete-à-Tete' is a miniature, 6- to 8-inch cultivar that bears one to three golden yellow blooms in early spring and rapidly establishes colonies. Zones 4-8.

Division VII. Jonquilla Hybrid Daffodils are hybrids and cultivars of *N. jonquilla.* They generally have fragrant ½- to 1-inch flowers with small cups and thin, reedlike leaves. 'Pueblo' grows 14 inches tall and usually blooms late with all-white blossoms. 'Quail' bears fragrant, golden yellow flowers with two or three blooms per stalk. 'Stratosphere' grows 24 inches tall, usually blooms late and has all-yellow flowers. 'Suzy' bears two- to four-flowered clusters of fragrant blooms with orange-red cups and broad yellow perianth segments. 'Trevithian' bears two- to four-flowered stalks of fragrant, lemon yellow blooms with broad, overlapping perianth segments. Flowers are borne atop 18-inch stems and appear in midspring. Among miniatures, 'Baby Moon' grows 6 inches tall, has yellow blooms and naturalizes easily; 'Chit Chat' grows 4 inches tall and usually blooms late with all-yellow flowers. Zones 4-8.

Division VIII. Tazetta Hybrid Daffodils are hybrids and cultivars of *N. tazetta,* and are sometimes called Poetaz or Polyanthus daffodils. Flowers are ½ to 1¼ inches across, have small cups, are usually fragrant and are borne in four- to eight-flowered clusters. The plants range from 12 to 18 inches in height. 'Avalanche' grows 16 inches tall, blooms in midseason and is white with a yellow corona. 'Geranium' produces fragrant, five- to six-flowered clusters of white blooms with small orange-red cups. 'Minnow' bears clusters of three light yellow flowers with darker yellow cups on miniature, 6- to 8-inch plants. 'Grand Soleil d'Or' is a nonhardy cultivar used in the North for forcing indoors on pebbles. It can be grown outdoors in gardens in Zones 7-10. It bears clusters of fragrant, golden yellow flowers.

Division IX. Poeticus Hybrid Daffodils are hybrids and cultivars of *N. poeticus.* They have pure white perianth segments and small, cuplike centers, or "eyes," that may be yellow with red margins or all red or may have greenish throats. All are fragrant and bloom in middle to late spring. 'Actaea' bears pure white, 3-inch-wide flowers with yellow centers edged in red atop 18-inch plants. 'Cantabile' grows 16 inches tall, blooms late and has white perianth segments and a red corona that is pale green at the base. Zones 4-7.

Division X. Species and Wild Forms includes all daffodil species and wild hybrids and forms. *N. asturiensis* is a 5-inch species with solitary, 1-inch-long, pale yellow flowers borne in early spring. The trumpets are longer than the perianth segments. Zones 5-9. *N. bulbocodium,* hoop-petticoat daffodil, bears small, bright yellow flowers in early spring with very narrow perianth segments and 1-inch-long trumpets. Plants range from 4 to 18 inches tall, have tubular-shaped leaves and naturalize easily. *N. bulbocodium conspicuous* is a large-flowered form. Zones 6-9. *N. cyclamineus* has narrow, 12-inch leaves and solitary, nodding, yellow flowers that are 1 to 2 inches long. Zones 6-9. *N. jonquilla,* common jonquil, grows to 18 inches and bears two- to six-flowered clusters of fragrant, 1-inch-long flowers. Blooms are yellow and have coronas that are half as long as the perianth segments.

N. × *odorus,* campernelle jonquil, grows to 12 inches and has fragrant, two- to four-flowered clusters of yellow, 2-inch blooms with ¾-inch cups. Zones 6-9. *N. poeticus,* poet's narcissus, pheasant's-eye narcissus, is an 18-inch species bearing fragrant, pure white flowers with small, shallow cups edged in red. Blooms are 2 to 3 inches across and appear in late spring. Zones 4-7. *N. pseudonarcissus,* daffodil, trumpet narcissus, produces solitary, yellow, 2-inch flowers with trumpets as long as the perianth segments atop 12- to 18-inch plants. *N. rupicola* is a 6-inch species with very short cupped, fragrant, yellow, ¾- to 1¼-inch-wide flowers borne one per stem. Zones 6-10. *N. scaberulus* is a 4-inch-tall species with deep orange-yellow flowers. Zones 7-10. *N. tazetta,* polyanthus narcissus, is an 18-inch species bearing clusters of fragrant, 1-inch flowers that are white with light yellow coronas. *N. tazetta papyraceus,* paperwhite narcissus, has all-white fragrant flowers that bloom in clusters. It is easily forced. 'Shelag' grows 24 inches tall and blooms early. 'Ziva' grows 18 inches tall and blooms very early. Zones 7-10.

N. triandrus, angel's-tears, has nearly round, 12-inch leaves and white, 1-to 1½-inch-long flowers with reflexed petals and cuplike coronas without wavy edges. The corona is half as long as the perianth segments. 'Albus' grows 4 inches tall and has all-white flowers that bloom in early to middle spring. *N. triandrus concolor* has pale yellow blooms. Collection in the wild has endangered many species in the genus; purchase from reputable dealers that sell only

NARCISSUS POETICUS 'ACTAEA'

NARCISSUS BULBOCODIUM

NARCISSUS CYCLAMINEUS

NECTAROSCORDUM SICULUM

NERINE BOWDENII

propagated bulbs. Zones 5-9.

Division XI. Split Corona Daffodils have coronas that are split at least one-third of their length. 'Cassata' grows 16 inches tall and blooms in early to middle spring; the blossoms are white with a yellow and white corona. 'Dolly Mollinger' grows 16 inches tall and blooms in midseason; the flowers are white with an orange and white corona. 'Orangerie' has a bright orange corona that lies against the white perianth segments. 'Valdrome' has bright yellow coronas that nearly conceal the pale yellow perianth segments. Zones 4-8.

Growing conditions. Grow daffodils in a site with full sun or light shade during the spring season, when the foliage is apparent. Soil should be rich in organic matter and well drained; bulbs will rot in wet soil. For best results, prepare the soil to a depth of 1 foot before planting and add generous quantities of compost. If drainage is a problem or if the planting is in wet clay soil, also add sand before planting. Plant bulbs in middle to late fall, but before the soil freezes so plants can develop roots before winter. In Zones 7-10, plant after the soil has cooled to under 70° F. Set bulbs at a depth of 1½ times the height of the bulb. Daffodils can be left undisturbed for years. They need dividing only when the plants become so crowded that flowering ceases. Mulch annually with well-rotted manure or compost. Daffodil foliage must be allowed to yellow naturally after the flowers fade if the plants are to produce blooms for the following season; do not mow it or cut it back.

Natal lily see *Moraea*

Nectaroscordum
(nek-ta-ro-SKOR-dum)

A genus of two or three species of bulbous plants in the amaryllis family that are native to southern Europe. Leaves are narrow and grasslike, and the bell- or funnel-shaped flowers are borne in a many-flowered umbel. *Nectaroscordum* species are closely related to onions, *Allium* species, and emit an onionlike odor when bruised. Zones 6-10.

Selected species and varieties. *N. bulgaricum* (formerly *Allium bulgaricum)* is a 4-foot plant with greenish white flowers that are tinged with pink. Flowers are borne in umbels, are nodding and ½ inch long and bloom in early spring. *N. siculum* (formerly *Allium siculum)* has narrow, 2-foot-long leaves and bears many-flowered, 4-foot-tall umbels of nodding, cup-shaped ½-inch flowers that are dull greenish red. Blooms appear in early spring.

Growing conditions. Plant nectaroscordums in full sun at a depth of two to three times the diameter of the bulbs. Space plants 6 to 18 inches apart, depending on the height of the species. Bulbs can be planted in spring or fall. Plants will grow in any good garden soil. Clumps may be left undisturbed in the garden for years; they require division only when crowding reduces flower production.

Nerine (ne-RY-nee)

A genus of about 20 species of bulbous, amaryllis-family members that are native to South Africa and bloom in autumn. Leaves are strap-shaped and borne at the base of the plant. Flowers are borne in umbels atop leafless stalks and are funnel-shaped, but with petal-like segments that are widely spreading. Blooms are white, pink or red. Nerines are grown in beds, borders and rock gardens. Zones 9 and 10; grown in greenhouses in the North.

Selected species and varieties. *N. bowdenii* is a 1- to 2-foot species. Blooms are pale to deep pink, 3 inches long and borne in eight- to 12-flowered umbels. *N. sarniensis,* Guernsey lily, is a 1½-foot plant whose narrow leaves appear after the flowers have faded. Blooms are bright red, 1½ inches long and and borne 10 per umbel. Cultivars with flowers ranging from rose-pink to deep red are available.

Growing conditions. Grow nerines outdoors in a location with rich, porous, well-drained soil. Nerines must have dry conditions during the summer dormant period and can be left undisturbed for many years without dividing. They may be hardy north of Zone 9 in a protected location, such as at the base of a south-facing wall, if heavily mulched. Plants can be grown in pots in rich, well-drained soil that contains coarse sand. Plant bulbs in late summer, when they are dormant. Water sparingly until flower spikes appear but do not allow the soil to dry out completely. Plants that are not hardy can be grown in a cool greenhouse that maintains temperatures above 50° F. Fertilize regularly once the foliage appears. When the foliage begins to yellow, gradually withhold water and store plants dry in the pots in a cool, dry place for four to five months. Plants should be repotted only every few years; replace the top third of soil annually with fresh soil. Plants bloom best if pot-bound.

Nodding onion see *Allium*

Notholirion (noth-o-LEER-ee-on)

A very small genus of lily-family members native to Asia. Leaves are very long and narrow at the base and shorter along the stem. Flowers are funnel-shaped, borne in spikes, and come in red, pink or lavender. Zones 7-9.

Selected species and varieties. *N. thomsonianum* is a 3- to 4-foot plant with 12-inch-long, 3/4-inch-wide leaves. Flowers, which are borne in spikes of 10 to 20, are fragrant, funnel-shaped, 2 inches long and pink to rose in color. Blooms appear in early spring.

Growing conditions. Notholirions are primarily grown in areas with mild winters and cool summers, such as the Pacific Northwest. They require moist, well-drained soil, protection from wind and a site with light shade. They can be grown in pots in cool greenhouses north of Zone 7.

Nothoscordum
(noth-o-SKOR-dum)
False garlic, grace garlic

A genus of amaryllis-family members closely related to onions (*Allium* species) but lacking the onionlike odor that most *Allium* species emit when foliage is bruised. Leaves are narrow and borne at the base of the plant. Flowers are borne in an umbel and are bell-shaped. Blooms have yellow or white petal-like segments that are united at the base. False garlic is used in rock gardens and in naturalized areas. Zones 8-10.

Selected species and varieties. *N. bivalve* is a 16-inch plant with narrow, grassy leaves and 1/2-inch-long flowers borne in few-flowered clusters. Blooms are yellowish or whitish and appear in early spring. May be hardy north of Zone 8 with protection.

Growing conditions. Grow false garlic in rich, well-drained soil and full sun. Plant the bulbs 3 inches deep.

One-day lily see *Tigridia*
Onion see *Allium*
Orchid amaryllis see *Sprekelia*
Orchid pansy see *Achimenes*

Ornithogalum
(or-ni-THOG-a-lum)

A genus of both hardy and tender species in the lily family that arise from bulbs. Leaves are borne at the base of the plant and can be narrow or broad. Flowers are borne in spikes and have six separate, spreading petals. Blooms may be white, yellow or orange-red. *Ornithogalum* species are used in naturalized areas or in beds and borders. Zones 5-10.

Selected species and varieties. *O. arabicum,* Arabian star-of-Bethlehem, is a 1- to 1½-foot species with narrow, 3/4-inch leaves. Flowers are white, 1 inch long and borne in six- to 12-flowered clusters in summer atop 1- to 2-foot stalks. Zones 8-10. *O. caudatum,* whiplash star-of-Bethlehem, is a spring- or summer-blooming species with white or green 1-inch flowers. Zones 8-10. *O. nutans,* nodding star-of-Bethlehem, has 8- to 12-inch stalks bearing three to 12 flowers that are white inside and green outside. Blooms are 1 inch long, nodding and fragrant. Zones 6-10. *O. saundersiae,* giant chincherinchee, bears strap-shaped, 1-foot-long leaves that are gray-green and 2 inches wide. Flowers are white, 1 inch across and borne in many-flowered clusters atop stalks that can reach 4 feet. *O. thyrsoides,* wonder flower, chincherinchee, has long, narrow leaves and 6- to 18-inch flowering stems that appear in late spring to summer. Blooms are 3/4 inch long, white or cream-colored, and borne in dense spikes of 12 to 18 flowers. All parts of

NOTHOLIRION THOMSONIANUM

NOTHOSCORDUM BIVALVE

ORNITHOGALUM NUTANS

ORNITHOGALUM UMBELLATUM

OXALIS RUBRA

the plant are poisonous. Zones 8-10. *O. umbellatum,* star-of-Bethlehem, nap-at-noon, summer snowflake, is a 1-foot plant with narrow leaves and white, 1-inch flowers borne in five- to 20-flowered spikes.

Growing conditions. Grow *Ornithogalum* species in naturalized areas in shade or full sun with ordinary garden soil. Hardy species will spread rapidly and aggressively, so plant them only in sites where spreading is not a problem. Tender species can be grown in beds and borders in Zones 8-10 or in pots in cool greenhouses. Pot-grown plants need a well-drained potting medium with sand and compost or leaf mold. Plant bulbs in fall or winter at a depth of 1 inch. Water sparingly until growth begins; keep soil evenly moist once the plants are actively growing. Feed with a balanced fertilizer when flower buds appear. Withhold water when the foliage begins to yellow after flowering. Store bulbs in a cool, dry place for bloom the following year.

Oxalis (OK-sal-is)

Oxalis, wood sorrel, lady's sorrel

A genus of annuals and perennials of worldwide distribution that generally arise from bulbs, tubers or rhizomes. Most species are from South America or South Africa; all have compound, cloverlike leaves with leaflets arranged finger-fashion. Leaflets often fold up at night and on dark days. Flowers have five petals and five sepals, are borne alone or in few-flowered clusters, and come in white, pink, red or yellow. The species listed below are all perennials. Oxalis is grown in rock gardens and woodland gardens. Zones 5-10.

Selected species and varieties. *O. adenophylla,* Chilean oxalis, is a 6-inch plant with tuberous roots. Leaves are umbrella-like clusters of nine to 20 blue-green leaflets. Flowers are 1 inch wide, rose-pink and borne throughout the summer on 2-inch stems. Zones 7-10. *O. bowiei,* Bowie oxalis, arises from thick, tuberous roots to a height of 12 inches. It is a native of South Africa and bears 1- to 1½-inch-wide flowers that are rose to purple in color. Blooms appear in summer. Zones 8-10. *O. braziliensis,* Brazil oxalis, is a 5- to 10-inch species that arises from small bulbs. In summer it bears one to three 1-inch flowers per stalk that are wine red or rosy purple in color. Zones 8-10. *O. corymbosa* is a tropical, 12-inch-tall plant arising from a swollen taproot that produces bulbils at the top. Flowers are ¾ inch across, purplish pink in color and borne in summer in many-flowered clusters. Zone 10. *O. deppei,* good-luck plant, is a 4- to 12-inch plant from Mexico that arises from a bulb and has four leaflets per leaf. Blooms are red or purplish violet and are borne in summer in five- to 12-flowered umbels. A white-flowered form is also available. Zones 8-10.

O. depressa is a 4-inch South African native that arises from a bulb and has solitary, 1¼-inch-long flowers that are white, pink or violet with a yellow throat. Zones 8-10. *O. lasiandra* is a 1-foot-tall, bulbous species from Mexico. The leaves have five to 10 leaflets and are marked with red underneath. The flowers, which are red to pinkish red and ½ inch wide, are borne in summer in many-flowered umbels. Zones 9 and 10. *O. pes-caprae,* Bermuda buttercup, is a 12-inch plant with three-leaflet leaves, thick roots and scaly bulbs. Despite its common name, it is native to South Africa. The blooms, which appear in early spring, are nodding, yellow and 1½ inches wide. Zones 9 and 10. *O. purpurea* is a bulbous South African native that blooms in fall. Plants reach 6 inches in height and bear leaves with three leaflets. Flowers are 2 inches wide, borne one per stem, and pink, red, purple or white with a yellow throat. Grand Dutchess series cultivars have large white, pink or rose-red blooms with yellow throats. Zones 9 and 10. *O. rubra* is a 6- to 12-inch plant with three-leaflet leaves and umbels of rose-pink flowers borne above the foliage. Blooms, which appear in winter, may be veined with violet or white and are ¾ inch long. Zones 8-10. *O. violacea,* violet wood sorrel, is a 10-inch, bulbous plant native to woodlands of North America. Flowers are ¾ inch long and rose-purple or pinkish white in color. Blooms are borne in few-flowered clusters in early spring.

Growing conditions. *O. adenophylla, O. braziliensis, O. corymbosa, O. deppei, O. lasiandra* and *O. rubra* are fine for rock gardens. They prefer well-drained, rich soil that is high in organic matter such as leaf mold. They generally do not relish hot summers or cold winters, and perform best in areas such as the Pacific Northwest. In the East, plant them in a north-facing site that is shaded during the hottest part of the day. They can also be grown in cool greenhouses in pots. Plant them in fall in well-drained potting medium that is neutral to slightly alkaline. Plants will bloom in winter; after bloom, store the tubers in a cool, dark place until the following autumn. *O. corymbosa* can become very weedy in tropical gardens.

Plant *O. bowiei, O. depressa, O. pes-caprae* and *O. purpurea* in full sun in a location with rich, well-drained soil that has been enriched with compost or leaf mold. Fertilize with 5-10-5 when the plants emerge and again a month later. In the South, plants can be mulched and left in the ground over winter. North of Zone 8, *O. bowiei* can be dug before the first hard frost. Shake off excess soil and allow plants to dry for several days in a cool, dry place out of direct sun. Store in dry peat moss or vermiculite at a temperature of 55° to 60° F. Plants can be started indoors and moved to the garden after danger of frost has passed. *O. pes-caprae* can become a troublesome weed and is often grown in pots or baskets to prevent it from spreading. *O. purpurea* makes a fine rock garden plant and is not weedy or aggressive.

Grow *O. violacea* in rich, well-drained soil in light shade. It makes a fine addition to a wild or woodland garden. All of the species except *O. violacea* can be grown indoors in pots as houseplants or greenhouse plants.

Pamianthe (pam-ee-AN-thee)

A very small South American genus in the amaryllis family. Plants arise from bulbs and produce umbels of one to four, tubular, white or greenish flowers. Blooms resemble those of basket flowers *(Hymenocallis* species), with a white, cuplike corona surrounded by long, narrow perianth segments. Zone 10.

Selected species and varieties. *P. peruviana* is a fragrant-flowered, 2-foot-tall species with 20-inch-long, 1-inch-wide leaves. Fragrant blooms are borne one to four per 2-foot stalk. Flowers have white, 5-inch-long perianth lobes and a 3-inch-long corona. Blooms appear in early spring.

Growing conditions. *Pamianthe* species can be grown outdoors in the warmest parts of Zone 10, where they prefer a sunny site with rich, sandy, well-drained soil. When they are grown outdoors, flowers appear in spring. In the North, plant bulbs indoors in pots in late fall or winter for late-winter bloom. Allow for a 2-inch space between the bulb and the edge of the pot, and plant the bulbs with the upper half above the soil surface. Use a rich, sandy potting soil to which bone meal has been added. Keep plants barely moist and in a warm, dark place until growth begins. Move plants to a bright spot out of direct sun for flowering. Remove stalks after flowering, feed twice a month with a weak fertilizer and keep watering until fall, when the leaves will begin to yellow. Store plants dry and repot in late fall or early winter.

Paramongaia
(par-a-mon-GA-ee-a)
Cojomaria

A one-species genus in the amaryllis family that is closely related to *Pamianthe.* Plants arise from bulbs, and the narrow, strap-shaped leaves appear with the flowers or after the flowers have faded. Flower stalks are 2 feet tall and carry a single, large bloom that is tubular and resembles a large daffodil. Zone 10.

Selected species and varieties. *P. weberbaueri* has 2½-foot-long leaves that are 2 inches wide. The blooms are fragrant, bright yellow, and borne one or sometimes two per stalk. They have 3-inch-long coronas, are 7 inches in diameter and appear in spring.

Growing conditions. Cojomaria can be grown outdoors in the warmest parts of Zone 10. Plant the bulbs in a sunny site with rich, sandy, well-drained soil. When cojomaria is grown outdoors, flowers appear in spring. In the North, plant bulbs indoors in pots in late fall or winter for late-winter bloom. Allow for a 2-inch space between the bulb and the edge of the pot, and plant the bulbs with the upper half above the soil surface. Use a rich, sandy potting soil to which bone meal has been added. Keep plants barely moist and in a warm, dark place until growth begins. Move plants to a bright spot out of direct sun for flowering. Remove stalks after flowering, feed twice a month with a weak fertilizer and keep watering until fall, when the leaves will begin to yellow. Store plants dry and repot in late fall or early winter.

Peacock orchid see *Acidanthera*
Persian violet see *Cyclamen*

PAMIANTHE PERUVIANA

PARAMONGAIA WEBERBAUERI

POLIANTHES TUBEROSA 'SINGLE MEXICAN'

PUSCHKINIA SCILLOIDES

RANUNCULUS ASIATICUS TECOLOTE GIANT

Peruvian daffodil see *Hymenocallis*

Peruvian jacinth see *Scilla*

Pineapple lily see *Eucomis*

Poison bulb see *Crinum*

Poison camas see *Zigadenus*

Polianthes (pol-ee-AN-theez)

A genus of about a dozen species, native to Mexico, in the agave family. Plants have bulblike bases and often thick rhizomes and roots. Foliage is grasslike; the flowers are tubular and borne in spikes. *Polianthes* species are grown in beds and borders, especially where their fragrance can be enjoyed. Zones 9 and 10; grown as annuals in the North.

Selected species and varieties. *P. tuberosa,* tuberose, is a 3-foot-tall plant with 12- to 18-inch leaves that are borne at the base of the plant. Flowers are extremely fragrant, waxy white and borne in loose spikes. Blooms appear in summer to fall. 'Excelsior Double Pearl' is a double-flowered cultivar. 'The Pearl' has clusters of double flowers on a 2-foot plant. 'Single Mexican' has fragrant, single flowers and grows 3 to 4 feet high.

Growing conditions. Tuberoses can be grown outdoors in beds and borders in Zones 9 and 10. Elsewhere they are generally planted outdoors when danger of frost has passed, then dug and stored indoors over winter. Plant the bulblike tubers in a site with full sun or light shade and rich, well-drained soil to which abundant amounts of compost have been added. Full-sized tubers should be planted 3 inches deep and 6 inches apart; smaller offsets should be planted 2 inches deep and 4 inches apart. Offsets will not bloom the first year. Healthy tubers will always show a green growing point. Mulch and water heavily through the growing season. Withhold water near the end of the season, when the foliage will begin to yellow, and dig and store the tubers indoors in a cool, dry place. Tubers can also be started indoors in February or March in 4-inch pots filled with porous, quickly draining potting medium. Lightly cover the tubers with peat or sphagnum moss. Place the container in a warm (60° to 70° F), bright place. Water sparingly until growth begins, then water more often. Do not set plants outside until danger of frost has passed.

Prairie onion see *Allium*

Puschkinia (push-KIN-ee-a)

A very small genus of spring-blooming plants in the lily family. Leaves are strap-shaped and borne at the base of the plant. Flowers are bell-shaped, white or blue, and borne in dense spikes. Zones 4-10.

Selected species and varieties. *P. scilloides,* striped squill, has 6-inch-long leaves that are ½ inch wide. Flowers are bell-shaped, ½ inch long and borne in spikes atop 6-inch stalks. Blooms are striped and bluish white.

Growing conditions. Grow striped squill in full sun or part shade in a location with rich, somewhat sandy, well-drained soil. Plant bulbs in fall at a depth of 3 inches and 3 inches apart. Plants do not need dividing and can be left undisturbed for many years. If plants become crowded and flowering diminishes, dig and divide after the foliage has ripened.

Quamash see *Camassia*

Rain lily see *Zephyranthes*

Ranunculus (ra-NUN-kew-lus)

Buttercup

The large genus from which the buttercup family, or *Ranunculaceae,* takes both its common and botanical names. Buttercups have fibrous or tuberous roots. Leaves are compound and deeply cut or divided. Flowers are generally yellow but sometimes red, and have five petals, five sepals and numerous stamens. Zones 8-10; grown in pots in the North.

Selected species and varieties. *R. asiaticus,* Persian buttercup, florist's buttercup, is a tuberous-rooted species that has been much hybridized. Leaves have three leaflets. Flowers are borne one to four per stem, are double or semidouble, and range from 1 to 4 inches across. Blooms may be yellow, white, orange, pink or red. 'Superbissima' has 1- to 4-inch semidouble flowers that are white, yellow, orange, red or pink atop 1-foot stems. Tecolote Giant hybrids have larger flowers with more brilliant colors than the species.

Growing conditions. Grow Persian buttercups in full sun in moist, compost-rich soil that is very well drained. Plant the tuberous roots in fall or early winter, with the pronglike roots pointing down, at a depth of 2 inches, spacing them 6 to 8 inches apart. Water thoroughly at planting time; do not water again until growth appears in about two weeks. Persian buttercups will not tolerate hot summer weather; they prefer night temperatures of 45° to 50° F. After flowering, let the plants dry out, dig the roots, cut off the tops of the plants and store the roots in a cool, dry place until the following fall.

Romulea (rom-yew-LEE-a)

This large genus of cormous iris-family members is closely related to both *Crocus* and *Gladiolus.* Plants are native to South Africa and southern Europe. Leaves are grasslike, and the flowers are borne on very short stalks, like those of crocuses. Blooms have tubular bases and long lobes. *Romulea* species are grown in rock and woodland gardens or in pots in cool greenhouses. Zones 8-10.

Selected species and varieties. *R. bulbocodium* is a 2- to 3-inch species with very narrow, 2- to 12-inch-long leaves. Flowers have outward-flaring lobes that may be cream-yellow at the throat and lilac to purple at the top, or may be predominantly yellow with purple only at the edges. Blooms are 1 to 1½ inches long and appear in early spring. *R. sabulosa* is a 4-inch plant with 4-inch leaves. The flowers are cup-shaped, 1½ inches long and resemble small rose-pink to bright red tulips. Blooms appear in late spring. Zones 9 and 10.

Growing conditions. In frost-free areas, plant *Romulea* species in the fall at a depth of 2 to 3 inches. They require a location with full sun and rich, well-drained soil. For best results they require cool temperatures (45° to 55° F) at night. North of Zone 9, they can be grown in pots in the greenhouse or in sunny windows.

Roscoea (ros-KO-ee-a)

A genus of ginger-family members with thick, fleshy roots and vaselike clusters of narrow, lance-shaped leaves. Flowers are borne in spikes and somewhat resemble orchids or open snapdragons. Blooms may be purple, blue or yellow. Zones 8-10.

Selected species and varieties. *R. alpina* is a 6-inch species with dark purple, 1-inch-long flowers that have a white tube. *R. purpurea* bears few-flowered spikes of white to purple flowers atop 1-foot-tall plants.

Growing conditions. *Roscoea* species are best grown only in areas with mild winters and cool, humid summers. Plant them in partial shade in sandy soil that is rich in organic matter and moist but not wet, and mulch to insulate the soil against heat.

Rosy onion see *Allium*
Scarborough lily see *Vallota*
Scarlet windflower see *Anemone*

Scilla (SIL-a)
Squill

A genus of bulbous lily-family members grown for their early-spring blooms. Narrow, grasslike leaves are borne at the base of the plant. Foliage usually appears with the flowers, which are small and bell-shaped. Blooms are borne in few- to many-flowered racemes and are blue, white or purple. Squills are grown in rock and woodland gardens, under deciduous shrubs and trees, and can be easily naturalized. Zones 4-10.

Selected species and varieties. *S. bifolia,* twinleaf squill, bears two or sometimes three narrow, 8-inch-long leaves. Flowers, which are borne in clusters of three to eight, are starlike, ½ inch wide and blue in color. 'Alba' bears white flowers. 'Rosea' is a pink-flowered cultivar. *S. litardierei,* meadow squill, is a 10-inch-tall species with three to six narrow, foot-long leaves. Flowers, which are borne in 12- to 35-flowered spikes, are blue, bell-shaped and 3/16 inch long. Zones 6-10. *S. peruviana,* Cuban lily, Peruvian jacinth, hyacinth-of-Peru, is an 18-inch plant with 1-foot-long, 1-inch-wide leaves. Flowers are ½ inch long, purple or reddish, although white forms also exist. Blooms are borne in spikes of 50 or more. Zones 9 and 10. *S. scilloides,* Chinese squill, Japanese jacinth, is a 1½-foot-tall species with

ROMULEA BULBOCODIUM

ROSCOEA PURPUREA

SCILLA PERUVIANA

SCILLA SIBERICA

SPARAXIS TRICOLOR

SPREKELIA FORMOSISSIMA

two 10-inch leaves. Flowers are ½ inch long, rose-purple in color and borne in dense 20- to 60-flowered spikes. Zones 6-10.

S. siberica, Siberian squill, is a 4- to 6-inch plant with deep blue, ½-inch-wide flowers that are nodding and bell-shaped. Blooms are borne three to five per cluster. 'Alba' is a white-flowered cultivar. 'Spring Beauty' is a large-flowered form with deep blue blooms. Collection in the wild has endangered the species; purchase from reputable dealers that sell only propagated bulbs. *S. tubergeniana* resembles *S. siberica* but is only 5 inches tall. Flowers are cup-shaped, 1½ inches wide, and white or pale blue. Zones 5-10. Collection in the wild has endangered the species; purchase from reputable dealers that sell only propagated bulbs.

Growing conditions. Grow squill in full sun or partial shade in a location with rich, well-drained, somewhat sandy soil. Siberian squill is able to grow under evergreens, where few other plants are able to survive. Plant bulbs in early fall at a depth of three times the height of the bulb. Plants will multiply rapidly, and benefit from an occasional fall mulching with well-rotted manure or compost.

Scilla see also *Brimeura; Endymion; Ledebouria*

Sea onion see *Urginea*

Sea squill see *Urginea*

Sego lily see *Calochortus*

Shell flower see *Tigridia*

Siberian lily see *Ixiolirion*

Snake's head iris see *Hermodactylus*

Snowdrop see *Galanthus*

Snowflake see *Leucojum*

Spanish bluebell see *Endymion*

Sparaxis (spa-RAK-sis)

Wandflower, harlequin flower

A small South African genus of cormous iris-family members with narrow, sword-shaped leaves borne at the base of the plant. The blooms are regular and funnel-shaped at the base with spreading, petal-like lobes. They are borne in loose spikes. Wandflowers blossom in late spring to summer and may be planted in beds and borders. They also can be forced in pots in cool greenhouses. Zones 9 and 10.

Selected species and varieties. *S. tricolor* is an 18-inch species with 1-inch-long, funnel-shaped flowers that are dark purplish red, yellow marked with brown-purple or white with purple. Blooms have yellow throats and yellow anthers.

Growing conditions. Grow wandflowers in a site with full sun and very well drained, rich soil. Plant corms in early to late fall at a depth of 3 to 4 inches and 1 to 1½ feet apart. Fertilize plantings with a balanced fertilizer annually in the fall. Mulch to protect the corms from cold. Wandflowers also can be forced in greenhouses or grown as annuals.

Spider lily see *Crinum; Hymenocallis; Lycoris*

Sprekelia (spre-KEE-lee-a)

A one-species genus native to Mexico and classified in the amaryllis family. Plants arise from bulbs and have long narrow leaves and solitary, two-lipped flowers. *Sprekelia* can be grown outdoors in beds or borders in the South and Southwest; grown indoors in the North. Zones 9 and 10.

Selected species and varieties. *S. formosissima,* Aztec lily, Jacobean lily, orchid amaryllis, is a 1-foot-tall species with narrow leaves that appear with the flowers. Blooms are bright red, 4 inches long and borne one per leafless, 12-inch-tall stalk. Flowers, which appear in summer, have three upright petal-like segments and three lower segments that form an orchidlike lip.

Growing conditions. *Sprekelia* species can be grown outdoors in the warmest parts of Zones 9 and 10, where they prefer a sunny site with rich, sandy, well-drained soil. When they are grown outdoors, flowers appear in late spring. In the North, plant bulbs indoors in pots in late fall or winter for late-winter bloom. Leave a 2-inch space between the bulb and the edge of the pot, and plant the bulbs with the upper half above the soil surface. Use a rich, sandy potting soil to which bone meal has been added. Keep plants barely moist and in a warm, dark place until growth begins. Move plants to a bright spot out of direct sun for flowering. Remove stalks after flowering, feed twice a month with a weak fertilizer and keep watering until fall, when the leaves will begin to yellow. Store plants dry and repot them in late fall or early winter.

Spring beauty see *Claytonia*

Spring meadow saffron see *Bulbocodium*

Spring starflower see *Ipheion*

Squill see *Scilla; Urginea*

Star grass see *Hypoxis*

Star lily see *Lilium; Zigadenus*

Star-of-Bethlehem see *Ornithogalum*

Stars-of-Persia see *Allium*

Sternbergia (stern-BER-jee-a)

A small genus of amaryllis-family members that arise from bulbs and have narrow leaves borne at the base of the plant. The flowers, which are solitary and funnel- or cup-shaped, closely resemble crocuses except that they have six stamens and crocuses have only three. Sternbergias are grown in rock gardens and are especially useful in hot, dry locations. Zones 7-10.

Selected species and varieties. *S. lutea,* winter daffodil, lily-of-the-field, is a 4- to 7-inch plant with narrow, ¾-inch-wide leaves that appear with the flowers. Blooms are yellow, goblet-shaped, 1½ inches long and appear in fall. The bulbs are poisonous. Collection in the wild has endangered the species; purchase from reputable dealers that sell only propagated bulbs. The cultivar 'Major' has larger flowers than the species.

Growing conditions. Grow winter daffodils in a location with full sun or light shade and well-drained, slightly dry soil. Plant the bulbs in midsummer in a sheltered place such as against a south-facing wall or other warm spot in the garden. Plant the bulbs 4 to 6 inches deep, with several inches of deeply prepared soil beneath the bases of the bulbs. The bulbs should be left undisturbed for as long as possible; divide only if flowering ceases. The foliage appears in autumn and persists over winter.

Streptanthera
(strep-TAN-the-ra)

A small genus of bulbous South African natives in the iris family. Foliage is sword-shaped and mostly borne at the base of the plant. Flowers have six petals and are either solitary or borne in small clusters. Zones 9 and 10.

Selected species and varieties. *S. cuprea* is a 9-inch species with very narrow, 2- to 5-inch-long leaves. Flowers are borne two to three per stem and are 2 inches wide. Blooms are pinkish copper-colored at the top, with a dark band separating a purplish and yellow-spotted base.

Growing conditions. Grow *Streptanthera* species in a site with full sun and very well drained, rich soil. Plant corms in early to late fall at a depth of 3 to 4 inches and 1 to 1½ feet apart. Fertilize plantings with a balanced fertilizer annually in the fall. Mulch to protect the corms from cold. They also can be forced in greenhouses.

Striped squill see *Puschkinia*

Summer hyacinth see *Galtonia*

Summer snowflake see *Ornithogalum*

Swamp lily see *Crinum*

Sword lily see *Gladiolus*

Tangut onion see *Allium*

Taro see *Colocasia*

Tartar lily see *Ixiolirion*

Tassel hyacinth see *Muscari*

Tecophilaea (tek-o-FY-lee-a)

A genus consisting of two species from the Chilean Andes. Plants arise from corms and have narrow leaves and bear one to three blue, bell-shaped flowers. *Tecophilaea* species are grown in rock gardens in areas with mild winters and cool summers. Zones 8-10.

STERNBERGIA LUTEA 'MAJOR'

STREPTANTHERA CUPREA

TECOPHILAEA CYANOCROCUS

TIGRIDIA PAVONIA

TRITELEIA LAXA 'QUEEN FABIOLA'

TRITONIA CROCATA

Selected species and varieties. *T. cyanocrocus,* Chilean crocus, is a 6-inch-tall plant with deep blue, 1½-inch-long flowers that have throats veined with white.

Growing conditions. *Tecophilaea* species are difficult-to-grow plants that prefer areas with mild winters and cool summers, such as the Pacific Northwest. Plant the bulbs in fall at a depth of 2 to 2½ inches. Soil should be well drained, fertile and rich in organic matter. Plants begin growth very early in spring and are often damaged by frost.

Tiger flower see *Tigridia*

Tiger lily see *Lilium*

Tigridia (ty-GRID-ee-a)

Tiger flower, shell flower, one-day lily

A genus of bulbous iris-family members native to Central and South America. Leaves are narrow and sword-shaped; cup-shaped flowers spread at the tips. Blooms last for only a day. Zones 7-10.

Selected species and varieties. *T. pavonia* is an erect, 2-foot-tall plant with rigid, 1½-foot-long leaves. Blooms are 3 to 6 inches across and are red spotted with yellow and purple in the cup-shaped center. Many cultivars with variously colored blooms are available.

Growing conditions. Plant tiger flowers in full sun in a location protected from high winds. Space corms 6 to 9 inches apart at a depth of 3 to 4 inches. Enrich the soil with compost and fertilize with 5-10-5 when the plants emerge and again a month later. North of Zone 7, tiger flowers can be grown provided the corms are dug before the first hard frost. Shake off excess soil and allow them to dry for several days in a cool, dry place out of direct sun. Cut back the tops of the plants and discard the remains of the previous season's corms. Store in dry peat moss or vermiculite at a temperature of 55° to 60° F. Plants also can be started indoors and moved to the garden after danger of frost has passed. They can be difficult to transplant, so start them in peat pots that can go directly into the ground or grow them in tubs. Propagate plants from the small cormels borne around old corms. Small corms take up to two seasons to bloom.

Triplet lilies see *Brodiaea*

Triteleia (try-TEL-ee-a)

A genus of North American amaryllis-family members that arise from corms and have narrow leaves and umbels of small, six-petaled flowers. In the West, they make fine additions to native plant gardens, naturalized areas and perennial borders. In the East, they can be grown in rock gardens. Zones 6-10.

Selected species and varieties. *T. hyacinthina,* wild hyacinth, has narrow, grasslike leaves and 2½-foot flower stalks topped with umbels of ½-inch flowers that are white, blue or lilac. *T. laxa,* grass nut, triplet lily, Ithuriel's spear, is a 2½-foot-tall plant with umbels of 1¼- to 1¾-inch flowers that are trumpet-shaped and violet-purple, blue or sometimes white. The cultivar 'Queen Fabiola' has deep blue or violet flowers with darker midribs. It grows 12 inches tall and has grasslike leaves.

Growing conditions. Plant triteleias outdoors in fall in a location with full sun and well-drained sandy or gritty soil. Plant the corms at a depth of 3 to 5 inches and space them 2 to 3 inches apart. These plants are easy to grow in the West, but are intolerant of wet eastern summers. In the East, keep the plants evenly moist while the flowers are in bloom and the foliage is green, in spring and early summer. After the foliage dies down, dig the corms and store them in a dry place over the summer. Replant in fall. In the West, plants can be left undisturbed for many years.

Tritonia (try-TOH-nee-a)

Blazing star

A genus of South African iris-family members once classified as *Montebretia* and closely related to *Gladiolus.* Plants arise from corms and bear narrow, grasslike leaves. Flowers are trumpet-shaped and borne on 1- to 2-foot spikes. Blazing stars are grown in beds and borders. In areas where they are not hardy, they can be dug and overwintered indoors. Zones 7-10.

Selected species and varieties. *T. crocata* grows 1½ feet tall; it has no branches, few leaves and spikes of

2-inch-wide flowers. Blooms are generally orange-red or yellowish brown, but scarlet and pale pink cultivars are also available. Flowers appear in late spring to summer.

Growing conditions. Plant blazing stars in full sun in a location protected from high winds. Space corms 6 to 9 inches apart at a depth of 3 to 4 inches. Enrich the soil with compost, and fertilize with 5-10-5 when the plants emerge and again a month later. North of Zone 7, blazing stars can be grown provided the corms are dug before the first hard frost. Shake off excess soil and allow them to dry for several days in a cool, dry place out of direct sun. Cut back the tops of the plants and discard the remains of the previous season's corms. Store in dry peat moss or vermiculite at a temperature of 55° to 60° F. Plants also can be started indoors and moved to the garden after danger of frost has passed. They can be difficult to transplant, so start them in peat pots that can go directly into the ground or grow them in tubs. Propagate plants from the small cormels borne around old corms. Small corms take up to two seasons to bloom.

Trout lily see *Erythronium*
Tuberose see *Polianthes*
Tulip see *Tulipa*

Tulipa (TOO-lip-a)
Tulip

A genus of hardy, spring-blooming bulbs in the lily family. Leaves are usually borne at the base of the plant but occasionally on the stem, and are generally thick and leathery. Most tulips have bluish green foliage; a few species and hybrids have mottled foliage. Flowers are showy, erect and cup-shaped. Each has six tepals (three petal-like sepals and three true petals) that are identical. Blooms come in most colors except true blue.

There are between 50 and 150 species of tulips as well as thousands of hybrids, which have been developed by breeders over the centuries. Hybrid tulips are much more commonly grown than the species. All of the species and hybrid tulips have been separated into 15 divisions according to bloom time, flower form and parent species. The divisions have been further organized into four groups: Species and their hybrids; Early; Midseason; and Late, or May-Flowering. By selecting a variety of tulips from several divisions and each of the four groups, gardeners can plan for a long spring tulip display. Tall hybrid tulips are grown in beds and borders. Species Tulips and their cultivars are grown as edging plants at the front of borders and in rock gardens. Most make fine cut flowers. Zones 4-10.

Selected species and varieties. Species Tulips. *T. acuminata,* Turkish tulip, is a 1- to 1½-foot-tall species with 4-inch-long flowers that are yellow or light pink. The tepals are very narrow and pointed, and blooms appear in late spring. Zones 4-8. *T. aucherana* is an 8-inch, early-spring-blooming species with strap-shaped leaves borne at the base of the plant. Flowers are starlike, 1 to 1½ inches long and pink with a brownish yellow central blotch and yellow stamens. Zones 4-8. *T. batalinii* is a 5- to 6-inch species with grasslike leaves and yellow, 2-inch-long flowers that appear in early spring. 'Bright Gem' has sulfur yellow blooms flushed with orange. 'Red Jewel' has red flowers. Zones 4-8. *T. clusiana,* lady tulip, candy-stick tulip, is 15 inches tall and has small, fragrant, 2-inch-long flowers that appear in late spring. Blooms are reddish purple at the base, white or yellowish at the tip, and striped with pinkish red on the outside. Zones 4-8. *T. humilis* bears 2½-inch-long flowers with pointed tepals atop 4-inch plants. Blooms are reddish green outside, pale purple with a yellow blotch at the base inside. Zones 4-8. *T. kolpakowkiana* is a 6-inch species that bears one or two early-spring flowers that are 2 inches long and yellow and slightly reddish outside. Zones 4-8.

T. orphanidea is an 8- to 12-inch species with narrow leaves and solitary flowers that appear in early spring. Blooms are orange to brown or yellow and marked with green outside. Tepals are pointed at the tips and the flowers are 2 inches long. Zones 5-8. *T. praestans* bears one to four 2-inch-long flowers atop 12-inch plants. Blooms are red without a central blotch and appear in early spring. 'Fuselier' bears stems of three or four scarlet-orange flowers. Zones 5-8. *T. pulchella* bears cup-shaped flowers that open flat atop 4- to 6-inch plants in early spring. Blooms are 1½ inches long and red to purple in color, paler inside. 'Persian Pearl' has blooms that are purple inside with a yellow base and magenta-rose outside. 'Rosea' has pale violet flowers with a yellow base. 'Violacea' has purple-red petals tinged with green

TULIPA HUMILIS

TULIPA ORPHANIDEA

TULIPA PRAESTANS 'FUSELIER'

TULIPA FOSTERANA 'PURISSIMA'

TULIPA GREIGII 'YELLOW DAWN'

TULIPA 'DUTCH FAIR'

on the outside and with a greenish black blotch inside. Zones 5-8. *T. saxatilis* produces bulbs at the end of creeping stolons and blooms in midspring. Flowers are borne one to three per 12-inch stem and are cup-shaped, fragrant, 2 inches long and pale pinkish purple with a large yellow blotch at the base. Zones 4-8. *T. sprengeri* is a 1-foot-tall species with orange or brownish red blooms that have a dark base inside. Blooms are 2 inches long, have very pointed tepals and appear in late spring. Zones 5-8.

T. sylvestris is an 8- to 12-inch-tall species with strap-shaped leaves and weak stems that blooms in late spring. Flowers are 2 inches long, somewhat starlike, fragrant and bright yellow in color. *T. tarda* has narrow, strap-shaped leaves and few-flowered clusters of yellow, starlike flowers edged in white. Blooms are 2 inches long and appear in early spring atop 5-inch plants. The species is long-lived. Zones 4-8. *T. turkestanica* is an 8-inch species that bears one to six 1¼-inch-long flowers that are white with an orange-yellow base. Blooms are star- or lily-like and appear in early spring. Zones 4-8. *T. wilsoniana* bears bright red flowers with a black blotch at the base of the bloom. Blooms are 2 inches long and appear atop 8-inch plants. Zones 4-8.

There are three divisions of tulips that have been developed from specific species and closely resemble the parent species. These are Fosterana Tulips, Greigii Tulips and Kaufmanniana Tulips.

Fosterana Tulips are hybrids and varieties of *T. fosterana,* a species with scarlet blooms marked with a black blotch edged in yellow at the base inside the flowers. Fosterana Tulips are early-flowering, 16- to 18-inch plants with three or four broad leaves and very large blooms. Cultivars with red, yellow, orange, white and rose-pink blooms are available. 'Red Emperor' is an 18-inch cultivar with flaming red blooms that are dark at the base inside. 'Purissima' is a white-flowered variant of 'Red Emperor' and is streaked with yellow at the base inside. Zones 4-8.

Greigii Tulips, hybrids and varieties of *T. greigii,* have large flowers that appear in midspring and attractive foliage mottled with maroon. They exhibit characteristics of *T. greigii,* a 6- to 9-inch species with broad, wavy-margined leaves that are mottled with purple-brown. The species has 3-inch-long, scarlet-orange flowers with a black blotch edged in yellow at the base inside the flower. 'Cape Cod' bears blooms that are apricot edged with yellow on the outside and darker with a black blotch at the base inside. Foliage is mottled with purple-brown. 'Red Riding Hood' is a 6-inch plant with scarlet flowers and green leaves heavily striped with dark, purplish brown. 'Yellow Dawn' has rose-red petals edged with yellow. Zones 4-8.

Kaufmanniana Tulips are hybrids and varieties of *T. kaufmanniana* and are commonly called water lily tulips because of the flowers' resemblance to water lilies. *T. kaufmanniana* is an 8-inch species with 3-inch-long flowers that open flat and are somewhat starlike. Kaufmanniana Tulips are generally the earliest tulips to bloom and range from 5 to 10 inches tall. Blooms may be white, pink, red or yellow, and have a yellow blotch at the base. Plants have three to five broad leaves that are pointed at the tip and may be solid green or mottled with maroon. 'Shakespeare' is a 7-inch cultivar with rosy red flowers. Zones 4-8.

Early Tulips, comprising both Single Early Tulips and Double Early Tulips, bloom in early spring and are good for forcing in pots. They are the first of the hybrid tulips to bloom and are somewhat shorter than other hybrids, ranging from 9 to 16, or sometimes 20, inches tall.

Single Early Tulips have large, long-lasting flowers that are single (six-petaled), cup-shaped, 2 to 4 inches long and often fragrant. Blooms come in a wide variety of colors, including red, yellow, orange and white. 'Bellona' has fragrant, golden yellow blooms. 'Princess Irene' has pale salmon tepals marked with orange at the base. Zones 4-8.

Double Early Tulips have many-petaled flowers that somewhat resemble peonies and come in a wide range of colors. Blooms are 3 to 4 inches wide. 'Electra' has double cherry red flowers atop 8-inch plants. Zones 4-8.

Midseason Tulips comprise the Mendel Tulips, Triumph Tulips and Darwin Hybrid Tulips. These bloom in middle to late spring.

Mendel Tulips are vigorous, 1½- to 2-foot plants that will stand up to early-spring wind and rain and come in a variety of colors. They have large, single, cup-shaped flowers that appear shortly after the Double Early Tulips.

Triumph Tulips are generally crosses between Single Early Tulips and later-flowering hybrids. They have large, strong, 1- to 2-foot stems and 2- to 4-inch-long flowers. Triumph Tulips come in a variety of colors and may be striped or edged with contrasting colors. 'Garden Party' is a 16-inch cultivar with white flowers edged in bright red. 'Golden Melody' has bright yellow blooms. Zones 4-8.

Darwin Hybrid Tulips are the result of crosses between Darwin Hybrids and *T. fosteriana.* They bear single, 3- to 4-inch-long blooms atop sturdy, 2-foot stems. Flowers come in a wide variety of colors and often have a dark central blotch. 'Daydream' has apricot-colored blooms. 'Dutch Fair' flowers are golden yellow streaked with scarlet, except at the base, which is bluish black. 'Elizabeth Arden' produces rose-pink blooms. 'Oxford' is bright red. Zones 4-8.

Late, or May-Flowering, Tulips include Darwin Tulips, Lily-Flowered Tulips, Cottage Tulips (also called Single Late Tulips), Rembrandt Tulips, Parrot Tulips, and Double Late Tulips (also called Peony-Flowered Tulips).

Darwin Tulips are 2- to 2½-foot plants with sturdy stems and single, 3- to 4-inch-long flowers that have a satiny texture and come in a wide variety of colors, including many pastels not available in other hybrid groups. In profile, the blooms look square-based and rectangular. 'Black Pearl' is a 24-inch cultivar with dark, nearly black blooms. 'Insurpassable' bears pale lilac blooms atop 28-inch stalks. 'Scarlett O'Hara' has bright red blooms. 'Sweet Harmony' has lemon yellow blooms. Zones 4-8.

Lily-Flowered Tulips bloom just before the Darwin Tulips and are crosses between Cottage Tulips and *T. retroflexa.* They bear single, 2- to 4-inch-long blooms with pointed tepals that curve outward. 'China Pink' has pale pink blooms. 'Queen of Sheba' has red blooms edged with orange atop 22-inch stems. 'West Point' has golden yellow blooms. 'White Triumphator' has pure white flowers. Zones 4-8.

Cottage Tulips, which are also called Single Late Tulips, have single blooms with rounded petals and are somewhat egg-shaped in profile. Flowers are generally 3 to 4 inches long. 'Blushing Bride' has creamy white blooms with a red band atop 26-inch stems. 'Halcro' has long-lasting red flowers. 'Maureen' has white blooms atop 28-inch stems. 'Mrs. J. T. Scheepers' has fine yellow flowers. Viridifolia-Type cultivars have green striping on the tepals. Fringed Cottage Tulips have tepals that have finely fringed edges. 'Burgundy Lace' has wine red blooms with fringed tepals. 'Maja' has fringed tepals and yellow flowers. Bouquet, or multiflowering, forms bear several flowers per stem. 'Orange Bouquet' is an orange-flowered bouquet-type cultivar. Zones 4-8.

Rembrandt Tulips are 1½- to 2½-foot plants with white, yellow or red blooms striped or marked with black, brown, purple, red or pink. Zones 4-8.

Parrot Tulips have fringed, ruffled tepals that give the flowers an orchid-like form. Blooms appear in late spring, are 6 to 7 inches wide and come in a variety of colors. The stems are often weak, so Parrot Tulips should be planted where they are protected from wind. 'Black Parrot' has very dark purple or nearly black blooms atop 20- to 28-inch stems. 'Fantasy' has salmon-pink flowers marked with green on the outside. Zones 4-8.

Double Late Tulips, also called Peony-Flowered Tulips, are from 1 to 2 feet tall and have long-lasting, many-petaled blooms that are 6 inches wide and come in a variety of colors. 'Angelique' has pale pink blooms with nearly white edges. 'Bonanza' has double red flowers edged in yellow. 'Clara Carder' has rose-purple flowers that are white at the base. 'Mount Tacoma' has white flowers. Zones 4-8.

Growing conditions. Tulips perform best when grown in sun, and require a minimum of five to six hours of full sun per day. Grow them in very well drained, deeply prepared soil that is somewhat sandy and rich in organic matter. Plant the bulbs in late fall, and be sure to store them in a cool place before planting. Bulbs exposed to temperatures above 70° F for even a short time will produce flowers that are one-half to one-third normal size. It is also a good idea to purchase from dealers who have proper cool-storage facilities. Set bulbs at a depth of 4 to 8 inches, depending on the size of the bulb. (Smaller bulbs are planted closer to the surface than larger ones.) Tulips planted at a depth of 1 foot will bloom for several years but will produce fewer offsets than bulbs planted closer to the surface. Feed plants in spring with a balanced fertilizer. Allow the foliage to ripen naturally to produce food for the following years' bloom. Bulbs can be dug and divided if they have become crowded after the foliage has faded.

Many gardeners treat tulips as annuals, because they tend to bloom less reliably after the first year. In that case, they are dug after the flowers have faded and are discarded. Tulips are eaten by mice and chipmunks. They can also be infected

TULIPA 'ELIZABETH ARDEN'

TULIPA 'WEST POINT'

TULIPA 'CLARA CARDER'

URCEOLINA PERUVIANA

URGINEA MARITIMA

VALLOTA SPECIOSA

VELTHEIMIA VIRIDIFOLIA

with virus diseases, which will cause the flowers to be striped with white or green. Infected bulbs should be dug and discarded. In Zones 9 and 10 tulips can be grown as annuals, provided the bulbs are stored for six to eight weeks at 40° to 45° F before planting in late fall or early winter.

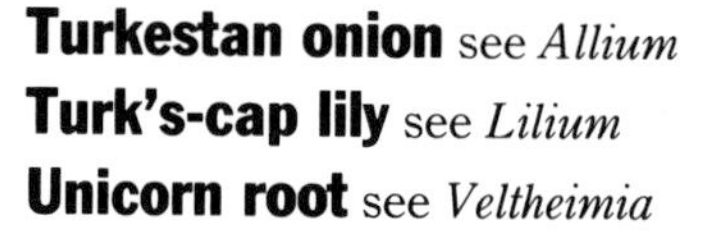

Turkestan onion see *Allium*
Turk's-cap lily see *Lilium*
Unicorn root see *Veltheimia*

Urceolina (er-se-o-LEE-na)

A small genus of bulbous amaryllis-family members from the South American Andes Mountains. Plants have oblong or lance-shaped leaves. The flowers are borne in few- to many-flowered umbels and are nodding and urn-shaped with short, spreading lobes. *Urceolina* species are usually grown as indoor plants, but can be grown outdoors in frost-free areas. Zone 10.

Selected species and varieties. *U. peruviana* is an 18-inch plant that has two- to six-flowered umbels of pendulous, bright red, 1½-inch-long flowers.

Growing conditions. Grow *Urceolina* species outdoors in the warmest parts of Zone 10. Plants prefer well-drained soil that is rich in organic matter and full sun. Pot plants in fall and grow in a cool (45° F) greenhouse until spring, when foliage appears. Keep soil moist but not wet until growth begins, then water regularly. The foliage will die down after the flowers appear in summer. Reduce watering and keep plants barely moist and repot in late summer or early fall.

Urginea (er-JIN-ee-a)
Sea onion, squill

A genus of lily-family members that arise from bulbs and have spikes of whitish, yellowish or pink flowers. Foliage is long and narrow and borne at the base of the plant. Individual blooms have three petals and three petal-like sepals. All parts of the plants are poisonous. Zones 9 and 10.

Selected species and varieties. *U. maritima,* sea onion, sea squill, produces a 5-foot-long flowering stalk densely covered with numerous ½-inch flowers that are whitish in color. Blooms appear in autumn.

Growing conditions. Grow sea onion outdoors in Zones 9 and 10, especially in areas with hot, dry summers. Plants require full sun and very well drained soil that is dry during the dormant season. Water frequently from the time growth begins until the foliage begins to die, then reduce watering as the plant becomes dormant. Plants can be grown in pots in a cool (45° to 50° F) greenhouse. Pot plants in midsummer for autumn bloom. Handle the bulbs carefully, because the sap can be irritating and may cause a rash.

Vallota (va-LO-ta)
Scarborough lily

A bulbous, one-species genus from South Africa in the amaryllis family. Leaves are strap-shaped and the flowers are trumpet-shaped and borne in umbels. Zone 10.

Selected species and varieties. *V. speciosa,* Scarborough lily, has 2-foot-long, 1-inch-wide leaves that appear with the flowers. Blooms are scarlet and appear from summer to autumn.

Growing conditions. Scarborough lily can be grown outdoors in the warmest parts of Zone 10. Plant the bulbs in a sunny site with rich, sandy, well-drained soil. North of Zone 10, grow bulbs indoors in pots for summer bloom. Plant the bulbs with the upper half above the soil surface. Use a rich, sandy potting soil to which bone meal has been added. Keep plants barely moist and in a warm, dark place until growth begins. Move plants to a bright spot out of direct sun for flowering. Remove the stalks after flowering, feed twice a month with a weak fertilizer and keep watering until the leaves begin to yellow. Store plants dry. Plants should be repotted only every five to six years.

Veltheimia (vel-THY-mee-a)

A very small genus of bulbous species from South Africa in the lily family. Leaves are strap-shaped and borne at the base of the plant. Flowers are pendulous, borne in dense spikes and shaped like narrow tubes. *Veltheimia* species are used in rock gardens and borders in areas where they are hardy and as potted plants in cool greenhouses elsewhere. Zones 9 and 10.

Selected species and varieties. *V. viridifolia,* unicorn root, has strap-shaped, 15-inch-long leaves that are 4 inches wide and have wavy margins. Flowers are borne in many-flowered, 6- to 10-inch-long spikes atop leafless, 2-foot stalks. Individual flowers are narrow, 1 inch long and pale pinkish purple spotted with pale yellow. Blooms appear in winter or early spring.

Growing conditions. Grow unicorn root outdoors in Zones 9 and 10 in a location with full sun and rich, well-drained soil. Indoors, pot bulbs in early fall and grow them in a cool (50° to 55° F) greenhouse. Keep the soil barely moist until growth appears in late winter; water more often once plants are growing actively. During the growing season, feed lightly with a balanced fertilizer. Once foliage begins to die in summer, reduce watering and keep plants barely moist until growth begins again. Repot plants only if flowering diminishes.

Wandflower see *Dierama; Sparaxis*

Watsonia (wat-SO-nee-a)

Bugle lily

A genus of plants in the iris family that arise from corms and are primarily native to South Africa. Foliage is sword-shaped and usually rigid. Flowers are tubular, often with flaring lobes, and are borne in spikes. Blooms are red or white in color. Bugle lilies are used in beds and borders. Zones 8-10; dug and stored indoors in the North.

Selected species and varieties. *W. marginata* is a 4- to 5-foot plant with many-flowered spikes of fragrant, rose-pink flowers. *W. pyramidata* grows 3 to 5½ feet tall and has spikes of 3-inch rose-pink flowers. Zone 8. *W. tabularis* reaches 5 to 6 feet in height and bears spikes of flowers that are coral red outside and pale salmon or rose-pink inside.

Growing conditions. Plant bugle lilies in full sun in a location protected from high winds. Space corms 6 to 9 inches apart at a depth of 3 to 4 inches. Enrich the soil with compost and fertilize with 5-10-5 when the plants emerge and again a month later. North of Zone 8, bugle lilies can be grown provided the corms are dug before the first hard frost. Shake off excess soil and allow them to dry for several days in a cool, dry place out of direct sun. Cut back the tops of the plants and discard the remains of the previous season's corms. Store in dry peat moss or vermiculite at a temperature of 55° to 60° F. Plants also can be started indoors and moved to the garden after danger of frost has passed. They can be difficult to transplant, so start them in peat pots that can go directly into the ground or grow them in tubs. Propagate plants from the small cormels borne around old corms. Small corms take up to two seasons to bloom.

White camas see *Zigadenus*
Wild hyacinth see *Camassia; Dichelostemma; Triteleia*
Wild onion see *Allium*
Windflower see *Anemone*
Winter aconite see *Eranthis*
Winter daffodil see *Sternbergia*
Wonder flower see *Ornithogalum*
Wood hyacinth see *Endymion*
Wood lily see *Lilium*
Wood sorrel see *Oxalis*
Yellow bell see *Fritillaria*
Yellow mariposa see *Calochortus*
Yellow onion see *Allium*

Zantedeschia

(zan-te-DES-kee-a)
Calla, calla lily

A very small genus in the arum family native to South Africa. Plants arise from thick rhizomes and have heart- or arrow-shaped leaves. The flowers are insignificant and borne on a fleshy spadix that is surrounded by a showy, petal-like spathe. Calla lilies are grown outdoors in beds or borders, or near water; they are also grown in greenhouses. Zone 10.

Selected species and varieties. *Z. aethiopica,* florist's calla, garden calla, is a 3-foot-tall species with arrow-shaped, 18-inch-long, 10-inch-wide leaves. The showy, petal-like spathe is milky white and flairs outward. The spadix is yellow and fragrant. 'Childsiana' is a heavy-flowering dwarf cultivar that

WATSONIA PYRAMIDATA

ZANTEDESCHIA AETHIOPICA

ZANTEDESCHIA ELLIOTTIANA

ZANTEDESCHIA REHMANNII

ZEPHYRANTHES GRANDIFLORA

ZIGADENUS ELEGANS

reaches 1 foot. *Z. albomaculata,* spotted calla, black-throated calla, has triangular, 18-inch leaves that are spotted with white. Spathes are 4½ inches long and whitish to pale yellow or pale pink. *Z. elliottiana,* golden calla, yellow calla, bears bright yellow, 6-inch-long spathes that are greenish yellow on the outside and curve outward. Plants are 2½ feet tall; leaves are 10 to 11 inches long and wide, and spotted with white. *Z. rehmannii,* pink calla, red calla, is a 2-foot plant with narrow leaves sometimes spotted with white. The showy spathes are 3 to 4 inches long and rosy purple to white with pink margins.

Growing conditions. Grow calla lilies outdoors in full sun with deep, moist soil that is rich in organic matter. Feed with a balanced fertilizer at the beginning of each growing season. Plants will thrive for years with little care and can be left undisturbed. Calla lilies also are grown in greenhouses for cut flowers.

Zephyranthes (zef-i-RAN-theez)

Zephyr lily, rain lily, fairy lily

A genus of bulbous species in the amaryllis family with grasslike leaves and solitary, funnel-shaped flowers that have flaring segments. Blooms may be white, yellow, pink or red. Zephyr lilies are planted at the front of borders and in rock gardens, and are used for naturalizing. Zones 7-10; in the North, bulbs can be dug in fall and replanted in spring.

Selected species and varieties. *Z. atamasco,* atamasco lily, fairy lily, has narrow, 12-inch leaves and white flowers that may be tinged with purple. Blooms are borne atop 12-inch stems and have flaring, lilylike perianth segments. Plants bloom in early spring. *Z. candida* bears grasslike, 1-foot-long leaves and white, 1-inch-long flowers that appear from summer to fall. Zones 9 and 10. *Z. citrina* has bright yellow, 2-inch-long flowers that somewhat resemble crocuses. Blooms appear from late summer to fall. Zones 9 and 10. *Z. grandiflora* bears 1-foot-long leaves and rose or pink flowers that are 4 inches across and 3 inches long. Blooms appear in late spring to summer. Zones 9 and 10. *Z. longifolia* is a 6-inch-tall species that has 1-inch-long flowers that are bright yellow inside and copper-colored outside. Zones 9 and 10. *Z. rosea* resembles *Z. grandiflora* but has broader leaves and rose-pink, 1-inch-long flowers. Blooms appear in fall. Zone 10.

Growing conditions. Grow zephyr lilies in full sun and rich, well-drained soil that remains moist while the foliage is above the ground. Plant the bulbs in spring (in fall in the Deep South and the Southwest) at a depth of three to four times the height of the bulbs. Space plants 2 to 3 inches apart. *Z. atamasco* requires a site that is very well drained in winter and should be planted in a warm, sheltered location near the northern limit of its hardiness. In the North, bulbs can be dug after flowering and stored in moist sand during the winter.

Zephyranthes

see also *Habranthus*

Zephyr lily see *Zephyranthes*

Zigadenus (zig-a-DEE-nus)

Death camas, poison camas, star lily

A small genus of North American lily-family members that may arise from bulbs or from rhizomes. Leaves are narrow, grasslike and borne at the base of the plant. Flowers are greenish white, yellowish white or purplish and are carried in spikes. Individual blooms are nearly flat or slightly bell-shaped. Some species are poisonous to livestock. Death camas are grown in native plant gardens. Zones 3-10.

Selected species and varieties. *Z. elegans,* mountain death camas, white camas, alkali grass, is a 3-foot species with 1-foot-long leaves and spikes of ½-inch flowers. Blooms are greenish or yellowish white. *Z. glaucus,* white camas, produces spikes of small, creamy white to greenish flowers that may have a brownish or purplish cast. Blooms appear in late summer to fall atop 3-foot stalks. Zones 5-10. *Z. venenosus,* death camas, is a 2-foot plant with narrow spikes of whitish, ⅛-inch-long flowers. Zones 4-10.

Growing conditions. Grow death camas in light shade and deep, fairly moist soil that is rich in organic matter. Plant the bulbs 3 to 4 inches deep and 4 to 8 inches apart. Do not dig or divide plants unless they become crowded and flowering ceases.

PICTURE CREDITS

The sources for the illustrations in this book are listed below. Cover photograph of *Lilium auratum* by Derek Fell. Watercolor paintings by Nicholas Fasciano and Yin Yi except pages 21, 22, 23, 86, 87: Catherine Anderson. 84, 85: Lorraine Moseley Epstein. Maps on pages 78, 79, 81, 83: digitized by Richard Furno, inked by John Drummond.

Frontispiece paintings listed by page number: 6: *Harold Gilman's House, Letchworth,* c. 1912 by Spencer Gore. Courtesy Leicestershire Museum and Art Gallery, Leicester. 32: *Amaryllis,* 1977 by Mary Frank. Courtesy The Metropolitan Museum of Art, purchase Stewart S. MacDermott Fund, 1977. 50: *Auratum Lilies,* 1935 by George Walter Dawson. Courtesy The Pennsylvania Academy of the Fine Arts, Philadelphia, gift of friends of the artist.

Photographs in Chapters 1 through 3 from the following sources, listed by page number: 8: Saxon Holt. 10: Karen Bussolini. 12: William D. Adams. 14: Horticultural Photography, Corvallis, OR. 16: Michael Dirr. 20: Steven Still. 28: Thomas Eltzroth. 30: Balthazar Korab. 34: © Walter Chandoha, 1989. 36, 38: Renée Comet. 40, 42: © Walter Chandoha, 1989. 46, 52: Thomas Eltzroth. 56, 60, 64: Horticultural Photography, Corvallis, OR. 66: Maggie Oster. 68: Michael Dirr. 70: Derek Fell. 72: Mark Gibson. 74: Horticultural Photography, Corvallis, OR.

Photographs in the Dictionary of Bulbs from the following sources, listed by page and numbered from top to bottom. Page 90, 1, 2: Breck's Dutch Bulbs, Peoria, IL. 3: Thomas Eltzroth. 91, 1: Pamela Harper. 2, 3: J. C. Raulston. 92, 1: Saxon Holt. 2: Pamela Harper. 3: Maggie Oster. 93, 1, 2: Pamela Harper. 3: Michael Dirr. 4: J. C. Raulston. 94, 1: Michael Dirr. 2: Horticultural Photography, Corvallis, OR. 3: Gillian Beckett. 95, 1: J. C. Raulston. 2: Breck's Dutch Bulbs, Peoria, IL. 3: Saxon Holt. 96, 1: Joy Spurr. 2: Steven Still. 3: Joanne Pavia. 97, 1: Robert E. Lyons/Color Advantage. 2: Emily Johnson/Envision. 3: Pamela Harper. 98, 1: Thomas Eltzroth. 2: Anita Sabarese. 3: Robert E. Lyons/Color Advantage. 99, 1: Thomas Eltzroth. 2: David M. Stone/Photo-Nats. 3: Pamela Harper. 100, 1: Pamela Harper. 2: Jane Grushow/Grant Heilman Photography. 101, 1: Steven Still. 2: Gottlieb Hampfler. 3: Maggie Oster. 102, 1: Joy Spurr. 2: Thomas Eltzroth. 3: © Walter Chandoha, 1989. 103, 1: Thomas Eltzroth. 2: Strybing Arboretum Society, Helen Crocker Russell Library of Horticulture, San Francisco. 3: J. C. Raulston. 4: Horticultural Photography, Corvallis, OR. 104, 1: Lefever/Grushow/Grant Heilman Photography. 2: Breck's Dutch Bulbs, Peoria, IL. 105, 1: Saxon Holt. 2: Breck's Dutch Bulbs, Peoria, IL. 106, 1: Thomas Eltzroth. 2: Roger Holmes/*Fine Gardening Magazine*. 3: Derek Fell. 107, 1: Joanne Pavia. 2: Ann Reilly/Photo-Nats. 3: Joanne Pavia. 108, 1: Thomas Eltzroth. 2: Pamela Harper. 3: Breck's Dutch Bulbs, Peoria, IL. 109, 1: Pamela Harper. 2: Jim Bauml. 110, 1: Runk/Schoenberger/Grant Heilman Photography. 2: Breck's Dutch Bulbs, Peoria, IL. 111, 1, 2: Breck's Dutch Bulbs, Peoria, IL. 3: Thomas Eltzroth. 112, 1: Derek Fell. 2: Michael Dirr. 3: Maggie Oster. 113, 1: Pamela Harper. 2: Trevor J. Cole. 114, 1: Gerald B. Straley/University of British Columbia. 2: Robert E. Lyons/Color Advantage. 3: Gillian Beckett. 115, 1: Robert E. Lyons/Color Advantage. 2: Joanne Pavia. 3: Wanda La Rock/Envision. 116, 1: Joanne Pavia. 2: Pat Toops. 3: Thomas Eltzroth. 117, 1: Jerry Pavia. 2: Pamela Harper. 3: J. C. Raulston. 118, 1: Pamela Harper. 2: Robert E. Lyons/Color Advantage. 3: Pamela Harper. 119, 1: Robert E. Lyons/Color Advantage. 2: Horticultural Photography, Corvallis, OR. 120, 1: Derek Fell. 2: Michael Landis. 3: Robert E. Lyons/Color Advantage. 121, 1, 2, 3: Pamela Harper. 122, 1: Pamela Harper. 2: Saxon Holt. 123, 1: Pamela Harper. 2: David M. Stone/Photo-Nats. 3: Pamela Harper. 124, 1: © Walter Chandoha, 1989. 2: Joy Spurr. 125, 1: James Compton/Chelsea Physic Garden. 2: J. C. Raulston. 126, 1: Breck's Dutch Bulbs, Peoria, IL. 2: Lefever/Grushow/Grant Heilman Photography. 3: Thomas Eltzroth. 127, 1: Gillian Beckett. 2: Cole Burrell. 3: Horticultural Photography, Corvallis, OR. 128, 1: Dwight Ellefsen/Envision. 2, 3: Breck's Dutch Bulbs, Peoria, IL. 129, 1: Gottlieb Hampfler. 2: J. C. Raulston. 3: Berry Botanic Garden. 130, 1: Horticultural Photography, Corvallis, OR. 2, 3: Pamela Harper. 131, 1, 2: Derek Fell. 3: Thomas Eltzroth. 132, 1: Derek Fell. 2: Horticultural Photography, Corvallis, OR. 3: John J. Smith/Photo-Nats. 133, 1: © Walter Chandoha, 1989. 2: Derek Fell. 3: Steven Still. 134, 1: Gillian Beckett. 2: William C. Aplin. 3: Gillian Beckett. 4: Derek Fell. 135, 1, 2: Thomas Eltzroth. 3: Pamela Harper. 136, 1: Thomas Eltzroth. 2: Lefever/Grushow/Grant Heilman Photography. 3: Trevor J. Cole.

ACKNOWLEDGMENTS

The index for this book was prepared by Lee McKee.
The editors also wish to thank: Sarah Brash, Alexandria, Virginia; Steven H. Davis, Alexandria, Virginia; Betsy Frankel, Alexandria, Virginia; Dr. Peter Goldblatt, Missouri Botanical Garden, St. Louis, Missouri; Kenneth E. Hancock, Annandale, Virginia; Brent C. Heath, The Daffodil Mart, Gloucester, Virginia; Jim Henrich, Missouri Botanical Garden, St. Louis, Missouri; Mary Kay Honeycutt, Crofton, Maryland; Malak Photographs Limited, Ottawa, Ontario, Canada; Thanh Huu Nguyen, Alexandria, Virginia; Jayne E. Rohrich, Alexandria, Virginia; Allison and Paul Ryan, Alexandria, Virginia; Candace H. Scott, College Park, Maryland; Zabriskie Gallery, New York, New York.

FURTHER READING

Bailey, Liberty Hyde, and Ethel Zoe Bailey, *Hortus Third: A Concise Dictionary of Plants Cultivated in the United States and Canada.* New York: Macmillan, 1976.
Barnes, Don, *Daffodils for Home, Garden and Show.* Portland, Oregon: Timber Press, 1987.
Brooklyn Botanic Garden, *Bulbs.* Brooklyn, New York: Brooklyn Botanic Garden, 1985.
Browse, Philip McMillan, *Plant Propagation.* New York: Simon and Schuster, 1988.
Calkins, Carroll C., ed., *Reader's Digest Illustrated Guide to Gardening.* Pleasantville, New York: Reader's Digest Association, 1978.
Catterini, Robert, ed., *Spring Flowering Bulbs, 1986.* Venissieux, France: Horticolor, 1985.
De Hertogh, August, *Holland Bulb Forcer's Guide.* Hillegom, the Netherlands: International Flower-Bulb Centre, 1985.
Fairchild, Lee, ed., *How to Grow Glorious Gladiolus,* Sun City, Arizona: North American Gladiolus Council, no date.
Fox, Derek, *Growing Lilies.* Dover, New Hampshire: Croom Helm, 1985.
Grosvenor, Graeme, *Growing Irises.* Kenthurst, Australia: Kangaroo Press, 1984.
Hamilton, Geoff, *The Organic Garden Book.* New York: Crown Publishers, 1987.
Hartman, Hudson T., and Dale E. Kester, *Plant Propagation Principles and Practices.* Englewood Cliffs, New Jersey: Prentice Hall, 1975.
Hill, Lewis, *Secrets of Plant Propagation.* Pownal, Vermont: Storey Communications, 1986.
Horton, Alvin, and James McNair, *All about Bulbs.* San Francisco: Ortho Books/Chevron Chemical Company, 1986.
Johnson, Hugh, *The Principles of Gardening.* New York: Simon and Schuster, 1979.
Leighton, Phebe, and Calvin Simonds, *The New American Landscape Gardener.* Emmaus, Pennsylvania: Rodale Press, 1987.
Miles, Bebe, *The Wonderful World of Bulbs.* Princeton, New Jersey: D. Van Nostrand Company, 1963.
Papworth, David, Bob Legge and Noel Prockter, *Concise Encyclopedia of Garden Flowers.* New York: Crescent Books, 1987.
Price, Molly, *The Iris Book.* New York: Dover Publications, 1973.
Reynolds, Marc, and William L. Meachem, *The Garden Bulbs of Spring.* New York: Funk and Wagnalls, 1967.
Rix, Martyn, *Growing Bulbs.* Portland, Oregon: Timber Press, 1983.
Rix, Martyn, and Roger Phillips, *The Bulb Book.* London: Pan Books, 1981.
Schauenberg, Paul, *The Bulb Book.* New York: Frederick Warne and Company, 1965.
Scheider, Alfred F., *Park's Success with Bulbs.* Greenwood, South Carolina: Geo. W. Park Seed Company, 1981.
Scott, George Harmon, *Bulbs: How to Select, Grow and Enjoy.* Los Angeles: HP Books, 1982.
Seddon, George, and Andrew Bicknell, *Plants Plus.* Emmaus, Pennsylvania: Rodale Press, 1987.
Smith, Michael D., ed., *The Ortho Problem Solver.* San Francisco: Ortho Books/Chevron Chemical Company, 1984.
Sunset Editors, *Bulbs for All Seasons.* Menlo Park, California: Lane Publishing, 1985.
Swindells, Philip, *Bulbs for All Seasons.* Topsfield, Massachusetts: Salem House Publishers, 1987.
Taylor, Norman, *Taylor's Guide to Bulbs.* Boston: Houghton Mifflin, 1986.
Wyman, Donald, *Wyman's Gardening Encyclopedia.* New York: Macmillan, 1986.

INDEX

Numerals in italics indicate an illustration of the subject mentioned.

M

N

O

P

Q

R

S

T

U

V

W

Y

Z

THE CONSULTANTS

C. Colston Burrell is the series consultant for The Time-Life Gardener's Guide. He is Curator of Plant Collections at the Minnesota Landscape Arboretum, part of the University of Minnesota.

Robert E. Lyons, consultant for *Bulbs,* is an associate professor of horticulture at Virginia Polytechnic Institute and State University in Blacksburg, Virginia, where he teaches courses in herbaceous plant materials. He has written numerous articles on flowering plants.

Library of Congress Cataloging-in-Publication Data
Bulbs.
p. cm.—(The Time-Life gardener's guide)
Bibliograpy: p.
Includes index.
1. Bulbs. I. Time-Life Books. II. Series.
SB425.B86 1989 635.9'44—dc19 89-4360 CIP
ISBN 0-8094-6636-8
ISBN 0-8094-6637-6 (lib. bdg.)

First printing. Printed in U.S.A.
Published simultaneously in Canada.
School and library distribution by Silver Burdett Company, Morristown, New Jersey.